Comparatively Speaking

SAGE ANNUAL REVIEWS OF COMMUNICATION RESEARCH

SERIES EDITORS

EDITORIAL ADVISORY BOARD

Books in This Edited Series:

Editors

Jay G. Blumler
Jack M. McLeod
Karl Erik Rosengren

Comparatively Speaking: Communication and Culture Across Space and Time

Sage Annual Reviews of Communication Research

Volume 19

SAGE PUBLICATIONS
The International Professional Publishers
Newbury Park   London   New Delhi

For information address:

SAGE Publications, Inc.
2455 Teller Road
Newbury Park, California 91320

SAGE Publications Ltd.
6 Bonhill Street
London EC2A 4PU
United Kingdom

SAGE Publications India Pvt. Ltd.
M-32 Market
Greater Kailash I
New Delhi 110 048 India

Printed in the United States of America

Library of Congress Cataloging-in-Publication Data

Comparatively speaking : communication and culture across space and
    time / editors, Jay G. Blumler, Jack M. McLeod, Karl Erik Rosengren.
        p.   cm. — (Sage annual reviews of communication research ; v.
    19)
    Includes bibliographical references.
    ISBN 0-8039-4172-2. — ISBN 0-8039-4173-0 (pbk.)
    1. Communication and culture.   I. Blumler, Jay G.   II. McLeod,
Jack.   III. Rosengren, Karl Erik.   IV. Series.
P91.C563   1992
302.2—dc20   91-33336

92 93 94 95 96 10 9 8 7 6 5 4 3 2 1

Sage Production Editor: Astrid Virding

CONTENTS

PART III: Conclusions

PART I

INTRODUCTION:

DIFFERENT APPROACHES

Chapter 1

AN INTRODUCTION TO COMPARATIVE COMMUNICATION RESEARCH

Jay G. Blumler, Jack M. McLeod, and Karl Erik Rosengren

COMPARATIVE RESEARCH could be called the communication field's "extended and extendable frontier." The metaphor echoes the advancing globalization of the Social Science Academy itself. As researchers' international contacts multiply—through professional associations, conferences, visiting appointments, and the learned literature—scholars from different countries naturally think of working together on common problems. However, it also reflects an increasing appreciation of three distinctive contributions to knowledge that only comparative research—however demanding to conceive, organize, and carry out—can offer.

First, at the level of observation, comparative inquiry cosmopolitanizes, opening our eyes to communication patterns and problems unnoticeable in our own spatial and temporal milieux. It helps us to see our communication arrangements in a fresh light, enriches the raw material sources of communication theory building, and deepens appreciation of communication policy issues, learning how they have arisen and been dealt with in other places and periods.

Second, only comparative research can overcome space- and time-bound limitations on the generalizability of our theories, assumptions, and propositions. Blumler's (1983, p. 359) point about election research applies without exception to all other communication institutions and practices: "Most election studies are culturally blinkered because they are confined to single countries. They cannot distinguish those features of campaign communication that are common to all democratic polities from those that are nationally exceptional." As Kohn (1989c, p. 93) has put it, "Any comparisons we make within a single country are necessarily limited to one set of political, economic, cultural and historical contexts represented by that particular country."

Third, only comparative analysis can explore and reveal the consequences of differences in how communication is organized at a macrosocietal level. As Nowak (1989, p. 38) makes the point for social theory more broadly: "These characteristics—being the properties of whole societies or their cultures—by definition cannot have intrasystemic variation and therefore their relevance for the tested relationship cannot be discovered or proved through intrasystemic . . . analysis."

This is not to maintain that there is yet a formed genre of comparative communication research. Before any such claim could be made, there would have to be

(1) more theories specifically fashioned to guide communication analysis across spatial and temporal boundaries, and
(2) more evidence of cumulativity in findings and their interpretation.

The present stage of comparative communication research is probably best characterized as an *exploratory* one: increasingly active, wide-ranging, and productive but also rather probing and preliminary. It is as if the scholars involved are pushing a variegated fleet of all manner of boats out into relatively uncharted seas, attuning their compasses to unfamiliar bearings, plumbing their depths with a miscellany of lines and bait, and beginning to learn what fish can be caught.

Other would-be comparative explorers can take heart, however, for on the evidence of this volume, the specimens of marine life available for inspection and consumption are both abundant and tasty. It presents a rich and varied collection of essays illustrating concretely the present state of the art in the conception, conduct, and outcomes of comparative communication research. In the remainder of this chapter we accordingly aim

(1) to introduce the reader to the book's contents,
(2) to indicate some of the things to be noticed about comparative communication inquiry, and
(3) to explain what we mean by such inquiry, including certain core features we associate with it.

ORIGINS OF THE COLLECTION

This book had its inception in the theme that was designated to give intellectual shape to the 1989 conference of the International Communication Association. Termed "Comparatively Speaking . . .," the three of us had collaborated over its definition and representation in the conference program.

Adoption of this theme reflected in part the personal involvement of two of us in large-scale comparative projects, one predominantly across space, the other predominantly across time, that had proved stimulating conceptually and fertile empirically. Blumler had coordinated a multilevel study (dealing with communicators, content, and audiences) of the role of television in the campaigns for the 1979 European Parliamentary elections in the nine different political and media systems of the member countries of the European Community (for comment on some of its features see Swanson's Chapter 2). While confirming certain characteristics of his outlook on the organization of political communication systems, the results also compelled some revision of it (Blumler, 1983). Meanwhile, from the mid-1970s, Rosengren had led a 15-year, mixed cross-sectional/longitudinal panel study of media uses and effects among Swedish children and adolescents in a small city and a medium-sized town. The analysis prompted a schematization of forms of stability and change in communication structures over time that should be applicable in organizing the findings of other lines of temporally oriented communication research (see Chapter 8 for an account). As a result, each of us emerged from these involvements as an enthusiast for the comparative approach.

More important, our commitment to the "Comparatively Speaking . . ." theme reflected our conviction that comparative research had much to offer communication scholarship that until recently had been little exploited. As stated in the Conference Call for Papers:

> Comparative inquiry may counter naive universalism—the implicit assumption that communication works everywhere as found in some single locale. It also can provide multiple testbeds for validating propositions of communication science. It can refine theory, pinpointing the circumstances in which its tenets apply, do not apply or take modified form. It can improve our understanding of how communication systems "tick," specifying the forces that differentially constrain the behaviors and attitudes of producers, processors and receivers of communication. It can clarify

policy problems, profiling their incidence and proposed solutions in different settings.

We thereby wished to give comparative research and analysis more priority and visibility; to encourage a wider awareness of its potential and more involvement in work of this kind; and to stimulate a critical discussion of what might be involved in doing it well.

In the event, the theme attracted a considerable and vigorous response at the 1989 ICA conference. Forty-three sessions were devoted to it, incorporating 168 formal papers and presentations. The range of topics open to comparative treatment is illustrated by their scheduling, not only in a number of special theme sessions, but also in the programs of nine of ICA's Divisions and Interest Groups: in Mass Communication; Political Communication; Intercultural and Development Communication; Information Systems; Human Communication Technology; Interpersonal Communication; Organizational Communication; Public Relations; and Philosophy of Communication. The theme's extensive international appeal is illustrated by the fact that the authors of the papers hailed, not only from the United States (where the ICA headquarters and the bulk of the membership are located), but also from more than 20 other nations.

Thus all the essays in this collection emanated from conference papers, which in most cases were extensively revised afterward in discussion with the editors. Four main criteria guided their selection for inclusion in this book:

1. *Quality.* This subsumed several attributes of fine comparative work. One was a considered adoption of the comparative approach—shown by the authors' awareness of why comparisons of a certain kind were worth pursuing and of what was involved in applying them. Another was a relatively high order of conceptualization in defining the nature of the comparative problem under examination and in theorizing about the phenomena to be compared. A third was the relative richness of the data being analyzed and of its treatment. Still another was evidence of a sustained effort having been made by the authors to interpret their evidence in imaginative yet careful ways, to provide explanations, and to draw inferences that should stand up for reasons explicitly given—including especially signs of a purposive engagement with any problematic elements in the analysis.

2. *Exemplary instructiveness.* By this criterion, we were looking for pieces of work that would highlight prospects and pitfalls of compara-

tive communication research, from which other scholars could learn by virtue of the readiness of the authors to explicate how they had faced these, and what solutions to problems they had adopted.

3. *Range of types of research and analysis.* We also wanted the collection of essays as a whole to represent as well as possible the variety of functions and utilities that comparative communication research could serve, the diverse theoretical and methodological strategies available for conducting it, and the range of possible entry points to it.

4. *Work in dynamic progress.* Finally, we very much wanted to mirror comparative communication research as it stands right now: in a phase of dynamic development. We wanted the promises of beginnings, not the polish of finished products. We therefore consciously sought out reports from ongoing research rather than final summaries of approaches and results that already have been well presented elsewhere (e.g., Edelstein, Ito, & Kepplinger, 1989).

COMPARISONS OF WHAT?

The proper use of terminology is ever a source of provocation in social science. We ourselves have no imperialist designs on the term *comparative*. As both James Beniger and Kjell Nowak in this volume and many others before them have noted, all scientifically conceived research is in some sense comparative. What then distinguishes the *kind* of comparative communication research that we have aimed to promote?

Our answer is that criteria can be specified that separate the form of comparative communication research presented here from the bulk of research that is comparative in a less restricted sense. Work is comparative for the purposes of this collection *when the comparisons are made across two or more geographically or historically (spatially or temporally) defined systems, the phenomena of scholarly interest which are embedded in a set of interrelations that are relatively coherent, patterned, comprehensive, distinct, and bounded.*

Three features inherent in the nature of comparative research when conceived in this way should be noted. First, it is system-sensitive. It is not just a matter of discretely and descriptively comparing isolated bits and pieces of empirical phenomena situated in two or more locales. Rather, it reflects a concern to understand how the systemic context may have shaped such phenomena. In Ragin's (1989, p. 67) words, "Characteristics of macro-social units appear in explanatory statements in all forms" of comparative social research. It thus creates a need to think structurally, to conceptualize in macro terms, to stretch vertically across levels and horizontally across systems. Comparative research obliges one to soften the focus of investigative attention somewhat, to adjust to the embeddedness of phenomena within a system, to keep an eye out for the relevant principles of its organization—entailing a sort of moving theory up a notch in abstraction and generality (for further discussion of the macrosocial level of communication systems, see McLeod & Blumler, 1987).

Second, comparative research thus defined is research conducted to a considerable extent as if "out of [one's own familiar] bounds"—or at least across bounds. This is why such research, involving a "leap in the dark" (into the relatively unknown), can be at once daunting and refreshing.

On the one hand, it can pose challenges to scholars' preconceptions and is liable to be theoretically upsetting. For those wedded to their own theory, it involves a certain amount of risk, for there is a good chance that one's theory could prove to be wrong or applicable only in certain limited conditions. If we hold to the traditional view that universal propositions are the only acceptable form of theory, then the uncovering of limiting conditions is a fatal blow to our theorizing. A more positive view, however, would hold that the specification of the conditions of applicability of a theory is the very stuff of realistic social science.

On the other hand, the contribution of comparative research is not confined only to testing, validating and revising existing theory. It also has a more creative and innovative role—opening up new avenues, shifting the intellectual focus, forcing a redefinition of existing concepts and a fashioning of new ones transportable across space and time, and a framing of new problems and questions (Gurevitch & Blumler, 1990, offer many examples of this "eye-opening" function in comparative political communication research). Such a contribution is more like that of theory *building* (the active if groping practice much in evidence in the following essays).

Third, comparative research in our sense implies the interpenetration of space and time. This relationship has been too little addressed by comparativists, who—possibly because they equate comparative work exclusively with spatial distinctions—often convey a static impression when comparing geographical systems, treating them almost as if frozen in time, presenting them more like snapshots than as moving films.

System features and patterns are not eternal but instead are in continual flux, increasingly brought about these days by influences from a larger world system of communication.

Some scholars take the view that comparative research is only spatial or that it is so different from temporal analysis that the latter should not be brought into the same camp with it (William Dutton, personal communication, 1990). This is to ignore the fact that even if we confined ourselves to geographical units we would necessarily be dealing with systems-in-flux. To understand either one of these dimensions properly, it is necessary to take account of the other. Space conditions time, and time conditions space. Without both, comparative spatial analysis, by "holding time constant," may appear to be static, while temporal analysis, by "holding space constant," may underplay the variance within and between systems.

All this suggests the desirability of combining comparative studies of time and space. Ideally, then, we would merge cross-space and cross-time research in designs that would more adequately handle the direction of causality and estimate rates of change in various systems and subscale-systems. Perhaps a combination of cross-space panel and cohort analysis is the ideal design for this purpose. In this volume, Rosengren presents examples of the payoffs that can accrue from such a design. Nowak (Chapter 9) has also deliberately blended temporal and spatial elements in his research. Even more telling about their interpenetration, however, is the fact that despite their predominantly spatial research focus, many of the other authors were ultimately obliged to incorporate a temporal dimension in order to tell their analytical stories properly. Overtly evident in the chapters by Chaffee and Chu, Dutton and Vedel, and Ito, this is also subtly manifested in the work of Hallin and Mancini, and of Liebes and Livingstone.

One of our authors, James Beniger, is comprehensively at odds with usual notions of comparative communication research. He apparently finds most such comparative research uninteresting, involving "the relatively narrow empirical study of categories of things: media systems, nations, historical periods." He regards it as essentially atheoretical, even antitheoretical, for "the more researchers are attracted to 'comparative analysis' in its usual sense of the narrow empirical study of categories of things, the less likely is general and interdisciplinary theory to advance." He contends that the term *comparative* is "rarely . . . applied to a theoretical enterprise." In its place he recommends a comparison by functions of the information control revolution. This would examine alternative ways of achieving desired ends through the control of informational means whether by bureaucracy and information processing or by rationalization and what he calls preprocessing—all with a view to generating "truly comparative theory and research on information and communication technology and its impact on culture and society."

To that onslaught, the offerings of the *other* contributors provide a fully effective contrast. Beniger seems to equate research across systems with an unreflective comparativism, which in fact none of our authors endorses. It may be true that many comparative studies in the literature have been based on rather unimaginative comparisons of "things," but the substantive chapters of this book certainly do not just compare things. Their authors' concern is rather to compare—over social systems separated by sometimes considerable stretches of time and space—the ever continuing interplay between macro and micro, social and cultural, structures and processes in the realm of communication. Far from exemplifying such work as a- or antitheoretical, most have evidently found the task theoretically stimulating and challenging. Judee Burgoon, for example, who was already in possession of a quite well developed theory about the violation of communication expectations in nonverbal social relations, was impelled greatly to extend it in response to our invitation to consider its cross-cultural implications. Dutton and Vedel report from their experience of conducting a three-nation study of the diffusion of cable television that, "Comparative research . . . *forces* scholars to develop theoretical explanations that can apply across social systems" (emphasis added).

At present, there is no single comparative theory that can be outlined, accepted, or critiqued. Regarded in this light, comparative research today "is best seen as a strategy for extending knowledge in two respects—in level (from the microindividual toward the macrosocietal) and in scope (extending the number of sites to which theoretical propositions might apply and in which they might be tested)" (Gurevitch & Blumler, 1990, p. 319). By means of that strategy, existing theories will be gradually refined, extended, and solidified.

A good example of such a strategy is indeed Beniger's extended work on the "information control revolution" (Beniger, 1986). No such process will ever manifest a uniform set of ends or means, however, *regardless of the structural and cultural features of the societies it permeates.* Indeed, systematically comparative research of the kind we advocate is best placed to identify the main common and differentiating patterns that can result from the entry into different societies of new technologies substitutive of, or additive to, the functions performed by more established ones. Dutton and Vedel's analogous study of the development of cable television in England, France, and the United States is instructive on this very point.

WHAT ROLES MAY GEOGRAPHICAL AND TEMPORAL UNITS PLAY IN COMPARATIVE COMMUNICATION RESEARCH?

For specifically cross-national research, Melvin Kohn (1989b, pp. 22-24) has generated a fourfold scheme for classifying varieties of comparative research (tolerably distinct but with shadings into each other) that we accept, albeit with certain extensions.

First, nations may serve as the *objects* of our analysis, where the interest is in the particular countries being studied for their own sake, rather than as settings for pursuing some more general hypothesis. As Kohn notes, this category also includes investigators who are interested in comparing particular institutions in the countries concerned. An example is Chapter 6, in which Liebes and Livingstone explore how the soap operas of Britain and the United States are dramatizing the role dilemmas that many women face in modern society.

Second, nations may be treated as *contexts,* where the primary interest is in the generality of findings regarding variables acting within or connecting institutions. We could further divide this second use between situations where the contexts serve as conditions for replicating findings, and where contexts themselves are the focus of comparison. In this book, Burgoon's review of how theory about violations of communication expectations might fare in different cultures well exemplifies the first subtype. Dutton and Vedel's search for overarching explanations of similarities and differences in policies and institutional arrangements for developing cable television in three countries represents the other contextual form.

A third comparative research type is one in which nations are the *units of analysis,* serving as different points on dimensions or scales of interest to the investigator. This conforms to Przeworski and Teune's (1970) recommendation for cross-national comparativists to strive to convert countries' proper names into variables. Index-approach studies of communication and national development (e.g., Lerner, 1957) were early specimens in our field. A more recent example appears in Blumler's (1983) and Thoveron's (1983) intercorrelations of communication, cultural, and political features of nine European Community countries in order to explain cross-national differences in the mobilizing power and substantive directions of the campaigns for election to the European Parliament in 1979. In the present collection, Nowak's examination of trends in Swedish magazine advertising from the 1930s to the 1980s uses temporal periods as units of analysis.

Finally, Kohn identifies a fourth approach in which nations are treated as *components of larger international systems.* Gurevitch and Blumler (1990, pp. 310-312) even regard "the dramatic globalization of the flow of political messages" today as "the most compelling argument" for prioritizing comparative communication research. If no country is any longer an island so far as its communication arrangements are concerned, national communication systems may have to be examined partly as subsystems of an emergent global one. In this volume such an approach is taken by Hallin and Mancini, who consider how the reporting of superpower summits may be planting the seeds of an international communication system and inducing change in the national communication systems of Italy, the Soviet Union, and the United States.

We thus accept Kohn's listing of four types of comparative studies. Noting that attempts have already been made to reorganize the list in terms of a more systematic typology (Ragin, 1989), for our part we would like to extend it in two ways:

(1) Nations are not the only geographical/spatial entities that may be compared in communication research, though admittedly most of the examples in our book, as in Kohn's, are cross-national. But, for example, communities could be compared (cf., Tichenor, Donohue, & Olien, 1980; Rosengren in this volume). Organizations, social movements and microsocial systems, such as families, provide other possibilities for comparison.

(2) The four-fold scheme can be applied to temporal comparisons as well:

  (a) As *object* of analysis—interest in time periods per se—for example, comparing broadcasting in the 1930s with the present day.

  (b) As *context of study*—for example, comparing potentials for mass media effects before and after the rise to leisure-time dominance of television.

  (c) As *unit of analysis*—in time-series of different types where, for instance, tracking sequential trends or cycles over time is involved.

(d)   Although a temporal correspondence to Kohn's notion of nations as components of a larger system unit is less easy to realize, we would tentatively suggest as a parallel concept "transcendent"—when conceptualizing over "megaunits" of time—as in the seminal work of Harold Innis (1950) and the periodizing of a Gutenberg galaxy and an electronic global village by McLuhan (1962).

PROBLEMS OF COMPARATIVE RESEARCH

An assumption held to underlie all meaningful comparisons is that the objects being compared are indeed comparable. As Beniger forcefully argues, however, comparisons of "apples and oranges" may actually be of great benefit in extending the scope of our generalizations. This may be done by moving the comparison up a level of abstraction. Even so, when very different systems or time periods are being analyzed, the extent of the differences may overwhelm meaningful comparison (but see how Chaffee and Chu have coped with such problems in Chapter 9). Furthermore, differences not only may be large, but multidimensional as well, for social systems and time periods are "block-billed" (to borrow a term from Rosenberg, 1968). They may be different in so many ways that any comparison on a given characteristic or relationship may be confounded by a host of other variables, making inference drawing correspondingly more hazardous. This may well be where scholarly creativity is put to its hardest test.

Another potential problem of comparative research may arise where, by focusing on differences between social systems or time periods, the investigator unwittingly understates the variance *within* the system or period. Nations and cultures are not typically homogeneous; they often encompass different language and ethnic groups, regions, and social classes that are in symbolic and pragmatic competition. (Ito in this volume criticizes certain theorists of intercultural communication differences for not taking sufficient account of such in-society distinctions.) The system may therefore be ill-represented by a single summary statement or index. More effort could be made than appears in the literature to capture such internal dynamics through measures of dispersion and inequality. Within-nation differences may also be regarded as subunits within the larger system that provide side-information to interpret more adequately across-nation studies (Eulau, 1986; Przeworski & Teune, 1970). Rather than being simply within-system error variance in the statistical sense, the subunits may reveal differences in the strength of the relationships being examined and hence become part of the interpretation.

Another problem stems from the need, in cross-space comparative research at least, to form often costly and difficult collaborative relations with scholars in other systems with often differing theoretical and methodological predilections (see both Swanson, Chapter 2, and Dutton & Vedel, Chapter 5, for useful analyses of such relationships). Due to the extended investment of time that may be required, project gestation may be more like that of an elephant than a rabbit!

This volume illustrates a related problem facing comparative research. It requires financial support and collegial contact that is more feasible in the more affluent Western nations than in the rest of the world. As a result, this book shows a preponderance of North American and European work (though the Japanese and Chinese Orient is also represented). Not surprisingly, this was also true of a recent sociological collection of cross-national studies (Kohn, 1989a). This situation was certainly not the wish of the editors in either case but reflects uneven support for scholarship in different parts of the world at this time. To the extent that there is an imbalance toward Western postindustrial nations in the origins of comparative research, there is the danger that the comparisons and judgments will be made through the eyes of the West, thereby marginalizing, or making deviant, patterns that do not fit "normal" expectations and sequences from that cultural vantage point. There are ways to lessen such biases but none better than building research teams balanced by area of origin. We hope that a similar volume of comparative communication scholarship, should one be constructed a decade from now, say, would show a more even span of worldwide contribution.

ON WHAT FOLLOWS

Whatever the difficulties, it is worthwhile confronting them, since communication is a particularly rich site for comparative analysis, offering a wealth of entry points and significant interrelations for exploration. Two properties of communication explain this potential:

(1) *The organization of communication within a Chinese-boxes-like set of levels.* Mass media systems, for example, are externally related to

surrounding political, economic, and cultural systems, as well as to a host of sources and clients, and internally divisible into institutional organization (ownership, management, production, distribution, etc.), professional cultures, content, and audiences.

(2) *The problematics of dependency/autonomous relations.* Communication is an aspect of all social phenomena. At the same time, in most human societies there are institutions especially focused on that aspect. Those communication institutions, structures, and processes may be seen as reflections, consequences, and products of, as well as sources of, intervention into and effects upon other social institutions, structures, and processes.

Each of the 10 chapters that form the body of this book manifests one or both of these properties and illustrates or elaborates upon some of the more general points made about comparative communication inquiry in this chapter.

In the second chapter of this section, David L. Swanson analyzes three basic strategies for dealing with the theoretical diversity often accompanying comparative communication studies. His exemplars are certain major projects of comparative political communication research, in which mass media characteristics have been treated as both "independent" and "dependent" variables in their relations to political system features. In the next chapter, completing the introduction, James Beniger mounts a scathing criticism of what might be called run-of-the-mill comparative communication studies and analysis. Beniger thus joins with considerable brio a series of illustrious humanists and social scientists who for at least half a century have raised warning fingers against mindless comparativism (cf., for instance, Macridis, 1955). He also calls for more imaginative theorizing about how technologies of information control impinge on political, industrial, and social organization in the widest sense.

The two chapters by Judee Burgoon and Youichi Ito, which open and close the next section of exemplars, stand out from the others for their interest in interpersonal communication styles. Yet they differ in perspective and methodology. Burgoon offers a meticulous overview and summary of more than a decade of experimental, quantitative, mainly social-psychological research on nonverbal interpersonal communication, distinguishing properties she would expect to be cross-culturally universal from those that could vary according to (be "dependent" on) different surrounding cultures. Taking a more critical and analytical approach, Ito daringly compares interpersonal and organizational communication within drastically different cultures around the globe. He also challenges the established literature's heavily psychologistic orientation and calls for more attention to those macrosocietal factors of economy, politics, education, and family organization that may be concomitants or "causes" of cultural differences.

Drawing on interviews with elite figures, policy documents, and other historical sources, William Dutton and Thierry Vedel compare the way in which a particular technological device—cable television—was finally incorporated along not dissimilar lines (despite different points of departure) into the media systems of Britain, France, and the United States. Although methodologically they apply the case study approach, they strive to reconcile its characteristic emphasis on a detailed understanding with the more spare and essentialist demands of comparative analysis. The fascinating paths that the innovation had to travel for decades across a two-dimensional conceptual space in the three countries give much food for thought about the reciprocal interplay between technology, economy, polity, and culture.

Whereas Dutton and Vedel thus focus on the comparative analysis of media structure, mass media content is the main center of interest of the two chapters by Tamar Liebes and Sonia Livingstone and by Daniel Hallin and Paolo Mancini—complemented in the latter piece by attention to a professional culture (that of journalism). Although both sets of authors deal with television content, the genres are different: soap operas and summit meetings; the worlds of popular culture and high politics; the roles of statesmen and media personalities, on the one hand, and those of mothers, wives, and everyday working women, on the other. Common to the two chapters, however, is an interest in ascertaining how societal script and mass media organization and traditions interact to produce considerable and highly significant differences in superficially the same forms of media content. As noted above, Hallin and Mancini also venture to explore the impact of emerging global influences on the various national communication patterns.

The three remaining chapters in this section draw on *time* as the dimension by means of which differences in sociocultural systems and their consequences for media content and related communication processes are subjected to analysis. Although they have the element of time in common, the three chapters are otherwise radically different in theory and methodology.

The first of these turns to the audience level of mass media systems. Drawing on a combined panel and cohort design stretching over some 15 years, Karl Erik Rosengren tries to tease out the amount of stability and change—and stability *in* change—to be found in children's, adolescents' and young adults' uses of such media as television, music, and VCR. Kjell Nowak deals with yet another category of medium and content—the purposively persuasive form of magazine advertising. He compares many features of rhetoric and imagery found in advertisements appearing in popular magazines in Sweden and the United States over a six-decade period. Its interpretive frame of reference regards magazine advertising as a cultural system that is affected by the wider economic, social, and cultural context prevalent at a particular time in a particular society, and Nowak usefully spells out some of the mechanisms by which the former may respond to changes in the latter. Both chapters suggest that in the last analysis only a combination of spatio-temporal comparisons can offer the insights essential for fully grasping the subtle interplay between societal structures and media processes at the macro and micro levels.

In the penultimate chapter of the section, Steven H. Chaffee and Godwin Chu make an ambitious, indeed heroic attempt to follow and explain the fate of Confucian cultural values in the modern world and particularly in mainland China. By means of all possible sources to hand (the ingenuity of which is only meagerly indicated by its methodologically technical label of "multioperationism"), they pursue the relative plausibility of three possible sources of change in people's conformity to Confucian precepts: deliberate counterstructuring (by the Communist authorities); modernization; and exposure to Western media. The journeys of these intrepid space- and time-travelers take them from pre-Communist to present-day China, to Taiwan, and even to the United States.

The 10 chapters forming the body of this book convincingly demonstrate the breadth, vigor, and imagination characterizing comparative communication studies undertaken on three continents today. Even in this exploratory phase much theoretical and empirical gold is evidently being mined successfully. In the final chapter of the book, we make an attempt to draw together the lessons to be learned from this collection for the future development of comparative communication research, venturing the conclusion that it may well be on the verge of leaving its present exploratory phase for a decidedly more formative one.

REFERENCES

Beniger, J. R. (1986). *The control revolution: Technological and economic origins of the information society.* Cambridge, MA: Harvard University Press.

Blumler, J. G. (1983). Electoral communication: A comparative perspective. In J. G. Blumler (Ed.), *Communicating to voters: Television in the first European parliamentary elections* (pp. 359-378). London: Sage.

Edelstein, A. S., Ito, Y., & Kepplinger, H. M. (1989). *Communication and culture: A comparative approach.* New York: Longman.

Eulau, H. (1986). *Politics, self, and society: A theme and variation.* Cambridge, MA: Harvard University Press.

Gurevitch, M., & Blumler, J. G. (1990). Comparative research: The extending frontier. In D. L. Swanson & D. Nimmo (Eds.), *New directions in political communication: A resource book* (pp. 305-325). Newbury Park, CA: Sage.

Innis, H. (1950). *Empire and communications.* Toronto: University of Toronto Press.

Kohn, M. L. (Ed.). (1989a). *Cross-national research in sociology.* Newbury Park, CA: Sage.

Kohn, M. L. (1989b). Introduction. In M. L. Kohn (Ed.), *Cross-national research in sociology* (pp. 17-31). Newbury Park, CA: Sage.

Kohn, M. L. (1989c). Cross-national research as an analytic strategy. In M. L. Kohn (Ed.), *Cross-national research in sociology* (pp. 77-102). Newbury Park, CA: Sage.

Lerner, D. (1957). Communication systems and social systems. *Behavioral Science, 2,* 266-275.

McLeod, J. M., & Blumler, J. G. (1987). The macrosocial level of communication science. In C. R. Berger & S. H. Chaffee (Eds.), *Handbook of communication science* (pp. 271-322). Newbury Park, CA: Sage.

McLuhan, M. (1962). *The Gutenberg galaxy: The making of typographic man.* Toronto: University of Toronto Press.

Macridis, R. C. (1955). *The study of comparative government.* New York: Random House.

Nowak, S. (1989). Comparative studies and social theory. In M. L. Kohn (Ed.), *Cross-national research in sociology* (pp. 34-56). Newbury Park, CA: Sage.

Przeworski, A., & Teune, H. (1970). *The logic of comparative social inquiry.* New York: John Wiley.

Ragin, C. (1989). New directions in comparative research. In M. L. Kohn (Ed.), *Cross-national research in sociology* (pp. 57-76). Newbury Park, CA: Sage.

Rosenberg, M. (1968). *The logic of survey analysis.* New York: Basic Books.

Thoveron, G. (1983). How Europeans received the campaign: Similarities and differences of national response. In J. G. Blumler (Ed.), *Communicating to voters: Television in the first European parliamentary elections* (pp. 142-162). London: Sage.

Tichenor, P. J., Donohue, G. A., & Olien, C. N. (1980). *Community conflict and the press.* Beverly Hills, CA: Sage.

Chapter 2

MANAGING THEORETICAL DIVERSITY IN CROSS-NATIONAL STUDIES OF POLITICAL COMMUNICATION

David L. Swanson

> When you leave your own country behind, and take your army across neighboring territory, you find yourself on *critical ground*. . . . When you penetrate deeply into a country, it is *serious ground*. . . . When there is no place of refuge at all, it is *desperate ground*.
>
> —Sun Tzu, c. 500 B.C.

RESEARCHERS WHO HAVE INVADED foreign lands to conduct cross-national studies know something about desperate ground. Only rarely do modern comparativists report to Sun Tzu's favored weapons of maneuver, fire, and spies, but the perils they face are nonetheless daunting in their

AUTHOR'S NOTE: Portions of this chapter are based on: D. L. Swanson (1987, October), *The construction of political reality as a focus for comparative international study of presidential election campaigns,* paper presented at a meeting convened to consider conducting a comparative study of political communication in the 1988 French and U.S. presidential campaigns, Paris; D. L. Swanson (1988, May), *Dealing with theoretical diversity in collaborative, comparative studies of political communication,* paper presented at the meeting of the International Communication Association, New Orleans; D. L. Swanson (1989, May), *Theoretical diversity and metatheoretical coherence in comparative cross-national research,* paper presented at the meeting of the International Communication Association, San Francisco; and D. L. Swanson (1991), Theoretical dimensions of the U.S.-French presidential campaign studies, in L. L. Kaid, J. Gerstlé, & K. R. Sanders (Eds.), *Mediated politics in two cultures: Presidential campaigning in the United States and France* (pp. 9-23), New York: Praeger.

own way. One such peril concerns the risks of theoretical diversity that arise almost inevitably when, as is common in cross-national research, groups of scholars with dissimilar viewpoints and approaches come together to conduct a comparative study. This chapter considers why cross-national researchers are likely to encounter theoretical diversity, discusses some problems that may result, and describes some strategies for managing theoretical diversity that have proven to be successful.

The following discussion is written in terms of political communication research with occasional references to its near cousins that boast more established traditions of comparative scholarship, the fields of comparative politics and cross-national studies of mass communication. Comparative research in political communication, although still a cottage industry, has become something of a growth stock in recent years. The work of Sauerberg and Thomsen (1977); Blumler, Cayrol, and Thoveron (1978); Miller and Asp (1985); the 1979 European parliamentary elections study group (Blumler, 1983a); the Euromedia research group (see McQuail & Siune, 1986); and the 1988 U.S.-French presidential campaign study group (Kaid, Gerstlé, & Saunders, 1991), as examples, has pointed the way and created a favorable outlook for cross-national studies of political communication. Some of what is said in this chapter may apply to other domains of comparative research, but political communication provides a useful context in which to explore the subject and is the field in which I have encountered problems of theoretical diversity.

SOURCES OF THEORETICAL DIVERSITY: INTERNATIONAL RESEARCH TEAMS AND THE CASE FOR CROSS-NATIONAL STUDIES

The reasons why theoretical diversity may arise in cross-national studies of political communication are bound up with the arguments for undertaking such research in the first place (Gurevitch & Blumler, 1990, provide a comprehensive statement of the case). For the most part, these arguments are applications to political communication studies of general claims that have supported comparative studies in several different fields. So, for example, it is argued that comparative studies may allow us to begin to distinguish "cross-nationally generalizable communication patterns from country-specific ones" (Blumler & Thoveron, 1983, p. 9), expand our data base to provide more secure grounding for generalizations, counteract "naive universalism" and "unwitting parochialism" (Gurevitch & Blumler, 1990, pp. 308-309), and thereby encourage the development of sorely needed alternative, national-system-level conceptions of political communication.

The case for cross-national studies of political communication is perhaps strengthened by one of the clearest lessons from comparative politics: Comparative research is most vigorous and valuable when it responds to and, ultimately, aspires to influence in a constructive way the direction of change. The history of studies of comparative politics can be read as a succession of high-water marks and paradigm shifts that reflect in each period efforts to point the way to achieving prevailing conceptions of the virtuous state, from formal-legal comparative studies inspired by nineteenth-century European constitutionalism to the emergence of corporatist, dependency, and Marxist approaches mirroring the decline of superpower hegemony (Apter, 1963; Eckstein, 1963; Wiarda, 1985). Similarly, the brief history of international mass communication research reflects the energizing influence of a desire to shape change in, for example, the long run of the development paradigm and, lately, the debate about a new information order (Hur, 1982).

As described in the cases outlined above, the contributions that comparative studies of political communication can make seem to be attuned to certain recent developments on the international scene. As Gurevitch and Blumler (1990, pp. 310-312) have pointed out, the globalization of the mass media, coupled with the emergence of "American-style 'video politics' . . . as something of a role model for political communicators in other liberal democracies," raises important questions for comparative research, such as: What are the consequences of the diffusion of the so-called American model of political communication? The causes? Are there improvements or local adaptations that can be made? Alternatives that ought to be considered? The timeliness and importance of such questions are underscored by the dramatic turn to democracy in Eastern Europe and elsewhere. Thus the stage appears to be set for a surge in comparative studies of political communication.

In order to see where theoretical diversity enters the picture, it is helpful to notice one striking feature of the case for comparative research: For the most part, the subjects of cross-national studies of politics and political communication are deeply embedded in cultural and social contexts. The attempt to compare political communication in different countries is likely to involve study of such matters as national political cultures and subcultures, local systems of interpretation by which citizens decode political messages, political agendas that link societal concerns and cultural values in nationally distinctive ways, and the historically defined and culturally specific webs of interdependence that link a country's particular institutions of politics, government, and mass communication. As students of comparative politics have long realized, abstracting these subjects from their indigenous settings for purposes of comparison may distort the objects of study and lose valuable, even essential information (see Badie, 1989, esp. pp. 342-343; Sutton, 1963, p. 70).

Comparativists in fields including politics (e.g., Macridis, 1963) and mass communication (e.g., Gurevitch, 1989) appreciate the problem of cultural specificity and have sought to overcome it in various ways. One successful approach has employed international teams of researchers so that scholars from each country studied are involved in the research. In this way, the rich store of nation- and culture-specific knowledge thought to be essential to a proper understanding of the objects of study is represented on the research team to moderate the distorting effects of incomplete information and abstraction from unique cultural contexts. Several recent cross-national studies of political communication have used international research teams, including the 1979 European parliamentary elections study (Blumler, 1983a), the work of the Euromedia research group (McQuail & Siune, 1986), and the 1988 U.S.-French presidential campaign study (Kaid, Gerstlé, & Sanders, 1991).

When international teams are constituted, theoretical diversity almost inevitably comes into play. As Blumler and Thoveron (1983) explain with reference to the 1979 European parliamentary elections study:

> Large-scale intellectual collaboration cannot be theoretically pure or normatively singleminded. No common set of value standards . . . and no single "theory" of political communication could have steered this investigation. Fifteen scholars from nine countries, whose past work reflected diverse concerns, emphases and traditions, could not have reached agreement on such sources of guidance had they tried. (p. 12)

With nine countries represented, the European parliament group may be an extreme case, but it is not an unusual one with respect to theoretical diversity. Researchers from only two countries made up the team studying the 1988 presidential campaigns in the United States and France, but included in the group were rhetorical and narrative critics, social-scientific media effects researchers, semioticians, linguists, quantitative media content analysts, and others.

The opportunities they provide for assembling nationally and theoretically diverse research teams have been cited as a special strength of cross-cultural studies (e.g., Hur, 1982; Verba, 1985). Meadow (1985, p. 172) applauds comparative research for providing a venue for the kind of collaboration between scholars of different national, intellectual, and theoretical traditions that can enrich our thinking about political communication. International teams, the argument goes, can exploit their diversity by approaching the same problems using different methods and theories, thus providing a "fruitful clash of alternative approaches" (Verba, 1985, p. 35). In the present context, theoretically diverse research teams can be seen as representing synecdochically both the lack of a settled, dominant paradigm for comparative studies of political communication (Gurevitch & Blumler, 1990) and the anti-hegemonic spirit that is common among some comparativists working in several different fields at present.

Certainly, not every cross-national study of political communication uses an international team. Not every international research team includes scholars of differing theoretical orientations. And, a theoretically diverse research team can be constituted as easily from a single country as by assembling an international group. The point is that the use of international research teams is common in cross-national studies and reflects much about the rationale for and state of the art in comparative research. Some claim that, by definition, comparative research requires international teams, at least in the case of television news (Gurevitch, 1989, p. 228). Typically, when international research groups are assembled, theoretical diversity arises as a concern that must be addressed.

THE PROBLEM OF THEORETICAL DIVERSITY

The aims of comparative research cannot be accomplished by atheoretical empiricism. It is no longer controversial in communication research to believe that theoretical commitments, empirical observations, and scholarly explanations are intertwined and, to some extent, mutually determining. We encounter this familiar observation writ large as the "crisis of culture" (for a brief account, see Carey, 1988) and writ small in most contemporary views of social-scientific and critical scholarship. The import of the observation is to deny to us the belief that despite the differences in our general perspectives and specific theoretical commitments, we all study some single reality that is obdurate and necessarily given in the same way to all observers, or that what counts as observation, evidence, and explanation for some will enjoy the same status for all, or that incommensurable conceptual differences can be tamed or managed if we all attend closely to the transparent, univocal empirical world.

The study of political communication is both theory-laden and referential, that is, an attempt to understand events and processes that are real but are perceived in their details through lenses that, in part, reflect our theoretical views and associated ways of seeing. This feature of research is perhaps nowhere displayed more clearly than in cross-national studies. Comparative research necessarily abstracts institutions, events, and processes from their unique social and cultural contexts. Inescapably, it is theory that, explicitly or implicitly, supplies justification and guidance for the process of abstraction that precedes comparison. As political comparativist Roy Macridis (1963) points out, "prior to any comparison it is necessary not only to establish categories and concepts but also to determine criteria of relevance of the particular components of a social and political situation to the problem under analysis" as well as "criteria for the adequate representation of the particular components" (p. 49; see also Heckscher, 1963, p. 36). Moreover, theory also must be relied upon to justify and guide comparison, determining such matters as what can be compared with what, along what dimensions, for what purpose, and interpreted in what way to produce useful conclusions. Reliance on theory may be especially visible in fields such as political communication where it usually is thought necessary to forge links between individual-level and institutional-level data (Scheuch, 1989, esp. p. 162).

The key role of theory in comparative studies has prompted Heckscher (1963) to argue,

> We all hold a great number of theories and assumptions, on which we base our reasoning. . . . Particularly when they seem to us (but not necessarily to others) to be self-evident, they may not at all appear on the surface. This is always a danger, but it is particularly dangerous where we move in an international setting or else under circumstances where it can be suspected that basic differences exist among writers on the same or similar subjects. Consequently, a special effort is required to

make implicit assumptions and theories explicit if we are to avoid serious misunderstandings and complications. (pp. 35-36)

Given the prominence of theory in comparative research, collaborative cross-national studies involving researchers who hold different theoretical views invite theoretical incoherence. A cognitive psychologist interested in how political messages are processed by voters, a cultural-critical analyst interested in press coverage of a political campaign, a political scientist interested in political representation, and a semiotician interested in campaign advertising may set out to conduct a comparative study, but the most likely outcome of their efforts will be a cacophony of voices representing conflicting and, to some extent, incommensurable perspectives. The researchers will not be able to agree on a set of "bedrock empirical phenomena" to be observed, or even whether such phenomena exist, much less how the phenomena ought to analyzed and interpreted. Unless theoretical diversity is managed effectively, the contributions of individual researchers holding divergent views cannot be related to each other in a way that allows the final product to emerge as a coherent study.

Ultimately, the problem need not be seen as how to avoid theoretical diversity in cross-national research. The arguments noted above for the use of eclectic teams of researchers have strong appeal, and such teams almost inevitably will include scholars having different backgrounds, general perspectives, and particular theoretical and methodological views. Rather, the problem may be seen as how to manage successfully this inevitable diversity, perhaps even how to convert diversity into a resource that can enrich cross-national studies. The following section describes some ways of solving this problem that have been shown to be effective.

SOME STRATEGIES FOR
MANAGING THEORETICAL DIVERSITY

Of the various ways of coping with theoretical diversity in cross-national studies, three particular strategies receive attention here because they have been used with success in recent comparative studies of political communication and represent quite different approaches to the problem. The descriptions of the two strategies that capitalize on theoretical diversity rely, in each case, on a single exemplar. This reflects both the limited experience of a nascent research area and the need for economy in the present discussion. Despite efforts to the contrary, no doubt the analytical descriptions of the strategies are conflated to some extent with the details of the exemplars. As more studies using these strategies are conducted in the future, we will have a clearer picture of the essential ingredients and alternatives associated with each strategy. The distinctive advantages of the three strategies are contrasted briefly at the conclusion of this section.

THE AVOIDANCE STRATEGY

The first, and simplest, approach to theoretical diversity is to side-step the issue by employing a team of like-minded researchers, thereby ensuring the theoretical coherence and consistency of the result. Examples of this approach include Converse and Pierce's (1986) highly praised study of political representation in France, portions of which are based on comparative analysis, and Miller and Asp's (1985) more narrowly focused comparative study of political learning from the media in the United States and Sweden. The threats to coherence posed by theoretical diversity are avoided altogether when members of the research team share a common outlook, which is perhaps one reason why this approach has been used so frequently, especially in studies of comparative politics. In evaluating the approach, we might recall that a standard argument for comparative research holds that cross-national studies uniquely can enrich understanding by bringing together scholars representing diverse views and traditions. This advantage is given up in the first approach as the cost of theoretical consistency.

THE PRETHEORETICAL STRATEGY

A second approach to managing the risks of theoretical diversity is represented by the work of the group that studied political communication in the first European parliamentary elections (Blumler, 1983a). This comparative study was an ambitious, closely coordinated effort, one of our best exemplars of how cross-national studies can succeed using a theoretically and nationally eclectic research team. The design of the study was based on a general orientation to thinking about national political communication systems that was proposed by Blumler and Gurevitch in 1975: "How does the articulation of a country's mass media institutions to its political institutions affect the processing of political communication content and the impact of such content on the orientations to politics of audience members?" (p. 169).

Through conceptual analysis, a series of empirical research questions was derived from the study's structurally focused orientation to political communication systems. These questions included: What were the roles, activities, and interrelationships of party officials, journalists, and citizens? To what extent were party resources used to mount the campaigns? Did politicians and broadcasters treat the campaigns within conventional routines or in innovative ways that recognized the novel features of the first Europe-wide elections? What groups of voters became most involved in the elections, why, and what role did communication play in their involvement?

The researchers placed a premium on the requirements of direct comparative analysis in deciding what sort of data to collect and what kinds of analytical and interpretive methods to employ. In analyzing the content of television messages concerning the campaign, for example, these requirements were taken to mandate that a strictly quantitative approach be used. Hence, content analysis was confined to coding such unambiguous, objective matters as who was speaking, what themes were mentioned, and what countries were mentioned (Blumler, 1983b, pp. 33-34).

The parliamentary elections study group managed threats to theoretical coherence quite satisfactorily. The coherence and close coordination of the research, especially, have been praised (see Meadow, 1985). The keys to their approach, at least in the view of an outsider, were these: The design and execution of the study were based not on a formal theoretical view, with which some members of any diverse group of 15 researchers surely would disagree, but rather on a general orientation to the subject that was chosen for its "serviceability to this particular inquiry" (Blumler & Thoveron, 1983, p. 12). This orientation was conceived as pretheoretical and as providing a theory-neutral framework for defining, collecting, and analyzing data. It is important to recognize this aspect of the study's design. In order to produce analytical descriptions of the content of political messages, to take one example, researchers who have quite different theoretical views can be given a common coding system with which to represent objective features of message content, and the researchers may be expected to produce results that are directly comparable. Empirical findings, produced in each country by using "uniformly structured and worded instruments"

insofar as possible (Blumler, 1983b, p. 28), guided the subsequent development of theory as "an active element in the process of theory
building" (Blumler & Gurevitch, 1975, p. 166).

Based on the foregoing description, it appears that the second approach to managing theoretical diversity succeeds by suspending, for a
time, most of the theoretical issues that may divide researchers. This is
not to say that the design of the parliamentary elections study had no
theoretical basis. On the contrary, the structural view of political communication systems implied in the study's general orientation clearly is
a theoretical conception. That conception, however, was treated as sup-
plying not a substantive theory but rather a pretheoretical orientation to
guide decisions about the form, collection, and analysis of data. As
noted in the preceding section, such decisions are part of the essential
work of theory but, in this study, formal theory per se initially was set
aside to address empirical questions and brought into play later on to
make sense of what had been observed. In this way, theoretical diversity was bracketed until a set of results was on the table to be explained,
at which point the clash of differing views held by the researchers was
welcomed to mold creatively the development of a theoretical account
of the findings.

THE METATHEORETICAL STRATEGY

The 1988 U.S.-French presidential campaign study (Kaid, Gerstlé, &
Sanders, 1991) illustrates a third approach to managing theoretical diversity. The researchers conducting this study also represented a variety of theoretical views, and they, too, wished to exploit their diversity as a resource to enrich the investigation. In order to do so, they
endeavored to design their project around a broad metatheoretical
orientation to the 1988 campaign in the two countries that would accommodate their individual theoretical commitments, focus their attention on some key features of political communication in the campaigns,
and allow their individual efforts to be related to each other at a metalevel (for a detailed discussion of the theoretical dimensions of the
U.S.-French campaign project, see Swanson, 1991).

The general orientation of the U.S.-French campaign study was stated
in the familiar proposition that political communication in campaigns
constructs reality for voters. This proposition encapsulates many of the
claims the field has offered to describe the nature and consequences of

communication in election campaigns. The proposition is one of the most malleable concepts around, having been given an array of different interpretations by various theoretical traditions that have taken it up. And, the concept travels well, having led to significant programs of research in both Europe and the United States.

Conceptual analysis of the ways in which the general proposition has directed research (e.g., Adoni & Mane, 1984; McLeod & Chaffee, 1972) revealed that, at a metatheoretical level apart from any specific theoretical interpretation, the proposition implies three subjects for analysis and directs attention to the relationships between them: "objective" political reality (the actual events and conditions that are the referents of journalists' and politicians' representations in campaign messages); "constructed" political reality (the content of the representations offered by journalists and political leaders); and "subjective" political reality (citizens' perceptions of political reality, including political attitudes, beliefs, impressions of political leaders, and so on).

Most of the approaches that investigate the construction of political reality proceed by focusing on two of the three subjects for analysis implied in the general proposition. For instance, ideological critics focus on the relationship of objective political reality (e.g., the material conditions experienced by groups in society) to media-constructed political reality, while media effects researchers focus on the relationship of media-constructed political reality to the perceptions of reality held by media audiences. As illustrated by these examples, however, the one constant seems to be that constructed political reality always is the focus of analysis. The decision about which of the other two analytical terms will be paired with constructed political reality to create the architecture of any given study is dictated by the requirements of the particular research questions and theoretical approach used in the study.

The U.S.-French team agreed not to impose on their members any theoretical or methodological restrictions, nor to set aside at any point their individual theoretical views. Instead, the general orientation stated in the proposition concerning the construction of political reality was given the more specific formulation described above, in which a variety of theoretical approaches could be accommodated by different pairings of the three analytical terms implied in the proposition. The principal forms in which, through communication, political reality was constructed in the two campaigns were identified and assigned for study to particular researchers (e.g., U.S. political party platforms and French candidates' *professions de foi,* news coverage of the campaigns,

French official television broadcasts, televised debates between the candidates in both countries, U.S. political advertising and French posters and "clips"). The researchers were encouraged to use the theoretical concepts and methods for analyzing constructed political reality that seemed to them to be most valuable and appropriate to their respective subjects, and given latitude to focus on whichever pair of the three analytical terms implied in the general proposition was appropriate to their theoretical commitments and interests. The resultant group of studies was, predictably, quite diverse.

The metatheoretical orientation of the project was employed to relate the individual studies to each other in a way that illuminated some common themes having to do with the construction of political reality in the U.S. and French campaigns. One theme that emerged from the studies concerned how to explain why campaign communication in the two countries had the attributes that were found. Despite their theoretical differences, almost every study explained features of campaign messages by pointing to the self-interests of actors historically situated in roles and contexts defined within institutions of politics and mass communication that both cooperate and compete for dominance. That is, institutional interests and roles loomed large as explanations for how political reality is constructed in both countries.

"Constructed political reality" covers a multitude of discourses and forms of messages in a campaign. A second theme emerging in the U.S.-French studies concerned alternatives for defining the domain of discourse that is of greatest interest and identifying the essential features to be sought in analysis. Three alternatives were presented focusing, respectively, on how large bodies of campaign discourse are unified and become plausible and persuasive by means of an underlying structure of coherence (narrative and argumentative forms of coherence were stressed), on the topics of campaign discourse as agenda formations, and on campaign discourse as moments of strategic choicemaking that integrate the resources of multiple codes and languages to create meaning. Each alternative shed a different light on campaign discourse, and the array of alternatives that were presented yielded a fairly broad-based analysis of how campaign discourse constructs political reality for voters.

A final theme emerging from the various studies concerned viewpoints for evaluating the reality constructed in the two campaigns. Explicitly or tacitly, most authors invoked the traditional regulative ideal provided by liberal democratic pluralism. Two authors dissented, however, claiming that the traditional republican ethic of political communication is inappropriate and irrelevant to the contemporary scene. On this question, too, the clash of alternatives provided a broad frame of reference for thinking about policy implications of contemporary campaigning.

As illustrated by the U.S.-French campaign study, the metatheoretical strategy achieves a much looser sort of coherence than is produced by the pretheoretical strategy, reflecting the difference between treating the question of connections between elements within a study as a theoretical issue (in the pretheoretical strategy) and elevating the question of connections to the metalevel (in the metatheoretical strategy). Whereas the pretheoretical strategy tends to focus most attention on empirical findings, the metatheoretical approach necessarily highlights theoretical ideas as much as empirical observations. As exemplified in the theme described above concerning alternatives for analytically defining campaign discourse in the U.S.-French study, the metatheoretical strategy allows comparative evaluation of different theoretical approaches to the same subject. And, this strategy, too, can be useful in theory-building. As is suggested by the first theme described above concerning the influence of institutional roles and interests on the creation of political communication, generalizations that are supported by findings produced using multiple theoretical approaches are especially robust.

COMPARISON OF THE THREE STRATEGIES

Each strategy for managing theoretical diversity offers some distinct advantages that are well-suited to particular goals and circumstances that are found in comparative research. The pretheoretical and metatheoretical approaches have much in common and may be contrasted to the first approach described, which avoids both the risks and the benefits of theoretical diversity. The pretheoretical approach, illustrated by the European parliamentary elections study, and the metatheoretical approach, illustrated by the U.S.-French campaign study, both attempt to exploit theoretical diversity as a resource. Both approaches design broad-based comparative projects not on the basis of a formal theory but rather by invoking a general conceptual orientation to the subject of study. In each case, the general orientation concerned states—in the form of a research question—a descriptive proposition about political communication that can be accommodated in several different theoretical accounts (this may be a prerequisite to using theoretical diversity constructively). In the two exemplars that were described to illustrate these approaches, the general orientation did some of the work of theory in cross-national studies—defining the subject to be investigated, sketching the boundaries of the study, specifying some key concepts to be featured in explanations of findings, and so on.

The essential difference between the second and third approaches, of course, is found in whether the study's general orientation is treated as pretheoretical or metatheoretical. As judged by the exemplars, the pretheoretical alternative has the advantage of consistency and close coordination in data collection, which facilitates straightforward comparative analysis. In contrast, the metatheoretical alternative has the advantage of mining the resources of an array of appropriate theories in each phase of the study, including defining what will count as data and how data will be interpreted. Both approaches benefit from the clash of different theoretical views in formulating the ultimate conclusions of the research, but the pretheoretical approach stresses the results of the clash (i.e., the clash itself presumably occurs in the research team's private deliberations about how to interpret their findings and eventuates in the explanation that ultimately is offered to account for the data), while the metatheoretical approach gives more public voice to the various theoretical views by presenting individual studies based on each view.

In general, the first or "avoidance" strategy seems well-suited to research questions that are more narrowly drawn and closely intertwined with a particular theoretical formulation. The pretheoretical strategy offers perhaps greater opportunities for theory development than the first strategy, while retaining the latter's commitment to collecting data in forms that support straightforward comparative analysis. The individual contributions of contrasting theoretical approaches are featured in the metatheoretical strategy but, because of inconsistencies between theoretical approaches in collecting and dealing with data, comparison is easier within theoretical approaches than across theoretical approaches. The metatheoretical strategy partially compensates for the increased difficulties of comparative analysis by allowing evaluation of alternative theoretical approaches and by creating the possibility of formulating robust generalizations based on findings of multiple theoretical approaches.

CONCLUSION

There is good news and bad news in all of this. The bad news is that
theoretical diversity ought to be added to the list of potential difficulties that need to be managed in comparative studies, a list that is already long enough to lead Gurevitch (1989) to write with reference to
mass communication studies that "comparative research is arguably
plagued by more constraints and difficulties than most other research
areas" (p. 221). The good news is that theoretical diversity can be managed effectively and even turned into an asset that is uniquely appropriate to cross-national research. It is hoped that the good news will be
seen to outweigh the bad, and that future comparative studies of political communication will profit from the lessons offered by what we
may some day call the "first generation" of comparative studies of political communication.

REFERENCES

Adoni, H., & Mane, S. (1984). Media and the social construction of reality: Toward an
    integration of theory and research. *Communication Research, 11,* 323-340.
Apter, D. E. (1963). Past influences and future development. In H. Eckstein & D. E. Apter
    (Eds.), *Comparative politics: A reader* (pp. 725-740). New York: Free Press.
Badie, B. (1989). Comparative analysis in political science: Requiem or resurrection?
    Political Studies, 37, 340-351.
Blumler, J. G. (Ed.). (1983a). *Communicating to voters: Television and the first European
    parliamentary elections.* London: Sage.
Blumler, J. G. (1983b). Key features of research design. In J. G. Blumler (Ed.), *Com-
    municating to voters: Television in the first European parliamentary elections*
    (pp. 25-37). London: Sage.
Blumler, J. G., Cayrol, R., & Thoveron, G. (1978). *La television fait-elle l'election?*
    Paris: Presses de la Fondation Nationale des Sciences Politiques.
Blumler, J. G., & Gurevitch, M. (1975). Towards a comparative framework for political
    communication research. In S. H. Chaffee (Ed.), *Political communication: Issues
    and strategies for research* (pp. 165-193). Beverly Hills, CA: Sage.
Blumler, J. G., & Thoveron, G. (1983). Analysing a unique election: Themes and con-
    cepts. In J. G. Blumler (Ed.), *Communicating to voters: Television in the first Eu-
    ropean parliamentary elections* (pp. 3-24). London: Sage.
Carey, J. W. (1988). Editor's introduction: Taking culture seriously. In J. W. Carey (Ed.),
    Media, myths, and narratives: Television and the press (pp. 8-18). Newbury Park,
    CA: Sage.
Converse, P. E., & Pierce, R. (1986). *Political representation in France.* Cambridge, MA:
    Belknap Press of Harvard University Press.

Eckstein, H. (1963). A perspective on comparative politics, past and present. In H. Eckstein & D. E. Apter (Eds.), *Comparative politics: A reader* (pp. 3-32). New York: Free Press.

Gurevitch, M. (1989). Comparative research on television news. *American Behavioral Scientist, 33,* 221-229.

Gurevitch, M., & Blumler, J. G. (1990). Comparative research: The extending frontier. In D. L. Swanson & D. Nimmo (Eds.), *New directions in political communication* (pp. 305-325). Newbury Park, CA: Sage.

Heckscher, G. (1963). General methodological problems. In H. Eckstein & D. E. Apter (Eds.), *Comparative politics: A reader* (pp. 35-42). New York: Free Press.

Hur, K. K. (1982). International mass communication research: A critical review of theory and methods. In M. Burgoon (Ed.), *Communication yearbook 6* (pp. 531-554). Beverly Hills, CA: Sage.

Kaid, L. L., Gerstlé, J., & Sanders, K. R. (Eds.). (1991). *Mediated politics in two cultures: Presidential campaigning in the United States and France.* New York: Praeger.

Macridis, R. C. (1963). A survey of the field of comparative government. In H. Eckstein & D. E. Apter (Eds.), *Comparative politics: A reader* (pp. 43-52). New York: Free Press.

McLeod, J. M., & Chaffee, S. H. (1972). The construction of social reality. In J. Tedeschi (Ed.), *The social influence process* (pp. 50-99). Chicago: Aldine-Atherton.

McQuail, D., & Siune, K. (Eds.). (1986). *New media politics: Comparative perspectives in Western Europe.* London: Sage.

Meadow, R. G. (1985). Political communication research in the 1980s [Review essay]. *Journal of Communication, 35*(1), 157-173.

Miller, A. H., & Asp, K. (1985). Learning about politics from the media: A comparative study of Sweden and the United States. In S. Kraus & R. M. Perloff (Eds.), *Mass media and political thought: An information-processing approach* (pp. 241-266). Beverly Hills, CA: Sage.

Sauerberg, S., & Thomsen, N. (1977). The political role of mass communication in Scandinavia. In K. H. Cerny (Ed.), *Scandinavia at the polls: Recent political trends in Denmark, Norway, and Sweden* (pp. 181-216). Washington, DC: American Enterprise Institute.

Scheuch, E. K. (1989). Theoretical implications of comparative survey research: Why the well of cross-cultural methodology keeps on being reinvented. *International Sociology, 4,* 147-167.

Sutton, F. X. (1963). Social theory and comparative politics. In H. Eckstein & D. E. Apter (Eds.), *Comparative politics: A reader* (pp. 67-81). New York: Free Press.

Swanson, D. L. (1991). Theoretical dimensions of the U.S.-French presidential campaign studies. In L. L. Kaid, J. Gerstlé, & K. R. Sanders (Eds.), *Mediated politics in two cultures: Presidential campaigning in the United States and France* (pp. 9-23). New York: Praeger.

Verba, S. (1985). Comparative politics: Where have we been, where are we going? In H. J. Wiarda (Ed.), *New directions in comparative politics* (pp. 26-38). Boulder, CO: Westview.

Wiarda, H. J. (1985). Comparative politics past and present. In H. J. Wiarda (Ed.), *New directions in comparative politics* (pp. 3-25). Boulder, CO: Westview.

Chapter 3

COMPARISON, YES, BUT— THE CASE OF TECHNOLOGICAL AND CULTURAL CHANGE

James R. Beniger

TO LABEL RESEARCH in the social sciences as "comparative" is to invite misunderstanding. *All* social science research is comparative. After we designate researchers who compare across time (historians) and across space (geographers), researchers who compare communications content (content analysts), organizations (organizational sociologists), institutions (macrosociologists), countries (international relations specialists), cultures (ethnologists), and languages (linguists), and researchers who compare individuals in terms of gender, race, social class, age, education, and religion, what remains? What social scientist is not a comparativist?

Even research that produces individual case studies is implicitly comparative. When ethnographers document a particular culture, for example, they cannot help but address topics and questions raised by earlier ethnography of other cultures. Similarly, the form that case studies now take at business schools has developed through decades of trial and error in studies of other industries and sectors as well as other companies. Each business case study, like each ethnographic monograph, is implicitly a dialogue with many similar studies of often vastly different subjects. If such explicitly noncomparative research is inherently comparative, what research could be otherwise?

Even more insidious than the label "comparative" is the designation "comparative analysis," which obscures what ought to be obvious: All analysis is comparative. Comparison is inseparable from the meaning of *analysis,* which implies the separation of a subject into its component parts. How, then, could any analysis be other than comparative? Even statistical analysis, the explanation of variation in terms of its systematic relationship to other variation, is inherently comparative.

To say that part of variation in income results from variation in education, for example, is to compare statistically the variance among individuals (or regions, countries, or some other unit of analysis) of education and income. All statistical analysis thus involves two comparisons: (1) a comparison of statistical variances as measured most primitively by covariance and correlation and more elaborately by, for example, some form of the general linear model (analysis of variance or regression); and (2) a comparison of two or more substantive variables across some unit of analysis.

The word *comparative* is thus redundant in the social sciences and the term *comparative analysis* is doubly redundant. Those who use these terms do more than reveal their ignorance of social science and analysis more generally, however. Such terms obscure from students, the general public, and other uninitiated what ought to be widely known as an essential feature of social science—that we social scientists gain understanding of *all* phenomena by means of their comparison with other phenomena. To do social science is to understand each instance in terms of all others or, when that becomes a cognitive impossibility, in terms of as many others as possible.

DEEPER PROBLEMS

Were terms like *comparative analysis* merely redundant, this chapter could be mercifully brief, the equivalent of a reminder to use proper grammar. Unfortunately, talk of comparison in the social sciences often conceals another deficiency of thought creating problems that run much deeper: Those who see comparison as a special activity also tend to have set ideas about the special categories of things that social scientists ought to compare. This problem is most succinctly expressed in the injunction, often issued to students, that "one cannot compare apples and oranges." In fact, it is through just such comparison of disparate things that social science has made its greatest advances.

One notable example is that of *generalized symbolic media of exchange,* first described for money beginning with John Stuart Mill's *Principles of Political Economy* (1848) and culminating in John

Maynard Keynes's *Treatise on Money* (1930). Certainly money, as a generalized measure of cost and price, is one means by which apples *can* be compared to oranges. Combined with the idea of a *market*, established by Adam Smith's *Wealth of Nations* (1776), the generalized symbolic medium of money allowed virtually anything to be compared to anything else—and all things to be compared simultaneously.

As described for money by Mill (1848) and Keynes (1930), a generalized symbolic medium has three essential characteristics:

(1) it has no value in use but only in exchange;

(2) it can translate value or meaning by making otherwise heterogeneous things comparable in terms of itself; and

(3) it can serve as storage or memory to preserve value or meaning over time.

This idea has gained wide application in the social sciences, for example, in anthropology following field work among the Trobriand Islanders by Bronislaw Malinowski (1922), who found a Kula or "circular exchange" of necklaces and armshells that meets the criteria for generalized symbolic media (Beniger 1986, pp. 97-100).

Claude Lévi-Strauss (1949) extended this reasoning to kinship, which he argued—against Frazer (1918)—is not economic but rather generalized symbolic or *ritual* exchange. Because necklaces and armshells have no economic value, they must be exchanged out of *social scarcity,* which differs from economic scarcity in that it is purely *symbolic* (Lévi-Strauss, 1949, pp. 32-35), that is, created by diminishing the value of one's own outputs relative to the economically equivalent outputs of others. A birthday gift we buy for ourself, for example, simply *means* less than the same item given to us by a friend. Similarly, Lévi-Strauss argued, it is not economic, but social scarcity—an artifact of rules concerning exogamy and incest—that governs kinship and the supply of possible spouses.

Were this not enough to illustrate that social science has made considerable advances through the systematic comparison of disparate things, sociologist Talcott Parsons has further found that "social systems and other systems of action" are controlled by "generalized symbolic media of interchange," which include not only money but language, political power, influence, value-commitments, and intelligence (Parsons, 1969, 1975). To this list George Homans (1961, p. 385) had already added the generalized exchange medium of "social approval." Whether we accept these arguments or not, the idea of generalized symbolic media of exchange has clearly come a long way in the two centuries since Smith and Mill wrote of markets and money—apples and oranges notwithstanding.

PRECLUDING MODELING

Were it not bad enough that many who use terms like *comparative analysis* harbor rigid ideas about what categories of things social scientists ought to compare, this particular mind-set also tends to impede research. This can be seen, for example, in the widespread opposition to meta-analysis on the grounds that it depends on unwarranted comparisons (the possibility notwithstanding that other objections to the method may have merit). As Mann (1990, p. 478) reports on meta-analysis,

> One reason for the lag in adopting the method is that it is deeply ingrained in all who use statistics that you can't compare apples and oranges—that data from different studies cannot be pooled. "There must be more than a dozen studies of the effects of TV on children," says Richard Light, a statistician at the Harvard Graduate School of Education and the Kennedy School of Government, who with David B. Pillemer, a psychologist at Wellesley College, wrote a well-regarded introduction to the field of meta-analysis. "Each one was done with a different protocol, with different sets of kids, and with different definitions. You simply can't throw all of them together." Meta-analysis, its proponents explain, does not throw together experiments. Rather, it groups many individual studies and uses them, collectively, to compare what has been observed with the null hypotheses.

Elaboration of criteria for "comparative analysis" also tends to preclude the building of comparisons into theoretical models. Almost always the term *comparative* serves to describe the relatively narrow empirical study of categories of things: media systems, nations, historical periods. Rarely is the term applied to a theoretical enterprise. Despite the universality of comparison in research, the social sciences tend to confine conscious and purposive comparison to atheoretical ghettos like the analysis of cross-polity time series or the Human Relations Area Files. On the few occasions when comparison has broken free of rigid categories (of comparing apples with apples), however, theoretical advances have been significant.

In the case of generalized symbolic media of exchange, for example, early contributions by François Quesnay (1758) and Leon Walras

(1874) served to ground the economic theory of Smith (1776) and Mill (1848) in a cybernetic model of material flows with feedback flows of money qua information. The material economy constitutes a self-regulating processing system from this perspective, elaborated by Colin Clark in his *Conditions of Economic Progress* (1940) and in the input-output analysis of Wassily Leontief (1941). In this flow model, the material economy sustains itself by extracting matter and energy from the environment, processing them through ever higher sectors like manufacturing (secondary) and services (tertiary), and distributing the resulting value-added products to final demand.

As we might expect, considering the widespread application of the idea of generalized media of exchange, material flow models can be found throughout the social and behavioral sciences. Energy flows have provided the foundation for ecology since the late 1920s (Elton, 1927; Tansley, 1935; Transeau, 1926). Demography has often been characterized (e.g., by Stinchcombe, 1968) as an accounting system for flows of people through various life stages, including societal inputs (birth, immigration), biological changes (menarche, menopause), social changes (marriage, divorce), and outputs (emigration, death). One behavioral scientist (Miller, 1978, p. 1027) has attributed the processing and flow model to "living systems" more generally: "They are open systems with significant inputs, throughputs, and outputs of various sorts of matter-energy and information. Processing these is all they do—a deceptively simple fact not widely recognized by the scientists who study them."

Unlike living systems, however, *social* systems are made up of relatively autonomous components—individuals, families, groups, organizations—that can act for different reasons and even at cross-purposes. Because system processes must depend on exchanges among such autonomous components, however, their coordination and control will demand that information processing and communication account for a relatively greater proportion of matter and energy flows than they do in single organisms (the actual proportion will depend on such factors as population size and spatial dispersion, complexity of organization, and volume and speed of processing). This suggests that the proper subject matter of the social and behavioral sciences ought to be *information* or, more specifically, its generation, storage, processing, and communication to effect control.

This vision of social science has been expressed in a variety of disciplines over the past half-century. Norbert Wiener (1950, p. 9) has argued that "society can only be understood through a study of the messages and the communication facilities which belong to it." Zoologist E. O. Wilson, after surveying the thousands of social species from colonial jellyfish and corals to the primates, including *Homo sapiens,* declared "reciprocal communication of a cooperative nature" to be what he called the "diagnostic criterion" of society as most generally defined (Wilson, 1975, p. 595). In the summary of sociologist Niklas Luhmann (1984, pp. 1-2): "The system of society consists of communications. There are no other elements, no further substance but communications."

It is unfortunate that such sweeping (and inherently comparative) models of process and flow, like the highly integrative idea of generalized media on which they depend, do not ordinarily attract social scientists drawn to "comparative analysis." Even more unfortunate, the categories and activities designated by this term effectively preclude the building of comparisons into any complex theoretical models. The more researchers are attracted to "comparative analysis," in its usual sense of the narrow empirical study of categories of things, the less likely is general and interdisciplinary theory to advance.

EMBRACING FUNCTION

Once research and analysis are both seen to be inherently comparative, and comparison is accepted as ubiquitous in the social sciences, these disciplines will have every incentive to adopt methods that facilitate comparisons of the widest possible scope. One obvious example is *comparison by function,* not to be confused with the widely discredited "functional theory" or "functionalism" (Davis, 1967; Merton, 1968).

The major objection to functional or "in order to" explanations is teleological—that their effects precede rather than follow their causes (Nagel, 1961, chap. 12; L. Wright, 1976). Teleology may be untenable in physics and inorganic chemistry, but not for systems that change through directed selection, whether the "natural" selection of living systems or the purposive selection of human beings. As biochemist Albert Lehninger (1975, p. 3) expresses the distinction: "In living organisms it is quite legitimate to ask what the function of a given molecule is. However, to ask such questions about molecules in collections of inanimate matter is irrelevant and meaningless."

A noteworthy example of comparison by function is the work of Charles Darwin. In 1872, 13 years after he wrote *On the Origin of*

Species, Darwin published *The Expression of the Emotions in Man and Animals,* a book that anticipated ethology by showing how signals evolve from behavior serving other functions and might be interpreted in motivational (teleological) terms. Ignorant of the 1866 paper (rediscovered in 1900) by Gregor Mendel, who himself knew nothing of genetics, Darwin blithely assumed—by functional comparison—that physiological and behavioral features might compete in evolution. Sexual advertisement affects a male's chances of being picked as a breeding partner; for example, bright coloration (physical) and courtship display (behavioral) compete in males of many bird and fish species even though both features appear maladaptive: The former increases conspicuousness to predators, the latter takes time and energy away from other essential activities.

Darwin's ideas preceded by more than a half-century biology's so-called Modern Synthesis: the work of Alfred Lotka, Vito Volterra, and other mathematical ecologists and geneticists culminating in Ronald Fisher's *Genetical Theory of Natural Selection* (1930), Sewall Wright's "Evolution in Mendelian Populations" (1931), and J. B. S. Haldane's *Causes of Evolution* (1932). Darwin's ideas preceded by nearly a century the first postulation of DNA structure by James Watson and Francis Crick (1953). Not until a century after *On the Origin of Species* did biologists begin to establish the genetic basis for specific behavior. The behavior of "hygienic" bees who fight disease by locating infected larva, pulling them from their cells, and pushing them out of the hive, for example, was shown in breeding experiments by W. C. Rothenbuhler (1964) to result from two genes: one for uncapping diseased cells, the other for removing diseased grubs.

Had Darwin known genetic theory but not about findings that behavior can be genetically determined, he might have hesitated to postulate the inheritance of behavioral features like courtship display for lack of any obvious means of transmission. Guided by comparison of function in evolution, however, Darwin could conclude—without consideration of genetic transmission—that animal characteristics like bright coloration and courtship display might play functionally equivalent roles in sexual advertisement and hence in the chances of a male bird or fish being picked as a breeding partner. Thus did such functional comparison lead Darwin to the then startling conclusion that physiology and behavior—apples and oranges—might be like things, equivalent in some functions, and that they might even compete in evolution.

INFORMATION TECHNOLOGY

Perhaps nowhere in the social sciences has comparison by function shown more impressive gains than in the study of information technology and technological change, thanks largely to Max Weber's development of the concept he called *rationalization*. Although the term has a variety of meanings, both in Weber's writings and in the elaborations of his work by others, there is an important sense in which rationalization might be seen as the universal information technology as well as the engine of technological change.

Technology has also been defined in a variety of ways, but certainly it involves purposive artifact as the means by which some desired end might be achieved. Thus *technology*, in a general sense applicable also to nonhuman species, is simply *that which can be done*, excluding only those capabilities that occur naturally in living systems. Achieving ends in turn demands the control of means, and control—as established by cybernetics (Wiener, 1948)—depends on information processing and communication. Although some technological innovations increase capabilities to detect, process, and move information, rationalization increases control of means by decreasing the amount of information to be processed.

The former approach to control of means (information technology), namely *information processing*, was realized in Weber's day mainly through bureaucratization, a subject for which he remains a leading theorist. Weber was first to establish—most notably in his *Economy and Society* (1922)—that bureaucracy is in essence a control technology. He included among the defining characteristics of bureaucracy several important aspects of any control system: impersonal orientation of structure to the information that it processes, guided by a predetermined, formal set of rules governing all decisions and responses. Today computerization, based on these same principles, continues to supplant bureaucratization as the primary technology by which means are controlled directly through increased capability to process information.

The other approach to control of means (information technology), achieved by decreasing the amount of information to be processed, was realized in Weber's day through more traditional forms of rationalization: division of labor, specialization, formalization, planning, quantification, standardization, routinization. Most general and pervasive was the increasing regulation of interpersonal relationships by means of a formal set of impersonal and objective criteria. Claude Henri Comte de Saint-Simon, a technocrat during the early stages of modern bureaucratization, saw such rationalization as a move "from the government of men to the administration of things" (Taylor, 1975, part 3). The reason why people can be governed more easily qua things, of course, is that the amount of information about them that needs to be processed is thereby greatly reduced, and hence the degree of control—for any constant capacity to process information—is greatly enhanced.

More recent examples of such rationalization include just-in-time manufacturing, uniform product codes and automatic inventory control, containerized transportation, credit cards and systems for the automatic transfer of funds, centralized credit ratings, standardized testing and grading of students, and the automation of direct home marketing via mail, telephone, and cable television. Increasing control merely by decreasing the amount of information to be processed, what computer scientists now call *preprocessing,* continues to supplant information processors like bureaucracy and computers as the primary technology for the control of means (information technology). Although computing and related information-processing technologies have attracted almost all of the attention from scholars, media pundits, and the public, advances in preprocessing—the complement of control through processing—have accounted for far greater gains.

Social scientists drawn to the "comparative analysis" of information technologies have noticed the computer but have almost universally missed the three key functional comparisons: (1) the relationships among computers, bureaucracy, and the human brain as the three major means of information processing available to modern societies; (2) the resulting interactions among human skilling and intellectualization, bureaucratization, and computerization as agents of social and cultural change; and (3) the trade-offs between information processing and preprocessing as complements and alternatives to the control of means—the essence of information technology. Such topics are only obscured by narrow empirical studies of the computer and a few other members (apples and apples) of the category of obvious information hardware technologies, whether the printing press (versus desk-top publishing), film (in animation), the telephone (in telecommunications), or journals and books (for the dissemination of scientific information).

COMMUNICATIONS RESEARCH

That understanding of information technology has been impeded by "comparative analysis" in its usual sense of narrow empirical study of categories of things can be seen in the recent history of the academic field of communications in the United States—especially in the contributions of the late Wilbur Schramm. Although not primarily a student of technology himself, Schramm published several simple chronologies of innovations in communications hardware—printing press, camera, telegraph, telephone, radio, television—during the field's early and formative years of the late 1940s to early 1960s. Because of Schramm's stature as a pioneer of the field, his chronologies were widely imitated and elaborated by a host of other American academics.

The major impact of the diffusion of Schramm's ideas was to deflect research on information technology from pioneering historical and comparative theories like those of Harold Innis, Marshall McLuhan, and the Frankfurt Institute of Social Research during its years of exile in the United States (Czitrom, 1982). Under Schramm's influence, the study of information technology in the field of communications increasingly focused on simple and often facile comparisons of the most obvious technological innovations as reflected, for example, in periodizations of history into "eras" like those of writing, printing, telecommunications, and interactive communication (a common practice in recent textbooks).

Evidence of communications current obsession with relatively few of the most obvious (though not necessarily most important) hardware technologies, to the virtual exclusion of subtler and nonhardware forms of rationalization, can be seen in the *International Encyclopedia of Communications* (Barnouw, 1989), the field's first multiple-volume reference work covering all major subfields. Of the 30 "major fields of interest" under which the *Encyclopedia* groups its 569 articles (Barnouw, 1989, vol. 4, pp. 361-368), 6 fields (20%) represent major hardware technologies: computers, motion pictures, photography, print media, radio, and television. A 7th category, "Media," embraces 33 articles (including 12 designated as "comprehensive" or "important"). Of these 33 articles, 13 (39.4%)—including 9 of those designated as important (75%)—represent major hardware technologies: cable television, computers (2), motion pictures, photography, printing, radio, telegraphy, telephone, television (2), video, and videotex.

Such preoccupation with media stems from communication's attempts to elevate engineer Claude Shannon's "Mathematical Theory of Communication" (1948) into a full-blown model of human communication during the field's struggle to gain academic acceptance in the early 1950s. From the outset, Shannon denied that his work had anything to do with human communication; he continues to shun academics in that field. Wilbur Schramm, however, who had just established the Institute for Communication Research at the University of Illinois when Shannon's paper appeared, took the initiative—as editor of the University of Illinois Press—to reprint Shannon's paper (with an introductory essay by Warren Weaver) as a small book (Dahling, 1962). Schramm also promoted his own version of Shannon's work in an early article on its implications for research on mass communication (Schramm, 1955).

The index of the *International Encyclopedia of Communications* lists 30 topics under "Technology" that supposedly cover all of communication's interests in technology theory (e.g., Marxist theories), theorists (Innis, McLuhan), and technology's role in communications subfields (development, political), particular places (Africa, Hollywood), and topical issues (copyright, library trends, media ethics, New International Information Order). Of these topics, 16 (53.3%) represent major hardware technologies: computers, fiber optics, graphic reproduction, interactive media, mass media, microelectronics, photography, printing, satellites, sound recording, telecommunications, telegraphy, telephone, television, video, and videotex (Barnouw, 1989, vol. 4, p. 446). If the 465 authorities who contributed to the *Encyclopedia* are any guide, in the field of communications, *technology* means primarily nine historically dramatic innovations in hardware: especially printing, photography, television, and computers, but also telegraphy, telephony, motion pictures, radio, and video.

So pervasive has this view of technology—as a small number of discrete and highly visible hardware innovations—become in communications that many in the field who read the previous three paragraphs may wonder why anyone would belabor something so obvious. Why indeed? To expose this particular view of information technology as not only not the only one possible, nor even the most obvious one, but one that does preclude the building of more complex theoretical models of technology and social and cultural change. In so doing, it also effectively abandons the pioneering ideas of Weber, Innis, McLuhan, and the Frankfurt School—among the field's more insightful and suggestive historical and comparative theories of information and communication technology.

TOWARD WIDER COMPARISON

To illustrate the potential for much wider comparisons of technologies than those that currently typify research in the field of communications, consider the work of Harold Innis. In the only 212 pages of his *Bias of Communication* (1951), perhaps his most important book on information technology and social and cultural change, Innis managed to treat the following technologies (among many others): Arabic numerals, artillery, bards, bronze, brushes, cathedrals, cavalry, chariots, coffee houses, contracts, daylight savings time, department stores, finance, gunpowder, holidays, the horse, infantry, iron, irrigation, kingship, knots, linen, marriage, medicine, minstrels, money, mummification, newsprint, planning, postal rates, prices, pyramids, rags, roads, stone, sundials, tariffs, taxes, temples, and concepts of time.

Of these topics, almost all of which Innis discussed under a comparative framework for the understanding of information and communication technologies, not one is listed in the 87-page index of the 1,800-page *International Encyclopedia of Communications*. Nor are the technologies drawn from any preexisting or obvious conceptual set. Clearly Innis did not adhere to "comparative analysis" in the usual narrow sense—he did not shrink from comparing apples and oranges to many other fruits and to much that was anything but fruit.

Similar potential for much wider comparisons of technologies can be found in the work of Marshall McLuhan, who owed much to the example set by Innis. In Part II of his *Understanding Media* (1964), for example, McLuhan devoted all or a large part of each of his 26 chapters to one of the following media: speaking and writing, roads and paper routes, numbers, clothing ("our extended skin"), housing, money, clocks, prints, comics, printing, the wheel, bicycle and airplane, photography, the press, automobiles, advertising, games ("extensions of man"), telegraphy, typewriters, telephony, the phonograph, movies, radio, television, weaponry, and automation.

This list includes seven of the nine historically dramatic innovations in hardware (printing, photography, telegraphy, telephony, motion pictures, radio, and television) identified above with the field of communications (writing in the early 1960s, McLuhan missed computers and video). The list also contains 22 less obvious information and communications technologies, including 7 (the bicycle, housing, money, paper routes, prints, roads, and the wheel) not indexed in the *International Encyclopedia of Communications*. Like Innis, McLuhan did not adhere to "comparative analysis" in the usual narrow sense.

A more recent example of comparison of technologies in a wider sense than that now usually found in communications is my own *The Control Revolution* (1986) and my continuing work on rationalization as a component of social and cultural change. Identifying the growth of modern information societies with the demand for technologies to control the increased speed and volume of material processing systems following industrialization, I find the most important information and communication technologies during the crucial period (the "Control Revolution" of the 1840s to 1930s) to include not only telegraph, power printing, telephone, and broadcasting, but a host of others.

Of these technologies, major nonhardware innovations include (among many others): large-scale formal organization, packaging, standardization, and commodity exchanges (1840s), postage stamps and formal line-and-staff control (1850s), paper money, fixed prices, and traveling salesmen (1860s), trademark law, mail-order, and streamlined factory design (1870s), uniform standard time (1880s), travelers' checks (1890s), market research, scientific management, franchising, and self-service (1910s), decentralized corporate organization (1920s), and quality control and survey research (1930s). The concepts of rationalization and control, combined with an appropriately inclusive definition of technology, have obviously led me far from "comparative analysis" in the usual narrow sense.

SUMMARY

The word *comparative* is redundant in the social sciences and the term *comparative analysis* is doubly redundant. All social science research is comparative and so too is all analysis. Those who do see comparison as a special activity tend to harbor preconceptions about what categories of things social scientists ought to compare, a mind-set that greatly impedes research. Elaboration of criteria for "comparative analysis" also tends to preclude the building of comparisons into theoretical models. On the few occasions when comparison has broken free of rigid categories, theoretical advances have been significant.

Once research and analysis are both seen to be inherently comparative, and comparison is accepted as ubiquitous in the social sciences, the field of communications will have every incentive to adopt methods that facilitate comparison in the widest possible sense. Perhaps nowhere is this more true than in the study of information and communication technology and technological change. Comparisons by function, for example, particularly those guided by the complementary concepts of rationalization and control, afford students of information and communications technology one means to break free of "comparative analysis" in the usual narrow sense. However this might be accomplished, though, it will be necessary before modern communications research can regain the promising paths blazed by Weber, Innis, McLuhan, and the Frankfurt School, among other pioneers of truly comparative theory and research on information and communication technology and its impact on culture and society.

REFERENCES

Barnouw, E. (Ed.). (1989). *International encyclopedia of communications.* New York: Oxford University Press.

Beniger, J. R. (1986). *The control revolution: Technological and economic origins of the information society.* Cambridge, MA: Harvard University Press.

Clark, C. (1940). *The conditions of economic progress.* London: Macmillan.

Czitrom, D. J. (1982). *Media and the American mind: From Morse to McLuhan.* Chapel Hill: University of North Carolina Press.

Dahling, R. L. (1962). Shannon's information theory: The spread of an idea. In W. Schramm (Ed.), *Studies of innovation and of communication to the public* (pp. 117-140). Stanford, CA: Stanford University, Institute for Communication Research.

Darwin, C. R. (1859). *On the origin of species.* London: John Murray.

Darwin, C. R. (1872). *The expression of the emotions in man and animals.* London: John Murray.

Davis, K. (1967). The myth of functional analysis as a special method in sociology and anthropology. In N. J. Demerath & R. A. Peterson (Eds.), *System, change, and conflict: A reader on contemporary sociological theory and the debate over functionalism* (pp. 757-772). New York: Free Press.

Elton, C. S. (1927). *Animal ecology.* New York: Macmillan.

Fisher, R. A. (1930). *The genetical theory of natural selection.* Oxford: Oxford University Press.

Frazer, J. G. (1918). *Folk-lore in the Old Testament: Studies in comparative religion, legend and law, Vol. 2.* New York: Macmillan.

Haldane, J.B.S. (1932). *The causes of evolution.* Ithaca, NY: Cornell University Press.

Homans, G. C. (1961). *Social behavior: Its elementary forms.* New York: Harcourt, Brace, & World.

Innis, H. A. (1951). *The bias of communication.* Toronto: University of Toronto Press.

Keynes, J. M. (1930). *A treatise on money: The pure theory of money.* New York: Harcourt, Brace.

Lehninger, A. L. (1975). *Biochemistry: The molecular basis of cell structure and function.* New York: Worth.

Leontief, W. W. (1941). *The structure of the American economy, 1919-1929: An empirical application of equilibrium analysis.* Cambridge, MA: Harvard University Press.

Lévi-Strauss, C. (1949). *The elementary structures of kinship.* Boston: Beacon.

Luhmann, N. (1984). *Modes of communication and society.* Bielefeld, FRG: Fakultät für Soziologie, Universität Bielefeld.

Malinowski, B. (1922). *Argonauts of the Western Pacific: An account of native enterprise and adventure in the archipelagoes of Melanesian New Guinea.* New York: Dutton.

Mann, C. (1990). Meta-analysis in the breech. *Science, 249,* 476-480.

McLuhan, M. (1964). *Understanding media: The extensions of man.* New York: McGraw-Hill.

Merton, R. K. (1968). *Social theory and social structure.* New York: Free Press.

Mill, J. S. (1848). *Principles of political economy, with some of their applications to social philosophy.* Boston: Little, Brown.

Miller, J. G. (1978). *Living systems.* New York: McGraw-Hill.

Nagel, E. (1961). *The structure of science: Problems in the logic of scientific explanation.* New York: Harcourt, Brace, & World.

Parsons, T. (1969). *Politics and social structure.* New York: Free Press.

Parsons, T. (1975). Social structure and the symbolic media of interchange. In P. M. Blau (Ed.), *Approaches to the study of social structure.* New York: Free Press.

Quesnay, F. (1758). *Tableau oeconomique.* Ann Arbor, MI: University Microfilms International.

Rothenbuhler, W. C. (1964). Behavior genetics of nest cleaning in honey bees. IV: Responses of F1 and backcross generations to disease-killed brood. *American Zoologist, 4,* 111-123.

Schramm, W. (1955). Information theory and new communication. *Journalism Quarterly, 32,* 131-146.

Shannon, C. (1948). A mathematical theory of communication. *Bell System Technical Journal, 27,* 379-423 & 623-656.

Smith, A. (1776). *An inquiry into the nature and causes of the wealth of nations.* Chicago: University of Chicago Press.

Stinchcombe, A. L. (1968). *Constructing social theories.* New York: Harcourt Brace Jovanovich.

Tansley, A. G. (1935). The use and abuse of vegetational concepts and terms. *Ecology, 16,* 284-307.

Taylor, K. (Ed.). (1975). *Henri Saint-Simon (1760-1825): Selected writings on science, industry, and social organization.* New York: Holmes & Meier.

Transeau, E. N. (1926). The accumulation of energy by plants. *Ohio Journal of Science, 26,* 1-10.

Walras, L. (1874). *Elements of pure economics.* London: Allen & Unwin.

Watson, J. D., & Crick, F.H.C. (1953). Molecular structure of nucleic acids: A structure for deoxyribose nucleic acid. *Nature, 171,* 737-738.

Weber, M. (1922). *Economy and society: An outline of interpretive sociology.* New York: Bedminster.

Wiener, N. (1948). *Cybernetics: Control and communication in the animal and the machine.* Cambridge: MIT Press.

Wiener, N. (1950). *The human use of human beings: Cybernetics and society.* Boston: Houghton Mifflin.

Wilson, E. O. (1975). *Sociobiology: The new synthesis.* Cambridge, MA: Harvard University Press.

Wright, L. (1976). *Teleological explanations: An etiological analysis of goals and functions.* Berkeley: University of California Press.

Wright, S. (1931). Evolution in Mendelian populations. *Genetics, 16,* 97-158.

PART II

EXEMPLARS

Chapter 4

APPLYING A COMPARATIVE APPROACH
TO EXPECTANCY VIOLATIONS THEORY

Judee K. Burgoon

EDWARD HALL, the well-known anthropologist, was traveling in Japan when he experienced an incident that mystified him. He returned to his hotel room in Tokyo one day, picked up his key, and opened his door only to find his room filled with another person's possessions. At first he was mortified, thinking he had entered someone else's room by mistake. But when he checked at the front desk, he was told that the room was reserved by someone else and that he had been moved. When he went to the new room he found all his possessions laid out just as he had arranged them previously. Although pleased to find his possessions so carefully restored to their same locations, Hall was at first disturbed by what he considered disrespectful treatment. He writes, "the whole matter of being moved like a piece of derelict luggage puzzled me. In the United States, the person who gets moved is often the lowest-ranking individual" and "to move someone without telling him is almost worse than an insult" (Hall, 1981, p. 61). What Hall only learned later was that he had been introduced to a core concept in Japanese culture: *belonging*. As a Japanese friend explained, "As soon as you register at the desk, you are no longer an outsider; instead, for the duration of your stay you are a member of a large, mobile family. *You belong*" (p. 65). The fact that Hall was being moved about was tangible evidence that he was being accorded the much prized status of a family member, rather than that of an outsider.

This story is one of countless illustrations of how cultures differ in their nonverbal practices and how misinterpretations can arise when cultures collide. Yousef (1976) presents several examples of where members of one culture consider those of another "funny" or peculiar because the other culture's behavior is at odds with their own. In fact, such anecdotes are the staple of lectures on intercultural nonverbal communication. What these anecdotes have in common is that most of them can be cast as violations of expectations.

This concept of expectancy violations is one that has intrigued me for almost two decades. My purpose here is to sketch the theoretical model that several colleagues, graduate students, and I have been developing over the years (see, e.g., Burgoon, 1978, 1983, 1986; Burgoon & Aho, 1982; Burgoon, Coker, & Coker, 1986; Burgoon & Hale, 1988; Burgoon & Jones, 1976; Burgoon, Stacks, & Burch, 1982; Burgoon, Stacks, & Woodall, 1979; Hale & Burgoon, 1984), and to consider some of its cross-cultural applications and implications.

All interpersonal exchanges can be placed along a continuum of participant homogeneity-heterogeneity (Sarbaugh, 1979). Intercultural exchanges fall toward the heterogeneous end. The differences in world views, values, and normative behavior patterns across cultures, coupled with people's relative ignorance about such differences, greatly increase the likelihood that heterocultural exchanges will entail violations of expectations. Thus the theoretical model I am about to describe should have great applicability in predicting and explaining the nature and consequences of *inter*cultural exchanges. Consider, for example, the Mexican-American émigré to the United States who, shortly after his arrival, barged up to a sales counter and barked out his request without regard for the other customers who were already standing there. Because that is how things were done in the polychronic culture from which he came, he did not realize that he had violated the "waiting your turn" rule of U.S. culture. Consequently, he was puzzled by the irritated mumblings and glares that greeted him from fellow shoppers. The German businessman traveling to the Middle East likewise will not understand why he is distrusted by his Iraqi business associate when he stands several feet away and averts his breath during conversation. What is a comfortable level of sensory involvement for the German engenders in his Iraqi host the suspicion that the German is "withholding something." The intercultural literature is rife with such illustrations that can be recast as one culture's normative behavior being a deviation from, or violation of, normative expectations within another culture.

Although expectancy violations theory would be quite apropos to explain the reactions to these encounters, a bigger challenge is determining whether the model explains *intracultural* communication within divergent cultures. Given that the empirical support for the model has been derived primarily from mainstream North American, white Anglo-Saxon society, a critical question to be asked is whether the key premises of the model are pancultural or culture-specific. Addressing this question is the focus of the remainder of the chapter. To address it, I will review the central assumptions and propositions of the theory and highlight those that I suspect are universal. Because I believe the basic tenets of the theory ultimately should hold within Afro-centered and Asian-centered as well as Euro-centered societies, I will speculate about some of the assumptions and claims that would need verification before concluding that the theory indeed "works" to explain interpersonal exchanges within disparate cultures.

As I outline some of the primary assumptions and propositions of the theory, it should be noted that the original theory arose out of an attempt to explain proxemic behavior and communication and has routinely been labeled "nonverbal expectancy violations theory." However, the theory has since been expanded to encompass a wide range of nonverbal and verbal behaviors (see, e.g., Booth-Butterfield, 1990; Buller & Burgoon, 1986; Burgoon & Aho, 1982; Burgoon, Coker, & Coker, 1986; Burgoon, Manusov, Mineo, & Hale, 1985; Burgoon, Newton, Walther, & Baesler, 1989; Burgoon & Walther, 1990; Burgoon, Walther, & Baesler, 1990; Lobdell, 1990; White, 1989), hence the change in name to expectancy violations theory. I further anticipate that the theory can account for an even broader array of phenomena than have currently been investigated. Nevertheless, most of the empirical work to date has centered on what are called nonverbal immediacy behaviors—those behaviors such as conversational distance, gaze, touch, body orientation, and lean that affect the degree of sensory involvement of participants and that signal approach or avoidance. Many of the examples to be discussed will therefore feature such behaviors.

ASSUMPTIONS

The propositional framework of the theory is predicated on several key assumptions about the nature of human social life and social behavior. By definition, these should transcend cultural boundaries.

(1) *Humans have competing approach and avoidance needs.* Running throughout ethological, anthropological, sociological, and psychological literature is the theme that humans are a social species with a propensity to affiliate with conspecifics. Yet an equally abundant body of literature confirms that extended physical contact or proximity is often aversive. Thus just as porcupines on a wintry night seek that distance that maximizes warmth from the group while preventing injury from each other's spines, humans strive for a balance between these opposing drives for closeness and distance, for affiliation and separation. The optimal levels of proximity and involvement with others are not fixed but fluid, changing according to the circumstance and relationship. Whether these adjustments originate from biologically based survival needs or from social-psychological needs for intimacy, privacy, and autonomy is less material than the fact that they are manifested in numerous nonverbal and verbal signals of approach and avoidance that appear to be universal in nature.

Although the signals themselves may be universal, a first critical question is whether their topography and frequency is the same across cultures. Cultures vary substantially in their interpersonal communication styles. Australians, Indians, Pakistanis, Iranians, Israelis, Italians, and Spaniards are more assertive, talkative, and expressive than Japanese, Koreans, Swedes, Norwegians, and the British, who are far more reticent and reserved conversationally (Ito, Chapter 11, this volume). Some of this variability can be analyzed by locating cultures along a few key dimensions such as individualism versus collectivism, homogeneity versus heterogeneity, or human-relations-oriented versus ideological (Gudykunst & Ting-Toomey, 1988; Ito, Chapter 11). Thus individualistic cultures such as the United States, Canada, and Australia may differ from interindividualist[1] cultures such as Japan and China not only in the degree of desired involvement with others but also in the mechanisms by which they achieve affiliation or privacy. Baker (1989) has confirmed, for example, that Japanese report being more inattentive, or what I would label more nonimmediate, and more verbally indirect than North Americans when regulating privacy. Too, cultures may differ in the thresholds that must be surpassed before they exhibit reactivity to excessive closeness or distance. But this does not negate the basic premise that all people will display reactivity in some form when confronted with a discrepancy between what they need or desire and what they are actually experiencing.

(2) *Communicators evaluate the reward potential of others.* Consistent with social exchange models of human interaction (e.g., Sunnafrank, 1986; Thibaut & Kelley, 1959), it is assumed that all people "size up" other actors according to the extent to which they serve as potential sources of rewards. Reward value may derive from such diverse considerations as one's access to resources, one's potential as a mate or ally, one's social status, or one's likability, among others. The evaluation process, which may be conscious or unconscious, should result in a net assessment of how desirable the other person is at that point in time, based on the combination of all the evaluated characteristics. This is communicator reward valence. The *process* of reward valencing, if not the specific contents, should be culture-invariant. That is, all people should hold implicit evaluations of others, and the quotient of all those various evaluations, weighted in whatever fashion is typical of their culture and in line with their personal preferences, should lead them to place the other on some underlying continuum that ranges from favorable to unfavorable regard.

(3) *Communicators develop expectations about the nonverbal (and verbal) behaviors of others.* Such expectancies are largely grounded in the normative nature of social behavior. The accumulating empirical observations of various nonverbal behaviors testify to the presence of identifiable norms that relate to characteristics of (1) the communicators, (2) the nature of their interpersonal relationship, and (3) the communication context in which they find themselves (Burgoon, Buller, & Woodall, 1989). Norms may operate at a molar, societal level or more microscopic, subgroup level. In interindividualist cultures, it is likely that people will hold different sets of expectations for ingroup versus outgroup members. Greeks, for example, expect outgroup members to be hostile, competitive, deceitful, and untrustworthy in comparison to ingroup members, who are expected to be highly warm, cooperative, polite, reliable, and truthful (Broome, 1990). It is also possible that ideological societies, which depend on rules and principles to bind them together and to minimize conflict, are less tolerant of deviations from the norm than human relations societies, which are more concerned with group harmony than with conforming to prescriptions and principles (Ito, this volume). This would mean that a wider range of behaviors falls within the accepted and expected range in the latter societies than the former. Conversely, human relations cultures may be more restrictive, given that "respect for authority calls for the obedience to specific rituals in communication between elders and their juniors and

between superiors and their subordinates" (Chu, 1988, pp. 127-128), so as to preserve the status hierarchy and maintain harmony. But in either case, there should be identifiable norms and latitudes of acceptable variability around those norms that are the basis for general expectations for communicative behavior.

General expectations become particularized as people acquire knowledge about another's personal characteristics and idiosyncratic communication style and as communicators jointly develop their own unique patterns of interaction. Nevertheless, the individualized expectations should be anchored by the norms governing the participants' roles, relationship, and situation. Although the specific expectancies *should* vary by culture, each culture doubtless has its own set of expectancies of how members will and should behave nonverbally. Thus noncontact cultures (Hall, 1966) may expect greetings that minimize physical contact, whereas contact cultures may expect prolonged touch, but each culture will have its own anticipations of how greetings are to be conducted.

(4) *Nonverbal (and verbal) behaviors have associated evaluations ranging from extremely positive to extremely negative.* These evaluations may be grounded partly in instinctive responses, as when one experiences fear when subjected to a threat display from a larger conspecific. They may be learned from one's culture, as when one regards public displays of affection as immodest. They may originate in personal preference, as when extroverts find close conversational distances more comfortable and desirable than do introverts. But regardless of their etiology, nonverbal behaviors and behavioral composites should have associated evaluative reactions. So, Latin and Mediterranean cultures find it not only acceptable but pleasurable for same-sex friends to hold hands or to link arms in public, yet disapprove of the same kind of public display by a heterosexual pair, whereas just the reverse is true among North Americans (Morris, 1971). Oriental societies may treasure silence whereas occidental ones prize loquacity. And equatorial cultures may prefer emotional expressivity, but northern cultures may prefer emotional reserve.

Our current state of knowledge of what valences are attached to various behaviors rests largely on an anecdotal and intuitive base, leading to a fair amount of guesswork in predicting people's reactions to various nonverbal behaviors. Nonetheless, in principle it should be possible to assess empirically the degree to which behaviors are desirable, appropriate, permissible, or taboo in each culture and under what circumstances. At the cultural level, such assessments would fall under the rubric of identifying display rules (Ekman & Friesen, 1969). Net valences should be a function of both the prevailing social norms and individual preferences. Applying expectancy violations theory in new cultural contexts therefore ultimately requires empirical verification of what the local communication norms and associated evaluations are. In one such investigation of sojourners returning to the United States after travel abroad, Lobdell (1990) found that friends of the sojourners were uncomfortable, surprised, and angry when the returning sojourners violated social norms for dress, appearance, eating habits, and conversational behavior. This underscores the prevailing expectation that people will adhere to the social customs of their home country.

An interesting comparative question that arises is the degree of consensus or variance that exists in evaluating particular behaviors within a culture. The greater the uniformity in valencing of a given behavior, the greater the predictive ability of the violations model. Cultures that are more explicit about what behaviors carry approbation or disapprobation should be especially amenable to explanation via the expectancy violations model. Those that have greater flexibility or tolerance for deviance may be more difficult to account for with the theory.

(5) *Nonverbal behaviors have socially recognized meanings.* Some behaviors or collections of behaviors may have unitary or unambiguous meaning, while others may have multiple and sometimes conflicting meanings, but it is assumed that the array of possible meanings is recognized and delimited within a social community. For example, a caress may convey sympathy, comfort, dominance, affection, attraction, or lust; it does not convey anger, detachment, distrust, or formality. The social meaning need not be consciously processed at the time of its enactment. It is merely assumed that upon inspection or reflection, conventional meanings can be assigned to many nonverbal behaviors.

What becomes worthwhile to consider from a cross-cultural perspective is the degree of ambiguity that is possible. Hall (1981) distinguishes cultures according to whether their communication patterns are high-context or low-context:

> A high-context (HC) communication or message is one in which most of the information is either in the physical context or internalized in the person, while very little is in the coded, explicit, transmitted part of the message. A low-context (LC) communication is just the opposite, i.e., the mass of the information is vested in the explicit code. (p. 91)

Gudykunst and Ting-Toomey (1988) contend that high-context, ambiguous, and indirect communication typifies collectivist (interindividualist) cultures, while low-context, explicit, certain communication typifies individualistic cultures. Similarly, Ito (Chapter 11) contends that homogeneous cultures are characterized by (a) more ambiguous language and (b) greater reliance on nonverbal cues, which in itself permits greater ambiguity. Research my colleagues and I have conducted in the nonverbal arena has demonstrated that even in our individualist, heterogeneous U.S. culture, numerous nonverbal behaviors are subject to multiple interpretations (Burgoon, Buller, Hale, & deTurck, 1984). The implication for the expectancy violations model is that there may be even greater room for multiplicity of meaning and ambiguity in interindividualist and homogeneous societies.

While there are some additional assumptions that refine and amplify the ones presented here,[2] these five provide the mortar that binds the propositions to follow.

PROPOSITIONS

(1) *Expectancy violations are arousing and distracting, diverting attention to communicator and/or relationship characteristics and behaviors.* Nonverbal behaviors that are noticeably discrepant from expectations are posited to prompt an alertness and orienting response that shifts attention from the ostensive content of the interaction to the social environment and the relational implicature. There is ample evidence that certain kinds of nonverbal violations are indeed arousing and distracting and result in finer grained processing of the novel stimuli. According to the expectancy violations model, the violator's characteristics and the implicit meanings of his or her nonverbal behavior should be made more salient and hence have greater impact than if no violation occurred.

In considering this proposition from a comparative standpoint, two intriguing questions arise. One, do cultures differ in how deviant a behavior must become before the behavior is recognized as a violation? Hofstede (1980) has identified uncertainty avoidance as a dimension that discriminates cultures. Those that are high in uncertainty avoidance are intolerant of deviant behavior. One might therefore expect that such cultures would be quicker to declare a given nonnormative behavior as a violation than cultures that are more tolerant of individual variability.

Second, do cultures differ in the salience of the relational implicature and hence, the impact of a shift in focus to the interpersonal relationship? According to Yum (1988), Eastern Asian cultures are more
oriented toward interpersonal relationships than are individualistic cultures. For example, one of the cardinal principles of Confucianism is
promoting warm human feelings and "proper social relationships" (cf.
Chaffee & Chu, Chapter 10 of this volume). Thus we might expect interindividualist, high-context cultures to place even greater importance on
relational message interpretation than occurs among North Americans.
Moreover, in such cultures, the use of indirection as a means of preserv-
ing face and minimizing conflict forces a greater reliance on nonverbal
behavior (Reischauer, 1977). Doi (1973) underscores this principle in describing Japanese culture: "What is most important for Japanese is to re-
assure themselves on every occasion of a mutuality based on *amae*. One
could say then that for Japanese verbal communication is something
that accompanies non-verbal communication and not the other way
around" (p. 181). The implication is that nonverbal violations will carry
even greater signification in collectivist cultures than in individualistic
ones.

Attention to violations in turn activates a two-stage cognitive inter-
pretation-evaluation process that may be moderated by reward valence.

(2) *Communicator reward valence moderates the interpretation of
ambiguous or multimeaning communicative behaviors.* In our recent
revisions and extensions of the theory, we have made a distinction between those nonverbal behaviors that fit a social meaning model and
those that fit a reward mediation model. We have found that some nonverbal behaviors, such as gaze aversion or increased conversational involvement, have rather unequivocal, consensual meanings, regardless
of who commits them. We have designated such behaviors as consistent
with a social meaning model. Reward valence is most likely to alter the
interpretations of those behaviors that are subject to varying meanings, such that more positive interpretations are assigned to behaviors enacted by high reward communicators, and more negative interpretations to low reward ones. For example, a personal space invasion
by a highly regarded person may be interpreted as a show of liking
or involvement, whereas the same invasion by a poorly regarded person
may be interpreted as excessive familiarity or aggressiveness.

(3) *Communicator reward valence moderates the evaluation of nonverbal behaviors.* Even behaviors that are interpreted in the same way
may be differentially welcomed. An affiliative overture from a high

reward communicator may be seen as quite desirable but from a low reward communicator as distasteful or discomfiting. Similarly, informality by a high reward person, especially one of higher status, might be seen as that person expressing a sense of equality and mutuality, whereas the same informality by a low status counterpart might be viewed as conveying disrespect.

My assumption is that this basic cognitive interpretation and evaluation process should be the same, regardless of a person's culture. Only the content of the actual interpretations and evaluations themselves should vary by culture. And in some cases, highly divergent cultures might even have the same evaluative reaction to a given behavior. Ma (1990) reports that Chinese and North Americans are highly similar in their expressions of discontent when wronged, disappointed, or faced with disagreement, for example. It seems plausible that many communicative acts that are negatively valenced in this culture—betrayal of a trust, insults, vehement disagreement, excessive familiarity by a stranger, to mention but a few—would be negatively valenced in most other cultures as well. Similarly, some positively valenced communication acts—such as compliments, gift-giving, humor, unexpectedly positive feedback—may likewise generalize beyond North American culture.

(4) *The ultimate evaluation of a violation is a function of the magnitude and direction of the discrepancy between the evaluation of the expected behavior and the evaluation of the actual behavior such that (a) enacted behaviors that are more positively valenced than expected behaviors produce positive violations and (b) enacted behaviors that are more negatively valenced than expected behaviors produce negative violations.* The point of this proposition is to designate how we arrive at whether a violation is a positive one or a negative one. Such a decision requires comparing what the violator actually does to what is expected. For example, suppose the expectation is that a person will be moderately immediate in conversation and the person actually is highly immediate. If high immediacy is more positively evaluated in a given culture than moderate immediacy, this will constitute a positive violation. If, however, high immediacy is less desired in a given culture than moderate involvement, this will constitute a negative violation. Similarly, if aggressive behavior is expected but negatively evaluated and the communicator actually behaves in a nonaggressive, receptive way, this should constitute a positive violation. But if cooperative behavior is expected and positively valued and the communicator instead behaves aggressively, this will constitute a negative violation.

Negative violations are easy to imagine and identify. Lobdell (1990) found that most of the instances of violations recalled by her respondents in her sojourner study were negative ones (engendering feelings of discomfort, anger, frustration, disillusionment, concern, disgust, or embarrassment), but one fourth were positive violations (engendering feelings of happiness or gladness). The concept of a positive violation may seem fairly novel. Most writings implicitly or explicitly treat all violations as negative (Burgoon & Walther, 1990). Yet it is possible to think of a variety of positive violations—the reputed boring speaker who is unexpectedly fluent and entertaining; the aggressive, pushy communicator who becomes more subtle and restrained; the sullen, impassive friend who suddenly shows animated interest in what you are saying; or the outgroup member who shows warmth and respect. Although each of these instances may not be universally recognized as positive, the validity of the model rests on the *potential* for each culture to recognize some communicative acts that not only are violations but also positively valenced.

(5) *Positive violations produce favorable communication outcomes, and negative violations produce negative consequences.* A requisite to testing this proposition is identifying what qualifies as positive or negative violations. If these can be specified, the prediction is that positive violations will lead to more favorable communication outcomes (such as increased credibility, attraction, persuasion, and comprehension) compared with adhering to the norms; negative violations are posited to be detrimental relative to adhering to the norms.

Our own program of research has provided considerable support for significant increases and decreases in proximity, gaze, conversational involvement, immediacy, and touch being recognized as violations (see, e.g., Burgoon & Hale, 1988). Only high reward communicators appear to achieve more favorable communication outcomes when using proxemic, gaze, and some forms of touch violations. Both high and low reward communicators benefit from the use of increased conversational involvement, immediacy, and some forms of touch, while both high and low reward communicators lose ground by using gaze aversion, reduced involvement, and nonimmediacy.

These findings have led Gudykunst and Ting-Toomey (1988) to contend that the violations model may be inapplicable cross-culturally because collectivist cultures that emphasize power differentials between members may react negatively if a high-status individual invades the space of a low-status individual. Although it is probably true that such a violation would produce anxiety and therefore not be advantageous, this doesn't negate the model, because such a violation would doubtless qualify as a negative violation in such a culture, based on the interpretations and evaluations assigned to extremely close proximity in that culture. The model would therefore predict detrimental effects by virtue of such behavior serving as a negative violation.

What this does raise, however, is the question of whether positive violations are possible in other cultures. Typically, scholars have treated all violations as if they are negatively valenced. Thus many writings about U.S. culture make the erroneous claim that deviant behavior carries negative consequences. The line of research I have been pursuing has begun to debunk that myth. It is therefore equally likely that systematic empirical investigations in other cultures might uncover forms of positive violations there. What would be especially interesting to examine is what behaviors, if any, serve as positive violations in cultures that have more rigid standards for public conduct, and whether positive violations might only occur in more private circumstances.

One final direction we have begun to take the expectancy violations model is in trying to predict and explain intimacy exchange in interpersonal interactions. Two alternative patterns have been widely documented in the literature: reciprocity and compensation (see, e.g., Burgoon, Olney, & Coker, 1987; Cappella, 1981; Hale & Burgoon, 1984). If Person A's increase in immediacy is matched by an increase from Person B, reciprocity has occurred. If instead A's increased intimacy is met by a decrease from B, compensation has occurred.

In applying the expectancy violations model, we have argued that communicator reward and the direction of the intimacy adjustment will determine whether reciprocity or compensation occurs. Specifically, increased intimacy by a highly regarded other should serve as a positive violation and prompt a reciprocal increase in intimacy, whereas decreased intimacy by the same partner should be a negative violation that prompts a compensatory effort to restore the previous level of intimacy. Conversely, increased intimacy by a poorly regarded other should be a negative violation that elicits a compensatory effort to "cool" the interaction, whereas decreased intimacy should prompt a matching decrease. We have also suggested that as regard for the partner lessens, there may be less accommodation to the partner's intimacy adjustments.

We have not yet established firmly that these patterns even operate in North American culture, so it is rather risky to speculate on what would happen elsewhere. One possibility, however, is that non-accommodation to a partner's interaction style may be more prevalent in some cultures. For example, Cody, Lee, and Chao (1989) observed more self-control and masking of negative affect among Chinese than North Americans, a pattern that is consistent with cultures that are simultaneously communal and inclined toward inaccessibility (see Altman & Gauvain, 1981). If cultures differ in the extent to which they are nonverbally explicit and expressive, or implicit and subdued, in signaling liking and immediacy (Gudykunst & Ting-Toomey, 1988), then we may see a bias toward public displays of moderate positivity, which would appear as attenuated or restrained accommodation to one's partner. That is, we might still see patterns of reciprocity and compensation, but in abbreviated form. Whether or not the reward level of the communicator would be less salient than cultural proscriptions for public communication behavior is a question worth considering. Equally important to consider is whether patterns differ in private as opposed to in public. Hall's (1981) observation that Japanese have both a high-context, warm, unceremonious side and a low-context, official, status-conscious side suggests that different situations may elicit radically different behavior patterns.

There are additional assumptions, propositions, and hypotheses of nonverbal expectancy violations theory that could be developed but for lack of space. Current work, for example, is exploring the extent to which expectancy disconfirmations are perceived, how persistent pre-interaction expectancies are, whether dispositional versus situational features of reward make a difference in moderating reactions to unexpected behavior, and how confirming or disconfirming expectations in positive or negative ways alter communication dynamics over time. It is hoped that some of these issues will be extended into other cultures to determine their relevance and validity.

CONCLUSION

The primary values of expectancy violations theory, as I see it, are these: First, it should encourage scholars to examine communication phenomena, both verbal and nonverbal, from the vantage point of expectancies. An expectancy orientation would seem to be useful in making both inter- and intra-cultural comparisons. Second, the theory should encourage a message orientation toward communicative acts and attention to the interpretations and evaluations associated with those acts. To the extent that we believe communication is a symbolic process, we need to delve more deeply into how we assign meanings to communication behavior. Expectancy violations theory offers a framework for examining the combined interpretations and evaluations that give communicative behavior its illocutionary force. Third, the theory serves to underscore the possible circumstances under which relational issues and messages move from contextual background into the foreground. If unexpected behavior causes an attentional shift that makes relational considerations more salient, and if this heightened salience occurs in all cultures, it will reinforce the importance of relational communication in framing our interpretations of, and reactions to, others' communication. Finally, the theory may prove to be a valuable heuristic if it can be demonstrated that the ultimate designation of communicative behavior as positive or negative violations and positive or negative confirmations improves our ability to predict, explain, and understand the consequences of that communicative behavior. If these basic principles prove to have universal applicability, they may contribute to more parsimonious explanations of interpersonal communication processes.

NOTES

1. I have used the term *interindividualistic* in place of *collectivist* because collectivism carries negative connotations in some cultures (Ito, 1989). Preferred terms are *groupism, relationalism, contextualism,* or *interindividualism.*

2. Four of these are that (1) humans are able to perceive gradations in nonverbal behaviors (which means they can recognize when some threshold of expectedness or acceptability has been passed), (2) the desire for affiliation may be evoked or intensified by the presence of rewards (i.e., the context may influence how strong the affiliative or avoidance drives are), (3) it is more rewarding to interact with positively evaluated others than negatively evaluated others, and (4) the location of communication behaviors or collections of behaviors on the evaluative continuum is a function of (a) the social community's values and meanings for the behavior and (b) the individual receiver's personal preferences. Further discussion of these, as well as other assumptions related specifically to proxemic behavior, can be found in Burgoon (1978, 1986).

REFERENCES

Altman, I., & Gauvain, M. (1981). A cross-cultural and dialectic analysis of homes. In L. Liben, A. Patterson, & N. Newcombe (Eds.), *Spatial representation and behavior across the life span: Theory and application* (pp. 283-320). New York: Academic Press.

Baker, J. M. (1989). *Privacy regulation mechanisms in Japan and the United States.* Unpublished master's thesis, Arizona State University.

Booth-Butterfield, M. (1990, May). *Perception of sexual harassment and source reward value: An application of expectancy violations theory.* Paper presented at the annual meeting of the Eastern Communication Association, Philadelphia.

Broome, B. J. (1990). "Palevome": Foundations of struggle and conflict in Greek interpersonal communication. *The Southern Communication Journal, 55,* 260-275.

Buller, D. B., & Burgoon, J. K. (1986). The effects of vocalics and nonverbal sensitivity on compliance: A replication and extension. *Human Communication Research, 13,* 126-144.

Burgoon, J. K. (1978). A communication model of personal space violations: Explication and an initial test. *Human Communication Research, 4,* 129-142.

Burgoon, J. K. (1983). Nonverbal violations of expectations. In J. M. Wiemann & R. P. Harrison (Eds.), *Nonverbal interaction* (pp. 77-111). Beverly Hills, CA: Sage.

Burgoon, J. K. (1986, February). *Expectancy violations: Theory, research, and critique.* Paper presented to the annual meeting of the Western Speech Communication Association, Tucson.

Burgoon, J. K., & Aho, L. (1982). Three field experiments on the effects of conversational distance. *Communication Monographs, 49,* 71-88.

Burgoon, J. K., Buller, D. B., Hale, J. L., & deTurck, M. A. (1984). Relational messages associated with nonverbal behaviors. *Human Communication Research, 10,* 351-378.

Burgoon, J. K., Buller, D. B., & Woodall, G. W. (1989). *Nonverbal communication: The unspoken dialogue.* New York: Harper & Row.

Burgoon, J. K., Coker, D. A., & Coker, R. A. (1986). Communicative effects of gaze behavior: A test of two contrasting explanations. *Human Communication Research, 12,* 495-524.

Burgoon, J. K., & Hale, J. L. (1988). Nonverbal expectancy violations: Model elaboration and application to immediacy behaviors. *Communication Monographs, 55,* 58-79.

Burgoon, J. K., & Jones, S. B. (1976). Toward a theory of personal space expectations and their violations. *Human Communication Research, 2,* 131-146.

Burgoon, J. K., Manusov, V., Mineo, P., & Hale, J. L. (1985). Effects of eye gaze on hiring, credibility, attraction and relational message interpretation. *Journal of Nonverbal Behavior, 9,* 133-146.

Burgoon, J. K., Newton, D. A., Walther, J. B., & Baesler, E. J. (1989). Nonverbal expectancy violations and conversational involvement. *Journal of Nonverbal Behavior, 13,* 97-120.

Burgoon, J. K., Olney, C. A., & Coker, R. A. (1987).The effects of communicator characteristics on patterns of reciprocity and compensation. *Journal of Nonverbal Behavior, 11,* 146-165.

Burgoon, J. K., Stacks, D. W., & Burch, S. A. (1982). The role of interpersonal rewards and violations of distancing expectations in achieving influence in small groups. *Communication, 11,* 114-128.

Burgoon, J. K., Stacks, D. W., & Woodall, G. W. (1979). A communicative model of violations of distancing expectations. *Western Journal of Speech Communication, 43,* 153-167.

Burgoon, J. K., & Walther, J. B. (1990). Nonverbal expectancies and the evaluative consequences of violations. *Human Communication Research, 17,* 232-265.

Burgoon, J. K., Walther, J. B., & Baesler, E. J. (1990, June). *Interpretations and consequences of interpersonal touch.* Paper presented to the annual meeting of the International Communication Association, Dublin, Ireland.

Cappella, J. N. (1981). Mutual influence in expressive behavior: Adult-adult and infant-adult dyadic interaction. *Psychological Bulletin, 89,* 101-132.

Chu, L. L. (1988). Mass communication theory: A Chinese perspective. In W. Dissanayake (Ed.), *Communication theory: An Asian perspective* (pp. 126-138). Singapore: Asian Mass Communication and Information Centre (AMIC).

Cody, M. J., Lee, W. S., & Chao, E. Y. (1989). Telling lies: Correlates of deception among Chinese. In J. P. Forgas & M. J. Innes (Eds.), *Recent advances in social psychology: An interactional perspective* (pp. 359-368). North Holland: Elsevier Science Publishers.

Doi, L. T. (1973). The Japanese patterns of communication and the concept of *amae. Quarterly Journal of Speech, 59,* 180-185.

Ekman, P., & Friesen, W. V. (1969). The repertoire of nonverbal behavior: Categories, origins, usage, and coding. *Perceptual and Motor Skills, 24,* 711-724.

Gudykunst, W. B., & Ting-Toomey (1988). *Culture and interpersonal communication.* Newbury Park, CA: Sage.

Hale, J. L., & Burgoon, J. K. (1984). Models of reactions to changes in nonverbal intimacy. *Journal of Nonverbal Behavior, 8,* 287-314.

Hall, E. T. (1966). *The hidden dimension* (2nd ed.). Garden City, NY: Doubleday.

Hall, E. T. (1981). *Beyond culture.* Garden City, NY: Doubleday.

Hofstede, G. (1980). *Culture's consequences.* Beverly Hills, CA: Sage.

Ito, Y. (1989). A non-Western view of the paradigm dialogues. In B. Dervin, L. Grossberg, B. J. O'Keefe, & E. Wartella (Eds.), *Rethinking communication* (pp. 173-177). Newbury Park, CA: Sage.

Lobdell, C. L. (1990, June). *Expectations of family and friends of sojourners during the reentry adjustment process.* Paper presented to the annual meeting of the International Communication Association, Dublin, Ireland.

Ma, R. (1990). An exploratory study of discontented responses in American and Chinese relationships. *Southern Communication Journal, 55,* 305-318.

Morris, D. (1971). *Intimate behavior.* New York: Random House.

Reischauer, E. (1977). *The Japanese.* Cambridge, MA: Harvard University Press.

Sarbaugh, L. E. (1979). *Intercultural communication.* Rochelle Park, NJ: Hayden.

Sunnafrank, M. (1986). Predicted outcome value during initial interactions: A reformulation of uncertainty reduction theory. *Human Communication Research, 13,* 3-33.

Thibaut, J. W., & Kelley, H. H. (1959). *The social psychology of groups.* New York: John Wiley.

White, C. H. (1989). *Effects of expectancy violations on uncertainty in interpersonal interactions.* Unpublished master's thesis: Texas Tech University.

Yousef, F. S. (1976). Some intricate and diverse dimensions in intercultural communication. In L. A. Samovar & R. E. Porter (Eds.), *Intercultural communication: A reader* (2nd ed.) (pp. 230-235). Belmont, CA: Wadsworth.

Yum, J. O. (1988). The impact of Confucianism on interpersonal relationships and communication patterns in East Asia. *Communication Monographs, 55,* 374-388.

Chapter 5

THE DYNAMICS OF CABLE TELEVISION IN THE UNITED STATES, BRITAIN, AND FRANCE

William H. Dutton and Thierry Vedel

IS COMMUNICATION TECHNOLOGY a cultural product? This issue has become central to the social study of technology, which has moved beyond a focus on the impacts of technological change to examine also the way social and political factors shape technology. Of course, people invent and construct technological systems and, in that sense, determine the shape of technology. The role, however, of particular actors and social or political structures in shaping technological change is problematic. To what extent can governments orient technological change and ensure that the design of systems promotes their values and interests? Or must the role of government be reduced to one of managing national resources in order to adapt smoothly to global economic trends? To what degree do economic conditions permit political choices to reflect the unique values and interests of national cultures?

The present research pursues this general issue of technology as a cultural product through comparative case studies of cable television policy in the United States, France, and Britain. At first glance, cable TV is a policy area where political determinism has prevailed over technological determinism. Its technology provides facilities for

AUTHORS' NOTE: This chapter is based on research supported by grants from the U.S.-France Cooperative Science Program of the U.S. National Science Foundation (INT-8414059) and the National Center for Scientific Research in France. We thank Kendall Guthrie, Johanna Zmud, Chris Spelius, and Jay Blumler for their comments.

the transmission of multiple channels of broadcast and interactive programming, including locally originated and public, educational, government, and entertainment services. In this form, it has been available since the early 1970s. Nevertheless, some countries, like France and Britain, chose to block cable development by limiting its use to the relay of over-the-air broadcast signals. Since the 1980s, however, cross-national differences in cable development have diminished, as if each country was heading, even if at different speeds, toward the same model. Cultural distinctions and political singularities have seemed no longer to exert so powerful a force as they once did.

THE CONVERGENCE OF CABLE POLICY

Are national cable policies unique or converging? The answer to this question depends on the way we define policy and the way we treat time in comparing nations. By focusing on functionally equivalent policies over time, we found the evidence to be more supportive of convergence.

National cable policies can be compared by the way in which each nation addresses two functionally equivalent policy issues. One is the degree to which cable system development will be promoted or restricted. The other is whether the public sector shapes cable system development to reach certain governmental policy objectives (e.g., economic development or social services) or whether market forces, particularly consumer demand and private initiative, are allowed to dictate the ways cable systems endure. The public versus market-led axis incorporates two ways in which the public sector can lead development.[1] One is by the direct involvement of public actors (e.g., municipal authorities, European PTTs[2]) in the ownership and operation of cable systems. The other is by the regulation of cable system operators, public or private. Each of these dimensions can be viewed as a continuum on which a nation's cable policy could vary within (i.e., over time) and across systems (i.e., cross-nationally).

Figure 5.1 shows our placement of each nation along these two dimensions. The figure illustrates more concisely than we could describe in narrative form that, despite a multitude of cross-national differences in the specifics of cable policy, U.S., British, and French cable systems have developed along markedly similar paths (Figure 5.1). Policy has traveled through four similar stages since the invention of cable.

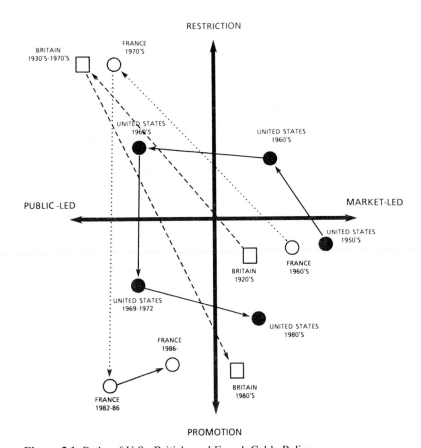

Figure 5.1. Paths of U.S., British, and French Cable Policy

NOTE: The placement of nations on each continuum represents a consensus based on the judgmental ratings of the authors, who discussed the ratings with other experts on cable policy. It aims to reflect the relative positions of each nation, rather than any absolute position.

STAGE 1: MARKET-LED INTRODUCTION

Initially, each nation witnessed a spontaneous, or market-led, introduction of cable television systems, originally as simple relay systems. Cable TV development initially engaged local entrepreneurs in a small business enterprise focused on consumer interest in the improved reception of radio signals. Even before the introduction of cable TV in Britain, as early as the 1920s, wired relay systems for radio began to import signals from the continent. In the United States, market-led development of cable TV began in the late 1940s. Similarly, early relay systems were built in France during the 1960s, without interference by the state (Hanicotte, 1978).

Governments allowed market-led development to proceed until it threatened broadcasters, telephone companies, newspapers, or politicians. When threatened, the groups at risk sought to restrict cable system development, albeit in nationally unique ways. As early as the 1920s, even before the invention of cable TV, the British Broadcasting Corporation (BBC) felt that wired relay operators jeopardized its monopoly on public broadcasting by importing foreign radio signals from the continent (Hollins, 1984). In France and the United States, cable posed threats to not only broadcasters, but also to the telecommunication monopolies, which sought to block cable system development in different ways. For example, American telephone companies often charged exorbitant fees for cable operators to attach their wires to telephone poles, and the French PTT reaffirmed its legal monopoly on any transmission by wire.

STAGE II: RESTRICTIVE PUBLIC POLICIES

Eventually, the threatened interests ushered in public policies that restricted cable system development in each nation. In 1936, the BBC persuaded the Post Office to adopt a restrictive policy toward the services of wired relay operators, protecting the retransmission of BBC (and later Independent Television), while placing limits on the retransmission of foreign programs (Hollins, 1984; Negrine, 1985). In the United States, restriction depended far longer on market forces through such mechanisms as poll attachment fees and the purchase of franchise rights by broadcasters, who often held back the construction of systems (Sparkes, 1985). Throughout the 1950s, broadcasters and telephone companies were unable to persuade the Federal Communication Commission (FCC) to assume jurisdiction over cable to restrict its development. Not until 1962 did the FCC accede to Congressional pressure and begin to restrict cable system development, albeit only in the major television markets.[3] In France, an interministerial committee chaired by the President of the Republic decided in 1975 to "suspend" experiments with cable that had begun two years earlier. Subsequent regulation limited the use of cable systems to retransmitting over-the-air signals.

Each nation based its restrictive policies on public interest arguments. In Britain, from the 1960s through to the early 1980s, public authorities sanctioned a few limited experiments with *multichannel cable systems,* but continued to view cable as a threat to public service broadcasting values.[4] During the early 1970s, when some nations, such as the Netherlands, Canada, and the United States, began or accelerated the development of cable TV, French authorities turned their efforts toward modernizing their basic telecommunications network. This preoccupation, as well as a wish to protect local newspapers from cable competition, diverted the DGT, the telecommunications branch of the PTT ministry, from building cable TV systems. French politicians also feared that cable TV might become a political tool that would undermine the structure of local power (Dondoux, personal interview, August 24, 1987; Flichy, 1980; Veyres, personal interview, August 7, 1987). In the United States, the FCC viewed cable as a threat to local broadcasters and therefore to the Commission's policy objectives, which included the promotion of localism, universal service, and equity in broadcasting (Negrine, 1985).

STAGE III: CABLE PROMOTION
BY PUBLIC AUTHORITIES

At different points in time, public authorities in each nation then moved to promote cable system development to meet broader public interest objectives. Beginning in the late 1960s and continuing through 1972, the FCC shifted its position to promote the development of local and interactive cable systems (Federal Communications Commission, 1972). The objectives of the FCC at this time were to break the commercial broadcasting oligopoly and to encourage more diversity in programming, including more local, public service, and educational programming. These policy objectives did not fit the French or British context. In both nations, broadcasters pursued a diverse range of noncommercial programming. Also, neither posited localism as a primary policy objective, though Britain's Independent Television service was organized on regional lines.

Britain did not promote market-led cable TV systems until the 1980s. In 1982, Prime Minister Thatcher's Information Technology Advisory Panel (ITAP) recommended the enactment of policies to permit the early development of private cable systems and services, initially supported and led by the market for entertainment offerings (Information Technology Advisory Panel, 1982). A broadcasting inquiry endorsed the thrust of this recommendation (Hunt Report, 1982). Even before passage of the Cable and Broadcasting Bill in July, 1984, the government launched a series of pilot cable franchises to speed the development of new cable systems (Home Office, 1983).

Like Britain, France restricted multichannel cable TV until the 1980s. In November 1982, the Ministry of PTT designed an ambitious plan, in collaboration with other ministries, to wire 6 million homes within 10 years. The telecommunications' directorate of the PTT, the DGT, would construct systems based on fiber optic technology arranged in a switched-star network. The plan placed commercial operation of cable systems under the control of municipal authorities.

STAGE IV: MARKET-LED EXPANSION

In the United States, the public promotion of cable system development was short-lived. Since the mid-1970s, the FCC has moved away from public policies that forced advanced technologies (e.g., interactive cable) or services onto the cable industry and entered a fourth stage, characterized by moves toward deregulation—constraining the regulatory authority of state and local governments and allowing the marketplace to set cable rates and offerings. From the mid-1980s on, both Britain and France have shifted policy in a similar direction.

In Britain, enthusiasm waned long before passage of the cable bill. From the start of the pilot projects through the remainder of the 1980s, Britain's emergent cable industry faced low subscription rates and difficulties securing investment funds, particularly from the British financial community.[5]

In France, the costs and delays of Plan Cable became apparent within a couple of years as its implementation fell increasingly behind schedule. After the general election of March 1986, a new right-of-center government suspended the plan and passed another communications law, which ended the PTT's monopoly over the construction and technical operation of cable systems. Since September 1986, local authorities have been free to choose whatever cable operator they wished, even if it was a foreign company. This permitted the development of a private cable industry in France.

The United States has remained the most supportive of market-led development. France has continued to be the most reliant on public initiatives of the three nations, despite the introduction of competition since 1986. The DGT remains as a major player in the construction of cable systems. Yet private cable operators have appeared. Policymakers expect them to invigorate cable diffusion by introducing more flexibility than would be provided by the DGT alone. More important, the DGT has now given up its attempt to impose a more technologically sophisticated system than the market demands in the short term. It has also become more flexible, offering more customized solutions to meet actual demand.

INSTITUTIONAL AND SYMBOLIC CONVERGENCE

Thus, if we look at the functions of policy over time—to restrict or promote cable TV and to use the public sector or the marketplace to shape its development—convergence prevails. Cable developed in the three countries along the same, four-stage path, although at different paces. Moreover, each nation has converged toward the others in other ways that are closely related to strategies for promoting market-led development. With respect to the legal-institutional arrangements surrounding cable TV, all three nations have restricted the role of local authorities and increasingly adapted to a cable industry structured along similar lines. At the symbolic level, all three are also converging toward remarkably similar social values.

THE ROLE OF LOCAL AUTHORITIES

Historically anchored institutional arrangements have led local authorities to play different roles in each nation's cabling process. But this is changing.

In Britain, the government initiated, debated, and implemented cable policy with almost a complete absence of participation by local authorities. The Cable Authority defined areas for cabling based on economic and market criteria, instead of local jurisdictional boundaries. Local authorities affected local cabling projects only in the sense that they could frustrate the work of the cable operator constructing systems within their jurisdiction.

In France, the 1982 cable plan assigned a major role to the local authorities. Not only were they to initiate plans for cabling their community, the cable plan obliged them to contribute financially to the PTT's expenses in constructing their cable systems. Local authorities were also to be closely associated with the operation of cable systems. This scheme was changed after 1984 when city officials more fully realized the financial implications of such commitments. Nevertheless, local authorities continued to play a critical role in deciding who would cable their community and who would operate the system for them. Moreover, mayors could influence national cable policy, particularly the details of regulation, through their ties to the national government.[6]

In the United States, cable policy conforms to many other policy areas in reflecting a sharing of authority among national, state, and local authorities. In some respects, the United States represents the most decentralized model of cable policy formation and implementation. During the first years of cable development, cable policy was essentially a local affair as the FCC chose not to view it as falling within its jurisdiction. The influence of local governments reached a peak in the late 1970s and early 1980s. In the franchise wars, competition between multiple system operators for the major urban cable franchises permitted cities to extract major concessions for public, educational, and government channels and facilities, such as public studios.

The United States and France, however, have moved toward national cable policies that constrain the role of local authorities. In the United States, this was one major goal and consequence of the 1984 Cable Communication Act that substantially reduced a city's influence over cable operators by, for example, deregulating the rates charged by cable operators (that had previously been carried out through negotiations between the city and the cable operator), and by allowing operators to renege on many promises made during the franchise wars.

In France, the government increasingly shifted cities into the role of franchising authorities. Even with respect to this more limited role, their influence is constrained by tacit agreements among cable operators that reduce competition among operators for the same territory. In addition, various competing systems, which are not under the jurisdiction of local authorities, such as Satellite Master Antenna Television (SMATV) within public housing complexes, are now developing.

This trend is likely to continue to the point that local authorities will play a minor role in cable TV. This is justified mainly by an economic argument. Cable operators seek economies of scale and scope associated with larger and compatible cable systems that overlap city boundaries. They also want to diminish the transaction costs associated with negotiating unique franchises with each local authority (Vedel, 1987).

THE STRUCTURE OF THE CABLE INDUSTRY

Historically, another major cross-national difference had concerned the degree to which private companies have owned and operated cable television systems. This distinction has also begun to vanish.

Since the 1940s, the United States has been the most privatized, Britain less so, and France the least. This difference continues to be reflected in the number of systems that are publicly owned and operated. In the United States, only a handful of local cable systems are municipally owned. In Japan and Western Europe, public ownership, particularly by the PTTs, but also by cooperatives and municipal authorities, is more common. In Britain, most relay operators were private entrepreneurs, often in the TV set rental business. The private ownership of cable TV was one feature that supported public service arguments for restricting cable system development. It is true that British Telecom owned and operated cable systems, while still a public body, such as in Milton Keynes, and has become a major player in cabling since 1984. Although now privatized, it is not fully privatized. That said, policy changes in Britain and France have moved both nations toward the development of private networks and services, in which private investors and operators are playing an increasingly central role. Additionally, France, following Britain and other European countries, is introducing elements of privatization to the DGT.

The convergence of industry structure goes beyond ownership. Overall, the cable industry has tended to develop along the same lines and to face the same issues in each country. Most cable systems are run by multisystem operators (MSO), although a number of independent operators exist in each nation. Many of the MSOs have also become involved in program production. From a technological point of view, the sharp distinction between the French and British models for cable system development, which emphasized star structured, fiber optic systems, and the "American" coaxial, tree-and-branch structured network, no longer makes much sense when comparing actual developments.

Cable operators in all three countries are implementing similar systems that employ a mix of fiber and coaxial cable that is more in line with traditional tree-and-branch than switched-star networks.

In each country, cable operators face the same issues for the future: the introduction of pay TV and other addressable and two-way capacities; the prospect of a market for high definition television (HDTV); the increasing globalization of the cable and broadcasting industry; and the marriage of cable and telecommunication systems. These issues, however, take different forms given different national settings. With respect to the latter issue, in Britain and France the public telegraph and telecommunication companies have played more central roles in early cable system developments, owning and operating major cable systems. In the United States, the FCC has barred telephone companies from owning cable systems within their service areas, with the exception of those rural areas that might not otherwise be cabled. Here again, this distinction may be breaking down, as telephone entry into video services is being seriously considered in the United States.

INSTITUTIONAL DISPERSAL
OF POLICY RESPONSIBILITIES

Cable policy in all three nations has been subject to a certain degree of incoherence due in part to the fragmented institutional arrangements for governing communications. Authority over cable—and more generally communications—is more or less partitioned among a number of agencies or ministerial departments in each country. This reflects the degree to which cable policy overlaps a number of other areas, such as industrial, cultural, local development, and budget policy considerations.[7] However, nations have partitioned authority over cable in quite different ways. In the United States, policy authority has been shared among national, state, and local governments. The Federal Communications Commission (FCC), an independent regulatory commission, remains a unique feature of U.S. institutional arrangements. The courts have also played an influential role in the U.S. communications policy setting, when compared to other nations. In France and Britain, the fragmentation is more a function of split authority across the departments and ministries of the national governments (Blumler, 1987).

Each nation has sought legal-institutional solutions to this fragmentation, such as the Cable Authority in Britain, the Mission Cable in France, and passage of the 1984 Cable Act in the United States, which sought to concentrate more authority within the FCC. These efforts have not erased this fragmentation, partly because all three nations face a similar problem. Cable system development is, in fact, entangled with a variety of separate policy sectors. As a consequence, cable policy is more the outcome of a complex ecology of games interlocking several policy sectors that yield changing coalitions of interests over time, than the outcome of a rational, comprehensive policy deliberation focused solely on cable concerns.[8]

Some legal-institutional issues have been almost inconsequential to cable policy in the United States but quite central in other nations. This distinction might also be declining. For example, whereas cultural considerations have shaped the course of cable in France, they have been almost irrelevant for U.S. policy. The French P&T won support for its cabling plan in part because cable offered a mechanism for gaining more control over the nature of the programming that would be aired. It would be easier, for example, to limit the transmission of undesirable foreign (i.e., American) programming on cable networks than on direct broadcasting by satellite systems.[9] Whereas First Amendment traditions are taken for granted in the United States, the absence of a comparable tradition in France and Britain has allowed content issues concerning such matters as programming standards, advertising, and the importation of foreign programs to be more prominent in policy considerations. In the United States, the First Amendment tends to drive out issues of content, forcing them to be dealt with indirectly, if at all, through structural regulation. Of course, other factors contribute to the lower salience of content issues in the United States. It is a larger country, with strong domestic film and television production industries, where foreign programming has yet to make a major inroad. Also, foreign ownership of production facilities was not a salient issue until the late 1980s.

But even in this area, each country is beginning to face similar problems of maintaining their cultural identities. Each nation has an interest in building and maintaining its own production industries, supporting a pluralistic array of video sources, and offering diverse programming to the public. Yet they are all faced with the same fundamental economic imperatives that are moving cable TV and broadcasting to become a more concentrated, consolidated, and global industry (Noam, 1989).

THE ROLE OF SYMBOLIC POLITICS

In each country, symbols—the socially constructed meanings of new technologies—have played a critical role in shaping cable policy. They did so by identifying technological development and public policy initiatives with positive and negative images that served to structure and simplify the issues at stake and to marshal the support or opposition of various actors and interests.[10] What cable is, and what role it could play in broadcasting and society more generally, has certainly varied over time in each country. But, cross-nationally, some common symbolic patterns can be identified.

First, cable TV has been positively received, almost as a white knight, particularly in periods when broadcasting has been the target of widespread criticism. At such times, it has offered an image that legitimated shifts from restrictive to promotional policies. In the United States in the late-1960s, for example, critics of the networks' broadcasting oligopoly were among the proponents of cable system development, since they envisioned cable as a means for accomplishing some of the goals that commercial, network broadcasting had failed to address: localism, greater competition, and higher quality—meaning more educational and cultural—programming. And it was in large part due to a belief that cable offered an opportunity to serve the public through greater choice, including local and interactive programming, that the FCC agreed in the early 1970s to open the major TV markets to cable system development (Smith & Cole, 1987).

In France in the early 1970s, some groups became interested in the local, alternative video programming that cable systems might enable. But local politicians were captured more by negative images of cable, primarily as an alternative avenue for political expression that might destabilize local political affairs. In the 1980s, however, cable attracted a more positive image as dissatisfaction mounted with public broadcasting, given its highly centralized character and its history of close state control.

In contrast, cable initially generated far more negative images in Britain, where public service broadcasting enjoyed relatively widespread support among elites and in the public in general (albeit not among important segments of the Conservative Party). It had a reputation for quality and high standards around the world. Nevertheless, a positive symbolism of cable as a technology that supported more choice and enhanced consumer sovereignty was central to the government's case for developing cable TV. Even more important to the outcome of cable policy in Britain was the image that cable TV was a strategic resource for developing an internationally competitive strategy of information technology development.

This leads to the second symbolic appeal that worked in favor of policies to promote cable system development. In the United States during the late 1960s, the electronics industry favored the development of cable TV. American electronic engineers and manufacturers were among the major proponents of a wired nation (Goldmark, 1972; Smith, 1970). As noted above, the impetus for developing cable TV in Britain emanated from a committee (ITAP) charged with developing a future-oriented industrial policy. Cable was also viewed as a positive industrial development in France—a high-tech project that would further the modernizaion of the country and solve its economic problems. In all three countries, this positive image emerged at a time when their respective cable industries were relatively young and immature. Therefore, prospects of new jobs, both on the manufacturing and the programming sides, were expected. In addition, the progress in cable technology in the 1980s made it possible to envision cable systems as related to telecommunications services, that is, to more business uses. Throughout most of the 1980s, Americans have been less receptive than the French or the British to "hi-tech" images of cable. But this difference narrowed by the end of the decade, as debate over high definition television and telephone entry into cable reinvigorated discussion of the industrial implications of cable and telecommunication systems. United States, Japanese, and European leaders in government and industry now tend to share similar visions of the role that communication infrastructures, such as cable, can play in international economic competition.[11] And this image provides a major impetus for promoting the market-led development of cable systems and services, since they are increasingly perceived as a national asset in a "global economic war."

Finally, a third common trend has been the way in which the social role of cable has been marginalized in each country. In the 1970s, cable TV was widely viewed as a way to foster community life, to encourage public participation in governmental affairs, to give voice to minority communities, and to foster consumer choice. During the 1980s, however, the image of cable as a local and interactive infrastructure of an electronic village—the wired city—has vanished (e.g., Smith, 1970; Smith & Cole, 1987). Dominant opinion in each country has judged public, educational, and governmental channels, with few exceptions, to have been exceedingly costly given the small audiences they attract. Cable came to be viewed instead as simply one of many competing entertainment media—a business more than a public service. Even in France, despite its historic cultural concerns, it has become acceptable to consider cable as simply one business among others. The stress is now on entertainment programming and pay-TV. The public service orientations, which stressed universal and equitable access to communication infrastructures, seem to have become obsolete in contemporary visions of cable. This radical change in the image of cable did not occur at the same time in each country, but was well advanced everywhere by 1990.

EXPLANATIONS FOR CONVERGENCE

Why is national cable policy converging? One possible interpretation is that communication technology is truly a cultural product, but that the advanced consumer-oriented nations, which certainly include our sample of nations, increasingly shared the same values, attitudes, and beliefs about communications. For example, all three societies might have a common affinity for a "quantitative consumerism" that would oppose any governmental restrictions on access to a greater amount and variety of a widely enjoyed consumer good or service.[12] Comparative research on public policy convergence, however, offers several alternatives to an explanation anchored in cultural convergence.[13]

One such interpretation would draw on *economic-cum-technological constraints* (Finnegan, Salaman, & Thompson, 1987). Features of cable technology might create a bias in favor of particular patterns of cable development. For example, the cost of wiring a nation tends to preclude the use of governmental revenues to fund its development as a universal, public infrastructure. Likewise, the cost differential between interactive or advanced switched-star technology and more conventional tree-and-branch cable networks tilts the scale against forcing advanced technology and toward a policy permitting the development of one-way, addressable systems, particularly since there is no proven mass market for cable services other than entertainment programming. More generally, similar solutions are likely to be chosen to address similar problems and opportunities posed by an essentially universal technology (Bennett, 1988).

Another interpretation explains convergence as a consequence of deliberate political strategy, placing more weight, then, on the politics of cable TV. Within this line of interpretation, a variety of convergent processes can be identified. One is that a *cable interest group regime* has exerted a major influence on policy in each nation. For example, Tom Forester (1985) has argued that British cable system operators and owners pressured public officials to permit the private, entertainment-led development of multichannel cable systems. This claim fails to account, however, for the weak position of the cable industry in each country at those moments when public-led development was promoted, such as in the United States in the late 1960s or in both France and Britain in the early 1980s (Dutton, 1987; Dutton & Blumler, 1988).

The convergence of cable policy might also be *one manifestation of partisan change,* the rise of conservative parties bent on privatization (Negrine, 1985). This interpretation overlooks, however, the broad partisan consensus that favored restrictive policies in each nation. Similarly, a degree of partisan consensus later formed around the promotion of cable system development. There has been a partisan politics of cable, but national political parties have divided primarily over the role that the public sector should play in cable system development. In each nation, right-of-center parties have favored market-led development under a light regulatory regime. Left-of-center parties have favored the development of cable systems along the lines of their respective telephone networks, either as public utilities or as privately owned systems regulated as a common carrier, largely because of their commitment to principles of universal and equitable provision.

In Britain, the Conservative Party's support for privatization of British Telecom and private cable systems was clearly opposed by labor. In France, right-of-center parties quickly opposed the 1982 cable plan as an extension of the state monopoly over communication. Their influence facilitated the introduction of private operators in 1986. In the United States, the promotion of cable TV systems during the late 1960s and early 1970s was tied to Lyndon Johnson's package of programs aimed at urban problems and supported by the Democratic Party. The wired cities plans of the late 1960s had many features in common with the French cable plan of the 1980s. In contrast, the deregulation of cable was spearheaded by Republican Senators although the first deregulatory moves were taken under the Democratic administration of President Carter.

Compared to Britain and France, however, American political parties have seldom placed cable TV policy near the center of their agendas. Partisan divisions over communications policy in the United States have seldom approximated the depth of cleavage among U.S. business rivals (e.g., IBM vs. AT&T; cable vs. telephone companies). Moreover, partisan differences over market versus public-led development have diminished in all three countries during the 1980s as a consequence of the increasing hold of neoconservative ideas within parties of both the left and right (Derthick & Quirk, 1985).

Penetration by the same transnational economic elites might account for convergence (Garnham, 1983). Foreign or transnational firms might export and impose their model in other countries. This explanation for convergence might be plausible within the nations that have fallen behind in cable system development. U.S. cable and telecommunications firms, such as U.S. West and Pacific Telesis, have been interested in the French and British cable TV markets as have firms from other nations, such as Japan and Canada. If they are pursuing long-term investment strategies in these countries, they might also attempt to influence the regulatory environment in them. Foreign firms, however, have often been challenged by industrial policies aimed at buttressing domestic industry. Their influence with national policymakers is problematic.

Another explanation is that national *elites happen to harmonize their policies* in order to enjoy various benefits, such as expanding the market for national industries. This might occur in Europe with the development of a single market and the strengthening of the European Commission in Brussels as a transnational policymaker. The Commission has produced a directive on audiovisual programming that could impact on cable system development. A similar process may be discerned in the American scene. Multiple system operators in the United States have backed certain national policies, such as rate deregulation and limits on local franchise fees, as a way to harmonize cable policy within the United States across the thousands of local governments in the country. But British and French elites did not attempt to harmonize their policies with those of the United States. Quite the contrary. For example, policy advocates often promoted cable TV systems that were at odds with American technology in order to create opportunities for domestic manufacturers.

Finally, *countries might imitate other nations,* such as by importing the American model. In the early 1970s, there were many references to the Canadian and Belgian experiences in France. Throughout the 1970s and 1980s, the American model was a frequent topic of discussion in Britain and France, but most often as a countermodel—an example of what could go wrong. At the symbolic level, however, discussions of cable TV have evolved into an increasingly international discourse that seems to have been built up through the imitation of themes and issues (e.g., consumer choice, competition) in one country after another.

Our comparison of three nations provides a basis for weighing the relative merits of these alternative explanations. As suggested above, each has some plausibility and can be viewed as more complementary than competing. Two explanations, however, seem most compelling. First, there is a case for some technological-cum-economic determinism in the sense that public authorities have been unable to mold cable technology and services in ways that fitted in with their early visions. In every country, market factors seemed to undermine public-led policies, particularly those aimed at promoting advanced technology and public services. Second, images of cable in other countries have shaped cable policies in France and Britain, but in less direct ways than suggested by notions of emulation. Generally, the symbols with which cable became identified had a major role in leading every nation first to restrict and then to promote market-led cable system development.

PROBLEMS AND OPPORTUNITIES FOR THE COMPARATIVIST

We would like to step back from the substance of our findings to reflect on some of the lessons that we have learned about the conduct of comparative inquiry. Our research has underscored the value of comparative inquiry, but also the problems that are inherent in most conventional research strategies.[14]

THE VALUE OF A COMPARATIVE APPROACH

We found cross-national, comparative research to be a natural laboratory for examining the role of culture in shaping communication technology. Comparativists can explore, in a broad way, the relative effects of universal factors, such as technological developments, and unique contextual factors, such as the legal and institutional arrangements of national political systems. While our studies alone cannot determine such effects, they do allow us to engage these issues.

Comparative research also forces scholars to develop theoretical explanations that can apply across social systems. The validity of explanations based on a case study is usually established by determining the degree to which the same patterns and themes emerge from other cases. For example, having found empirically that symbolic politics played a critical role in each nation, we were encouraged to put more emphasis conceptually on the role of symbols in shaping cable policy. Our case studies also identified a variety of patterns and themes that were not always cross-nationally uniform. The fact that there were no analogues in France or Britain to the role of cable interest groups in the United States, for example, caused us to question explanations anchored around the activities of such groups. Thus comparatively grounded theory will look different from theory that is generated by a single case.

At a more pragmatic level, communications is increasingly becoming transnational, if not global. For this reason, it is becoming necessary for students and professionals of communications to understand communications in countries other than their own. Our own analysis of cable indicates the degree to which the strategies of communication firms transcend geopolitical jurisdictions. Moreover, policymakers often use the experiences of other nations as models or countermodels for their own approaches to development of a new media technology like cable.

Finally, comparative analysis offers communication policy researchers a rare opportunity to assess the technical arguments that are often used to legitimate policies. Policy analysts in every country are often confronted with justifications based on technological principles or expertise (i.e., claims that a particular application necessitates a specific technology, or that technological change necessitates a given regulatory framework), which they have difficulty assessing. By revealing a variety of experiences and solutions to similar problems, comparative research allows one to draw a distinction between what *can* be done and what governments or interest groups *want* to do.

PROBLEMS OF COMPARATIVE RESEARCH

The arguments for comparative analysis are many, but the difficulties of this enterprise are also formidable. A first problem is one of locating

an equivalent object for comparative study. Cable technology and policy are rapidly moving targets. Given the seniority of the cable industry
in the United States, it was problematic to compare the politics of cable
in 1984 there, with almost half of the nation wired, simultaneously with
France or Great Britain, where cable was only being launched in 1984.
Instead of comparing systems at similar points in time, we therefore
focused on the development processes of cable. This led us to illuminate the dynamics of policy convergence. Otherwise, we might have
over emphasized the importance of nationally unique factors.

Yet, even if we compare policy processes over time, we leave a variety of alternative explanations for any cross-national patterns we discover. For example, policy decisions in Britain and France during the
1980s were influenced by American experiences in the 1970s. The
emergence of cable did not occur in the same technological and symbolic environments in the United States and in Europe. Also, the size of
countries had a dramatic impact on the social and political significance
of cable policies. For example, the 1982 cable plan can be considered,
in financial terms, as a major public venture for French society. But
compared to the United States, it was just equivalent to a local, short-
term public project such as the upgrading of the subway system in New
York City.

Another problem was that the data we could gather, including the
analysis of secondary sources, government documents, hearings, and
interviews with major participants and observers, were not strictly
equivalent cross-nationally. We were able to obtain a wealth of information about French and British decision-making processes surrounding their shifts from restrictive to promotional policies, since these
events occurred in the 1980s. For the U.S. case, however, we needed to
rely more on the historical record and the recall of participants. In the
former case, the information was fresher but also more entangled with
on-going justifications of actions offered by the participants. In the latter case, we had to avoid the simple duplication of well-established,
ready-to-wear interpretations.

Finally, we had to cope with a common problem in comparative research, that of sampling the countries to be investigated. On the one
hand, as many countries as possible should be studied in order to discover general findings and identify transnational trends. On the other
hand, because our approach was qualitative in nature, it necessitated
the analysis of a considerable amount of rich historical detail. Until we
conducted a substantial amount of field research, we could not be

confident of our understanding of each national case. Thus we were continually obliged to balance our need for thick descriptive detail with our desire to be comparative. This required that we progressively narrow our sample and focus. We began by considering advanced industrial democracies, as defined by their economic and political systems, then those nations that had adopted public policies aimed at developing cable television—primarily the United States, Canada, Britain, France, West Germany, and Japan. This preliminary stage provided us with background and environmental information, which proved useful in the subsequent stages of our project. Finally, we restricted our sample to the three countries where we were able to secure the resources and collaborative support to do intensive field research. As we built the detail of each individual case, we progressively moved toward a comparison of the cases.[15]

THE CASE FOR A MIXED STRATEGY

What is truly comparative research? As Macridis put it a long time ago, some "comparative" research hardly deserves this label since much is "essentially non comparative . . . essentially descriptive . . . essentially parochial . . . essentially static . . . essentially monographic" (Macridis, 1955). Ideally, comparative research should avoid the simple juxtaposition of national accounts.

Among the numerous ways to conduct a cross-national, comparative analysis, two approaches seem to dominate. In the first one, a single team undertakes case studies of alien nations; the second one consists of cooperative projects involving a number of national teams that study their own respective countries. Each of these approaches has both advantages and disadvantages in terms of: coherence of approach, field research costs, access to information, and the quality of observations (Table 5.1).

In order to overcome their respective limitations, while combining their advantages, we mixed these two strategies. Each case study was conducted by two investigators, one of whom was foreign and the other native to the country studied. This certainly enhanced our project in many respects. For example, the national investigator could save time in locating sources of information and making arrangements for interviews that were eventually conducted with the foreign investigator (to overcome any tendency towards ethnocentrism or any bias stemming

TABLE 5.1 Advantages and Disadvantages of Two Common Approaches to Comparative Research

	I	II
Definition	A single team conducts case studies of foreign nations	Several national teams cooperate on studies of their own countries
Coherence of Approach	Unified theoretical and methodological approach	Problems can arise from different backgrounds, research agendas, and interests
Research Costs	High costs to access information: travel, language barriers, difficult to identify pertinent sources and participants	Costs concentrated in communication to coordinate research and exchange information among teams
Quality of Observations	• Important factors may be discovered by a "fresh," naive observer	• Some factors may be underestimated for they are "naturalized" by the indigenous researcher
	• Difficulty in fully understanding all the parameters, the historical background, the real social significance of an event or institution	• Ability to provide thorough case studies
		• Risk of "capture" by your subjects
	• Tendency to focus on legal and institutional factors	
Common Shortcoming	The values, or issues, of the investigator's own country are overrated (ethnocentrism)	Juxtaposition of national, descriptive studies

from being acquainted with the interviewee). In a final stage, transcripts were jointly analyzed so that all implicit elements could be taken into account. More generally, such a strategy allowed a constant, reciprocal challenging of each investigator's views.

Although the mix of strategies we employed has several advantages, it depends on international communication among researchers. This reliance raises a final issue that is generally left out of the comparative texts: the human dimension of comparative research. International collaboration brings home the realization that researchers are human beings as well as cultural products. Doing comparative research involves spending months in a foreign country; cutting yourself off from your familiar world and routines; speaking or trying to speak languages other than your own; and adapting yourself to the working habits of others. This entails an emotional as well as an intellectual commitment. To succeed, a comparative research team must not only agree on a problem and approach, they must enjoy working with one another. It might well be that many comparative research teams fail, not because the countries were foreign, but because their international colleagues remained alien to them.

NOTES

1. A similar distinction has been drawn by other comparative communication researchers (e.g., Homet, 1979; Straubhaar, 1987).

2. PTT is the generic label for any public "post, telegraph, and telecommunications" authority, e.g., the French P&T is one of the European PTTs. The French P&T stands for the "French Ministry of Post and Telecommunications." The DGT is the "Direction Générale des Télécommunications"—the directorate within the French P&T that is in charge of telecommunications.

3. In 1962 the FCC found a basis for regulating cable through its authority to regulate the licensing of microwave relays to cable operators. Its regulatory authority was extended in 1965 by the FCC's First Report and Order to include all cable systems (FCC, 1965).

4. The Annan Committee's report (1977) on broadcasting provides one of the most comprehensive critiques of cable TV from a public service broadcasting perspective. The Committee argued that Britain could not afford to develop a cable system that could provide universal and equitable service throughout the nation. A market-led "patchwork" development of cable would be economically viable but not compatible with the universal nature of public service broadcasting (Annan Report, 1977).

5. British cable entrepreneurs received greater support from U.S. banks and communication firms, including telephone companies, than from the British financial community.

6. Mayors of large French cities are also members of the Parliament. In addition, the French Senate assumes a major role in representing the concerns of local authorities.

7. In France, cable investments by the PTT ministry have required approval by the Ministry of Finance and have therefore been dependent on general economic policy. In the United States, local governments have used cable franchise fees to support their general funds.

8. For a discussion of the ecology of games as applied to the study of communications policy, see Dutton (1992), Dutton and Mackinen (1987), and Vedel and Dutton (1990).

9. At the inception of the 1982 Cable plan, DBS systems were derided as the "Coca-Cola" satellites, which left little doubt about the low status they were accorded.

10. The notion of symbolic politics was developed by Murray Edelman (1971). For a discussion of its application to communications policy, see Dutton and Blumler (1988).

11. This theme has emerged from a comparative study of national visions of communication futures in the United States, Japan, and Western Europe (Dutton, 1991).

12. The term *quantitative consumerism* was suggested by Jay Blumler (personal communication, 1990).

13. We draw from Colin Bennett's (1988) summary of this literature in outlining the alternative interpretations presented in this section.

14. For a more general discussion of the value of comparative inquiry in communications, see Macridis (1955) and Gurevitch and Blumler (1990).

15. In this chapter, we have focused on cross-national comparisons. More detailed case studies of each nation can be found in other reports of our research (e.g., Dutton, 1987; Dutton & Blumler, 1988; Martin, Dutton, & Vedel, 1988; Vedel, 1983; Vedel, 1984; Vedel & Dutton, 1990).

REFERENCES

Annan Report. (1977). *Report on the Committee on the Future of Broadcasting.* London: HMSO, Cmnd 6753.

Bennett, C. J. (1988). Different processes, one result: The convergence of data protection policy in Europe and the United States. *Governance: An International Journal of Policy and Administration, 1*(4), 415-441.

Blumler, J. G. (1987). Live and let live: The politics of cable. In W. H. Dutton, J. G. Blumler, & K. L. Kraemer (Eds.), *Wired cities: Shaping the future of communications.* Boston: G. K. Hall.

Derthick, M., & Quirk, P. J. (1985). *The politics of deregulation.* Washington, DC: The Brookings Institution.

Dutton, W. H. (1987, September). *The politics of cable in Britain.* Paper presented at the meeting of the American Political Science Association, Chicago.

Dutton, W. H. (1991). *Technological visions shaping communication policy: Comparing the United States and Japan.* Unpublished working paper of visions project. Los Angeles: University of Southern California.

Dutton, W. H. (1992). The ecology of games in telecommunications policy. In H. Sapolsky, R. Crane, R. Newman, & E. Noam (Eds.) *The telecommunications revolution.* New York: Routledge & Keagan Paul.

Dutton, W. H., & Blumler, J. G. (1988). The faltering development of cable television in Britain. *International Political Science Review, 9,* 279-303.

Dutton, W. H., & Mackinen, H. (1987). The development of telecommunications: The outcome of an ecology of games. *Information & Management, 13,* 255-264.

Dutton, W., & Vedel, T. (1991). *The ecology of games.* Unpublished manuscript, Annenberg School for Communication, Los Angeles.

Edelman, M. (1971). *Politics as symbolic action.* Chicago: Markham.

Federal Communication Commission. (1965). *First report and order, rules re: micro wave-served CATV.* 38 FCC, 683-760.

Federal Communications Commission (1972). *Cable television report and order.* 36 FCC 2d, 143-325.

Finnegan, R., Salaman, G., & Thompson, K. (Eds.). (1987). *Information technology.* London: Hodder & Stoughton.

Flichy, P. (1980). *Les industries de l'imaginaire.* Grenoble: Presses Universitaires de Grenoble.

Forester, T. (1985). The cable that snapped. *New Society, 24,* 133-135.

Garnham, N. (1983). Public service versus the market. *Screen, 24,* 6-27.

Goldmark, P. C. (1972). Communication and the community. *Communication.* San Francisco: Freeman.

Gurevitch, M., & Blumler, J. G. (1990). Comparative research: The extending frontier. In D. L. Swanson & D. Nimmo (Eds.), *New directions in political communication* (pp. 305-325). Newbury Park, CA: Sage.

Hanicotte, R. (1978). *De la radiodiffusion a la teledistribution dans le droit de la construction et de l'urbanisme.* Unpublished doctorat de droit thesis, University of Lille 2.

Hollins, T. (1984). *Beyond broadcasting: Into the cable age.* London: Broadcasting Research Unit, British Film Institute.

Home Office, Great Britain. (1983). *The development of cable systems and services.* London: HMSO.

Homet, R. S. (1979). *Politics, cultures and communication.* New York: Praeger.

Hunt Report. (1982). *Report of the inquiry into cable expansion and broadcasting policy.* London: HMSO.

Information Technology Advisory Panel, Cabinet Office. (1982). *Cable systems.* London: HMSO.

Macridis, R. C. (1955). *The study of comparative government.* New York: Random House.

Martin, D., Dutton, W. H., & Vedel, T. (1988, May). *Cable television policy in the American federal system.* Paper presented at the annual meeting of the International Communication Association, New Orleans.

Negrine, R. M. (Ed.). (1985). *Cable television and the future of broadcasting.* London: Croom Helm.

Noam, E. M. (1989, May). *The "iron law" of media Americanization: An economic analysis.* Paper presented at the meeting of the International Communication Association, San Francisco.

Smith, R. L. (1970). The wired nation. *The Nation,* May 18.

Smith, R. L., & Cole, B. (1987). The American way of wiring a nation. In W. H. Dutton, J. G. Blumler, & K. L. Kraemer (Eds.), *Wired cities: Shaping the future of communications* (pp. 124-130). Boston: G. K. Hall.

Sparkes, V. (1985). Cable television in the United States. In R. M. Negrine (Ed.), *Cable television and the future of broadcasting* (pp. 15-46). London: Croom Helm.

Straubhaar, J. D. (1987, May). *An international comparison of market-driven vs. policy-structured cable television systems.* Paper presented at the meeting of the International Communication Association, Montreal.

Vedel, T. (1983). De la telematique a la videocommunication: Continuites et ruptures d'une politique publique. Actes des 5emes Journees internationales de l'IDATE, *Bullentin de l'Idate,* Octobre, *13,* 239-252.

Vedel, T. (1984, May). Pourquoi la France n'a-t-elle pas ete cablee plu tot? *Proceedings of the "Forum International sur les Politiques des Nouvelles Technologies de la Communication,"* Fondation Nationale des Sciences Politiques, Paris.

Vedel, T. (1987). Orientations et strategies des collectivities territoriales en matieres de reseaux de videocommunication: Une premiere comparaison de politiques locales de cablage. *Culture Technique, 17,* Mars, 1987, 225-230.

Vedel, T., & Dutton, W. H. (1990). New media politics: Shaping cable television policy in France. *Media, Culture and Society, 12,* 491-524.

Chapter 6

MOTHERS AND LOVERS: MANAGING WOMEN'S ROLE CONFLICTS IN AMERICAN AND BRITISH SOAP OPERAS

Tamar Liebes and Sonia M. Livingstone

Look, me and Lofty, we were just a couple of kids, brought up on promises of instant happiness as soon as we got married, had kids, and a place of our own. I mean, we were just doing what we thought we were supposed to, that's all. . . . And then we realized the promises weren't true, that life's not really like that.

—Michelle, in *EastEnders,* to Cindy on her wedding day.

WHAT MAKES WOMEN HAPPY? Many of woman's problems in modern society concern the conflict among the different roles she is supposed to fulfill. Without giving up the roles of wife and mother, she is expected to have a career and, no less important, to remain available for and interested in romance, to keep the husband from looking elsewhere. Although the relative emphasis on these roles may vary across cultures, no society would consider itself modern without expecting women to perform in all three domains. The conflicts among these demands, each of which can be considered a full-time job, present a

AUTHORS' NOTE: The authors wish to thank UNESCO and, for the second author, The Leverhulme Trust, U.K., for their support. Elihu Katz, Daniel Dayan, Jay Blumler and Suzanne Pingree provided helpful comments on earlier versions of this paper, which was first presented at the International Communication Association Annual Conference, San Francisco, May 1989.

formidable challenge to the modern woman. Does happiness mean choosing among or trying to reconcile the various roles?

Putting aside the feminist literature in which role conflict is much discussed, this dilemma is expressed in the various media of popular culture that explicitly address women, notably women's magazines, romance novels, and soap operas. It is through these media that most women encounter the formulation of their problem and available ways of coping with it. Soap opera is a very popular and visible genre allegedly dealing with the problems facing the modern woman. This chapter will examine the expression of contemporary feminist concerns in the crisis-laden, never-ending, forever-reversible soap opera.

Our analysis focuses on the expression, and sometimes the repression, of conflict between mother, lover, and career woman in four popular and long-running British and American soap operas. Most writing on the subject of soap opera treats only the American variety, taking its universality for granted (Allen, 1985; Cantor & Pingree, 1983; Fiske, 1987).[1] Our argument, however, is that images of the female condition projected by soap operas on either side of the Atlantic differ in terms of a set of related oppositions that express two different worlds and world views. To anticipate, the British soap opera portrays a world that is communal, inclusive, and systemic, while the American soap opera world is individualistic, exclusive, and dyadic. Woman's roles are differently constructed in the two kinds of narratives. We will examine the ways that each deals with the problem of motherhood, as this poses a major feminist problematic. The different images of women within the two soap-opera worlds will then be related to the liberal (unisex) and women-centered (sisterhood) models of feminism and their distinctive approaches to these role conflicts. We will ask, finally, whether the messages in these two kinds of soap opera are feminist or hegemonic. This has been the subject of much recent debate (Ang, 1984; Curti, 1988; Fiske, 1987; Kuhn, 1984; Seiter, Borchers, Kreutzner, & Worth, 1989).

Our analysis is based on interpretations of two American daytime soap operas, *The Guiding Light* (*GL*) and *As the World Turns* (*ATWT*), and on two British soap operas, *Coronation Street* (*CS*), and *East-Enders* (*EE*), as shown in 1987-1988.[2]

METHODOLOGY

Soap operas, of course, are about kinship. A good way to reveal the place of women in these family dramas is by analyzing the kinship structures, including all family and romantic connections. Methodologically, therefore, we have chosen to base our study on a quasi-ethnographic mapping of the extent to which characters are interrelated by blood, marriage, and romance. We first compare the maps of the two cultures—as represented by their texts—in terms of the interconnectedness of their characters, the structure of families (nuclear or extended), the generational structure, and so on. Against this background, as a second step, we analyze the ways in which the narratives "activate" these ties and give them role definitions. We ask which of these social constructions serve as loci for functions such as role-modeling and socialization, support and advice, romantic love, competition. Thus we try to identify the conditions under which the kin-in-the-map are present or absent on the screen, the situations that bring them together, the rules that attribute "mothering" to non-kin, or that transform mothers into lovers (sometimes, even in competition with their daughters). Rather than assuming that mothers do the mothering, we ask where does mothering take place; rather than assume that mothering is a fixed function, we trace its circulation.

Analytically, this allows us to propose generalizations about the stories these cultures choose to tell about themselves, such as the preference for dyadic versus pluralistic relationships, the acknowledgment of relationships other than blood and romance, the relative importance of family versus community, the nature of relations across generations, the implicit division of labor among generations. We chose this analytic method in preference to the more traditional method of content analysis. In their comparative analysis of European soap operas, Silj (1988) and colleagues found that although the soap operas seemed superficially similar, the underlying differences were so great that a strict comparative content analysis proved impossible. The very categories and categorical structures of interest differed and an a priori content analytic scheme could not be applied. Of course, content analysis can be used in comparative analyses—indeed this is its main purpose, having been developed originally for historical comparisons. However, a highly detailed set of categories would be needed to index the many features of interest in the diverse programs concerned.

For example, to index our finding (see below) that in the American soap operas it is more often biological mothers who "mother" their children, whereas in the British programs it is unrelated and often single women in the community who mother others, one should not count the frequencies of mothers in each program, but instead categorize and quantify aspects of mothering behaviors performed by different kinds of persons. We do not here attempt this more detailed content analysis but limit ourselves to the prior stage in the analytic process, namely interpretation of the programs so as to reveal the nature of the qualitative differences between British and American serials in the meanings and conditions of use of key categories such as "mother," "romance," and "baby." The rich pictures of the two subgenres presented below are anchored analytically by mapping the kinship structures for each. These provide starting points for investigating the significance of differences in the range of mothers, the exclusivity of mothering, or the generation gaps between mothers and daughters.

KINSHIP PATTERNS

Strikingly different patterns are evident in Figures 6.1 and 6.2, representing respectively the American *As the World Turns* and the British *Coronation Street,* two of the longest running soap operas. In the American serial, as shown by Figure 6.1, all the characters are highly interconnected by past and present ties—biological, marital, and romantic. Consequently, the boundaries between the central families are hard to identify as the characters move back and forth among the different families. All characters are connected to the others by birth, marriage, or affairs.

In the British soap opera, the central families stand alone, with few marriages or affairs to connect them, as Figure 6.2 makes clear. The interconnections among the characters are dramatically different. In terms of familial and romantic relationships there are numerous unattached characters, mainly aging women—widows and spinsters—without evident men or children. The British programs, however, connect the characters in an equally powerful although very different manner. Ironically, perhaps, the differentiation and interdependence of Durkheim's "organic solidarity" apply to the British serials while the "mechanical solidarity" of similarity and interchangeability applies to the American.[3] In both types of program, business connections generate

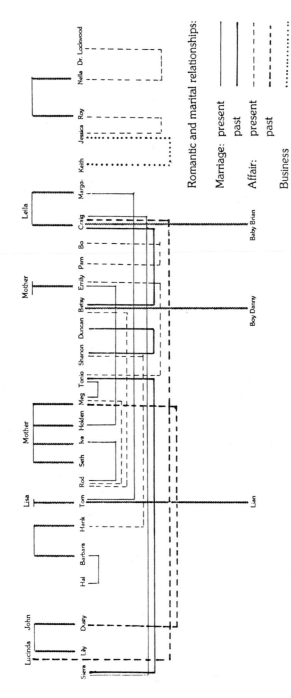

Figure 6.1. *As the World Turns* (1988)

NOTE: Keith, Jessica, Roy, Nella, and Dr. Lockwood form a cluster not directly connected to the other 30 characters.

some interrelationships, but in the British soap operas, most characters are related through their common membership of the local community. They meet in the pub, the launderette, the shops, and the cafes. These public places are major centers of interaction in which troubles are discussed, gossip is spread, and advice is given. The discussions are inherently public, with many characters joining in without formal invitation.[4] In contrast, the American conversations occur either at home, where privacy is assured, or in restaurants and nightclubs where formal invitations to participate are required. The kinship network of the American characters operates primarily through dyadic and "horizontal" (i.e., intragenerational) links and encounters in contrast with the more multipersonal and vertical (i.e., multigenerational) encounters in the networks of characters in the British soap operas.

THE EXCLUSIVE OR
THE GENERALIZED MOTHER

Although often not biologically connected, all of the women in the British soap opera communities, and particularly the lone elderly women, take turns in "mothering" whoever is in need. In *CS*, for example, several surrogate mothers came to aid Gail when she was vulnerable, divorced by her husband while pregnant, and neglected by her flighty mother. Ivy, her mother-in-law; Phyllis, the elderly widow with whom she worked; and Emily, Rita, and Betty, all elderly widows in the community—each came to offer advice and sympathy. In the similarly structured *EE*, the young single parent, Mary, is the object of continual mothering by most of the women in the community at different times. Biological connections are subordinated to the communal mothering that connects the female characters. Typically the plight of these women goes unnoticed by the men, who are outside this female network (Livingstone, 1989).

Generalized mothering is little seen in the American soap operas, where the mother-daughter relationships seem more exclusive and specific. Each woman in trouble tends to turn to her own, conveniently available mother for support. As the mothers are generally supportive, no wider networks are needed. This results in the "symbolic annihilation" of those women who are neither mothers nor lovers; they are without social function and are thus excluded from the soap opera (Tuchman, 1979).

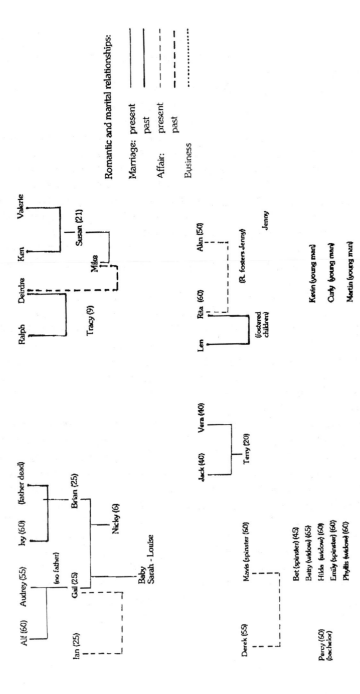

Figure 6.2. *Coronation Street* (January 1987)
NOTE: Ages are approximate

In *ATWT*, Meg, betrayed by her husband Tonio who is now Emily's lover, turns to her own mother for comfort. In the same episode, Emily turns to her mother when her marriage to Holden is in trouble, although this has not been a good relationship in the past. In each case, no other women are told or involved; the mothering relationship is an exclusive and specific one and the mothers do not let their daughters down. Even when Shannon proposes marriage to the virile owner of the castle, Duncan, with whom she has been involved for some time, a comforting mother-substitute is hidden in the next room, as if in a closet, waiting to celebrate or console as appropriate. When Duncan reveals himself as "not the marrying kind" and goes upstairs to change, hoping that "when I come down maybe you would have come back to your senses," the mother-substitute promptly emerges to comfort and distract Shannon. This seems an idealized conception of motherhood, in which mothers are available and supportive, when they are around. But, as we shall see below, there are characteristic periods when the American mother disappears (Emily's mother previously has been an example of this).

In contrast, the British mothers are often fallible, unsympathetic, or too preoccupied with problems in their own lives to support their daughters, and the mothering function is taken on by others. Thus different themes structure the programs: in the American there is a heavy focus on who the real mother is, and the problem is typically the daughter's male partners, whereas the British focus, instead, on who mothers whom and why.

The American men seem less in need of support from biological mothers and are more often supported by women of their own age with whom they have been, or may yet become, romantically involved. Thus in *ATWT* when Craig's wife Sierra is missing and feared killed in South America, a stream of past and potential lovers (for example, Betsy and Lily) in addition to his mother, Leila, come to mother not his young son but Craig himself. After the ceremonial peek at the baby, all collect downstairs to support the poor father. Lucinda, his mother-in-law and former lover, also arrives, but is less supportive than the other women. In the British soap operas, the sons are rarely mothered at all, being more likely to enact their independence and leave the community, as is rarely possible for the women. In *EE* several young men have left: Mark (Pauline's son), Nick (Dot's son), and Kenny (Lou's son).

THE RANGE OF MOTHERS

The generalized versus exclusive mothering issue raises a further point about the range of mothers portrayed in soap opera. For example, *EE* includes numerous other mothering positions in addition to the relatively few "normal" mother/father/child combinations (for example, Arthur, Pauline, and Michelle). There is the single-parent, Catholic, teenage prostitute mother, Mary; the formerly single parent, Michelle, now unhappily married to Lofty; the alcoholic, soon-to-be-divorced, adoptive mother, Angie; the currently infertile Sue, whose baby died a crib death; Dot, the religious, elderly mother of the local criminal; the matriarchal grandmother, Lou; the spinster, Ethel; Lofty's surrogate mother, his aunt; Naima, the ambitious, determined nonmother; and so forth. A similar range can be found in *CS*, where the number of spinsters and widows is even greater. Here there are several couples mothering children of previous marriages (for example, Audrey and Alf with Gail, Ken and Deirdre with Tracy and Susan, and Rita with her series of foster children).

In the American soap operas, the range is more limited. Mothers are biological, exclusive, and (mostly) available, although they do mother those whom they believe are their daughters (hence the who-is-the-mother issue) until they discover they are not (for example, Lily and Lucinda in *ATWT*). This exclusivity derives from the prioritization of romantic relationships in the American soap operas, where private and dyadic relationships are the norm, in contrast to the communal pattern of the British. The mother-daughter dyad of American soap operas also seems remarkably standardized; it is hard to tell one dyad from another. This is equally true, we shall see below, for the dyadic relationships of romantic couples.

THE SHRINKING GENERATION GAP

One reason for the more exclusive and limited range of mothers in the American soap operas is the age range of the characters. Because the American soaps "annihilate" all characters outside the reach of new romance, there is an absence of children and teenagers, on the one hand, and elderly mothers or grandmothers, on the other. The role of babies is very prominent in negotiating relationships, but the babies themselves are absent and their daily care is unproblematic.[5] Any grandmothers who are present (for example, Lucinda or Lisa in *ATWT*, or Miss Ellie in *Dallas*) are notably attractive and remain eligible for romance. The generation span appears to have shrunk, and the middle range is broadened and without distinction. All characters in the story may become romantically involved, and their ages seem irrelevant. This creates a tension between mothers and daughters, as they may compete with each other for the same men. (In *Dynasty*, for example, both Alexis and her daughter Fallon have an affair with and consider marrying Cecil Colby.) At the same time, the mothers' romantic experiences provide a resource for their daughters: They advise their daughters on their romantic problems and understand them perfectly. This fits with Chodorow's (1978) idea of merged ego boundaries between mothers and daughters: Mother and daughter are interchangeable.

The British soap operas abound with teenagers, babies, and grandmothers, and generational distinctions are marked. This makes for intergenerational conflict as a salient issue in the programs. The roles of mother and daughter are not interchangeable. For example, the mothers of teenage children such as Kathy and Pauline in *EE* will rarely become involved in romance and certainly not with men of a different generation. Their roles are those of mother, wife, neighbor, worker. This mirrors Alexander's (1988) notion that only if you have no other problems do you have time for romance.

In the British soap operas, the characters face a wide range of serious but humdrum problems (unemployment, marital conflict, managing daily chores, illness) and indeed have difficulty finding time for romance. The processes of everyday life are portrayed in detail: We follow the woman borrowing tools to mend her roof; we see the young mother washing the nappies and finding a babysitter. A typical scene in *EE*, for example, begins with Pauline telling her daughter, Michelle, "I'm off to do the shopping before I go to the launderette." In the next scene we witness these activities, which are never seen in American soap operas. Each step of these processes provides opportunity for neighborly interactions. Portraying the details of the characters' lives emphasizes both their differentiation from each other and their interdependence.[6] As the community is primary, each character is firmly anchored in her particular communal position, with each occupying a different but connected role. For the Americans, characters are more equivalent, each facing similar problems and following a similar life path, although at different times. Because the Americans are upper middle class, everyday management of their lives is taken care of, and romance and business take center stage: The processes of daily life are invisible. The quality of the romantic relationships is also not revealed. We witness only the crises and transition points, as when a couple is preoccupied with a third person who has been abandoned or is threatening the relationship. Conversations between mother and daughter focus on the endless makings and unmakings of the daughter's involvement with men. As this is all we know of these relationships, it is unclear why characters continually change partners, for one relationship is very much like another. One thing that can be said is that American soap operas don't leave their women alone: They must be seen to be actively engaged in a relationship and to move from one to another without intermission. Take, for example, Meg in *ATWT*, who has just discovered that her husband, Tonio, is having an affair. She runs to her mother's home where she happens to meet Rod, who is having his own problems with Betsy and is ready for a new involvement. Similarly, Chelsea in *GL*, who had a major fight with her lover at lunchtime, is persuaded by her boss at the nightclub to return and sing that evening in order to escape her depression.

ROMANCE, MOTHERHOOD, AND CAREER: ARE THEY COMPATIBLE?

What, then, makes the women in the soap operas happy? How do soap operas address the conflict between motherhood, romance, and career? Do they choose one over the other? On examining the two forms of soap opera, we would argue that neither resolves this problem, but each, because of its different historical development, prioritizes one form of feminine fulfillment over the other. The British soap operas, which derive in part from the conventions of social realism (Dyer et al., 1981), are committed to portraying the everyday problems of ordinary people's lives. Young mothers, who might be eligible for romance, are hindered by the responsibilities of childcare that leave little room for other activities. They have neither the time nor the freedom. No mother can leave the house without arranging for a babysitter and determining the time of return. They are exhausted by the daily drudgery of childcare. Happiness becomes irrelevant: Their quest is for successful, crisis-free management. Fulfillment must thus be found in motherhood, if at all. The romantic ideal cannot be sustained, for romance is clearly shown to lead to the everyday drudgery of motherhood. For example, teenager Michelle's half-hour fling with Den, the married publican of *EE*, has left her with the daily care of a child who fills her life thereafter. In the British soap operas, then, romance is subordinated to motherhood.[7] The plots are created through conflicts of gender and generation rather than romantic entanglement.

In the American soap operas, the converse is the case. The idea of babies is used as the expression of love, but real babies are in the way, for romantic relations are by nature exclusive. The women draw boundaries between self as mother and self as lover, and when in conflict, the former is subordinated or put aside. Babies become a part of the bargaining between lovers: The man provides security, the woman a baby (for example, Sue Ellen and J.R. in *Dallas*). The reality of child care is invisible. The dyadic nature of the relationship seems to be based on a model of exchange where each partner can weigh what he or she gives and gets. Brown (1987), as quoted by Fiske (1987), claims that the women in soap operas often use their pregnancy to get the father to marry them, thereby fulfilling their need to be looked after. Brown's suggestion, that women use their bodies to achieve their own ends, implies that dyadic relationships are based on exchange. The central concern of the characters is with new romances. In this sense, soap operas are one version of Cavell's (1981) "comedy of remarriage." Characters are continually trying to disentangle themselves from marriages and relationships in order to try again with someone new.

The continual disappearance of the central characters (for example, Margo and Sierra in *ATWT*; Bobby in *Dallas*; Fallon in *Dynasty*) provides a means of freeing characters and permitting recombinations. As disappearance leaves the remaining partner heartbroken, the new relationship centers on the missing person. The return of the missing character creates a further conflict. As noted before, the relationship is occupied with a third party, and the return of the missing person raises the question: With whom will I be most happy? The genre is more like Harlequin romances than is sometimes thought, because the possibility of the happy ending remains real, although always elusive. In this we would take issue with some writers (Allen, 1985; Fiske, 1987; Seiter et al., 1989) who argue that the absence of narrative closure in American soap operas, unlike romance novels, is evidence of a challenge to the romantic ideal. Certainly, relationships never conclude "happily ever after," but in American soap operas the ideal of romance is nonetheless retained as a goal for all characters. In British soap operas, however, there is no happy ending in sight: The ideal is destroyed by the portrayal of the everyday.

The phenomenon of soap opera incest, noted by Fiske (1987),[8] is facilitated by the disappearances of the mother and other characters, and by the equal eligibility of all characters for romance, regardless of age. Thus Fallon in *Dynasty* is about to marry Cecil Colby when her mother reveals him to be her real father. These relationships correspond to the current American preoccupation with father-daughter incest.

The third role held out for women is that of a career builder. In the working class collectivism of the British soap opera, social or professional ambitions would take the character out of her role in the community. As each character is needed to hold the whole system together, social advancement is punished or prevented (for example, in *EE* Michelle's attempts to leave her neighborhood were variously prevented, ultimately by pregnancy). In American soap operas, the individuality of the characters allows for some career development: Many women are reported to have careers, such as doctors, lawyers, nurses, business executives. Nonetheless, characters are sometimes punished for their ambitions (an extreme case is that of Lucy in *Dallas,* who was raped while trying to become a model) and Swanson (1982) develops the idea that *Dallas* punishes women for straying from their assigned family roles. Also note how differently the "villainess" Alexis Carrington is treated compared with her counterpart J. R. Ewing. More important, when women in American soap operas are labeled as independent professionals, we rarely see them involved in their work, and indeed their actions often seem to undermine this strong and independent image. Radway's (1984) analysis of the Harlequin romance also finds that the independence of the characters is only nominal; their actions reinstate their femininity.

The British and American soap operas offer women different compensations for this undermining of career ambitions. The British offer women a role in the stable community; the Americans offer the love of a man. Further, the concept of career or business plays a different role. In the American case, business, like babies, is bound up with romantic exchange, and business deals are often personally motivated, say, by jealousy or revenge. Thus Sue Ellen goes into the movie business to show her independence from her estranged husband, J. R., making a hostile film about him as an act of revenge. In another example, Holden in *ATWT* plans to buy his wife's lover, Tonio, out of business in order to revenge himself on his wife, Emily. In the British soap operas, the businesses play an integrating role in the community, typically providing the meeting places for neighborhood interaction. They rarely change hands for personal reasons.

THE DIALECTIC OF THE
MOTHER-DAUGHTER RELATIONSHIP

In American soap operas, women generally have an ideal, available mother on whose shoulder they can cry. At the same time, babies seem to be without mothers, and the heroines often grow up without a mother—or without their real mother. For example, Pam, Sue Ellen, and Lucy in *Dallas* all resemble the Cinderella syndrome of the Harlequin romances and the motherless girls of much children's fiction. The adult women form close relationships with their mothers as compensation for early neglect, though their early unrequited need is never fully satisfied. In the British soap opera, the reverse is true: Adult women did not lack mothers when they were children, and consequently their later relationships with their mothers are less salient and less dependent.

The dependency relations between mother and daughter have been analyzed by Chodorow (1978), who draws upon both psychoanalytic and feminist theory. For Chodorow, mothers' relationships with daughters and sons differ in two crucial ways. Daughters are less nurtured and yet kept more dependent, as mothers extend their ambivalence about their own status as women to their daughters. Sons, on the other hand, can be loved unambivalently and so encouraged to be independent, to take up their valued roles as men in society. Men are nurtured but are not taught by women to nurture others. As husbands, they fail to give their women the love and support they need. Mothers therefore seek nurturance from their daughters instead, and they teach their daughters, through the "reproduction of motherhood," to bring up their children similarly.

Chodorow's observations help to explain the erratic nature of soap opera mothering. Because mothers feel ambivalent about the resolution of their own female roles, and in consequence feel ambivalent toward bringing up their daughters to face the same conflicts, certain American characters may be led to abandon the role of mother at the crucial moment, seeking romance instead (including nurturance from men).[9] Furthermore, the mothers suspect that their daughters will fall into the same trap, choosing romance, knowing that the mothers have no solutions for the conflict. Once the daughter has discovered her fate, reenacting the same experiences, the mother can reemerge and try to help (Katz, 1988).

When characters support the unisex ideal of individual self-fulfillment and independence they can find little benefit in motherhood; conveniently, then, American soap opera makes babies invisible and undemanding. Somehow, they are being cared for. Romance—with its consequences of motherhood—is not directly in conflict with professional achievement. In fact, American soap operas frequently use the woman's career as a pretext or locus for romance. A career becomes another opportunity for asserting feminine sex appeal.

Although the British women characters do not escape the demands of motherhood, they do gain some of the benefits. They live within a woman-centered community (or sisterhood) in which a stable and collective ideal is actively fostered and in which motherhood is appreciated as a connecting force and a model for other female relationships. Self-fulfillment is not favored, especially when it involves being independent, whether within the community, or worse, outside it.

Chodorow's (1978) theory argues that the merged ego boundaries between mothers and daughters create mutual dependencies: At a certain point, daughters must mother their mothers. This creates ambivalence and often severe tensions between women, as is clear from the mother-daughter relationships in the British soap operas. For example, the relationship between Lou and Pauline in *EE* becomes increasingly tense as the mother, Lou, gets older. Yet the problems Pauline suffers as a daughter are reversed with her own daughter, Michelle, who is also called upon to mother her overworked mother.[10] By keeping all mothers indefinitely young and glamorous, American soap operas repress this problem that must face all women in some form. Instead, once the mothers become incapable they disappear from the screen. Older, powerful, and attractive women like Alexis Carrington or her daytime equivalent, Lucinda, deny the possibility of aging, and hence of dependence on their daughters.

THE CONTENT OF THE
MOTHER-DAUGHTER RELATIONSHIP

How do mothers relate to their daughters? The narrative structures of the two kinds of soap opera dictate different kinds of relationships. In the American soap operas, the story-line develops through information exchange. In scene after scene, different people come to acquire, to transfer, or to withhold information about others, and tension is generated through sharing or denying information. The centrality of secrets reflects the priority of romance over motherhood. Whereas mothering demands external participation and is publicly shared, the role of lover is by definition private, even secretive. Furthermore, the dyadic structure of American soap opera encounters based on romantic and biological links does not make room for women friends but rather constructs the mother as the confidante. Often the first or only character to hear her daughter's secrets, the mother is drawn into the private space of the couple. This concept of information exchange is part of an individualistic conception of relationships: All are equivalent but for their knowledge, and information is the power that links people. Knowledge creates allies, enemies, inequalities. The visual expression of this is the archetypal scene in which a couple is talking while a third character listens behind the door.

Once the mother is in the know, the American soap opera ethic demands that she should support her daughter uncritically. The mother has no conflicting independent opinions; in fact, she acts as sister or friend rather than as someone with greater experience. When, in *ATWT*, Emily and Holden's marriage faces problems, Emily's mother is simply there, supportive, but offering little advice or opinion. When, in another strand of the same episode, Shannon is rejected by Duncan, her mother offers dinner and a sympathetic ear but neither constructive advice nor judgment regarding the actions of either party. Possibly, the early neglect of daughters leads mothers of adult women to be wholly supportive, to allay their guilt for having subordinated motherhood to romance. Maybe, too, this reflects the American ethic of "letting it all hang out": It is the mother's role to provide a forum for the daughter to express herself, but not to exert influence or accept responsibility for her.

The independent identity of the British mothers, who have authority as members of the community in their own right, leads to less supportive, more conflictual interactions. For example, when in both *CS* and *EE* a central character had an abortion, each (Susan and Michelle) received considerable condemnation from her mother (or mother-substitute) and, indeed, from most of the women (generalized mothers) in the community. British interactions involve little information exchange but more expression and discussion of divergent opinions. This is due in part to the public life that the characters lead: Although there are certain significant secrets, generally everyone knows everyone else's business through the function of gossip, and the plot is advanced through the conflicts of everyday acts and talk.

IS THE SOAP OPERA FEMINIST?

It is currently fashionable to think of the soap opera as an open forum that represents women's problems and invites reflexive reactions from its women viewers. Allen (1985) argues that soap opera is an important "site of gender struggle," and Fiske (1987) concurs, emphasizing that non-prime time programming can escape hegemonic control more easily. Degraded as feminine entertainment, these programs are broadcast when most self-respecting members of the society are at work, in America at least (some British soap operas are broadcast in early prime time). One might add that this ghettoized time slot encourages a feeling of solidarity among women and that the multistranded, forever-open narrative permits exploration of various alternatives without the finality of a linear plot. This contrasts with earlier arguments that the message of soap opera was to pacify and flatter women for staying home. Warner and Henry (1948) argued that the genre stabilized the family by presenting the outside world as evil and by reinforcing the idea that the female listener's place is in the home. Content analyses of soap opera (summarized by Cantor & Pingree, 1983) show, for example, how nontraditional mothers are portrayed as evil characters, whereas the traditional mothers are rewarded. Perhaps things have changed: The locus of the programs, at least, is often outside the home, even if the British soap operas remain still within the neighborhood. And the issues with which they deal certainly seem contemporaneous (Katzman, 1972; Livingstone, 1988).

But can the soap opera be considered to contribute to feminist awareness? Are Allen and Fiske correct in postulating a new consciousness in the soap opera?[11] From our readings of these British and American soap operas we would answer in some ways yes, but more often no.

Undoubtedly, some of the things that soap operas are doing can be considered feminist. First, there is the fact that soaps address women's problems, overcoming what Hirsch (1981) notes as the cultural invisibility of women's issues, especially those related to motherhood and female-female relationships. We would argue that the British soap operas address women's problems more consciously and more explicitly, inasmuch as the various characteristics of the British soap operas, such as the clear differences across gender and generation, provide opportunities for discussing social and moral issues within a political framework. Characters frequently discuss events as exemplifying the nature of men and women or teenagers and the elderly.[12] More than with other issues, the characters seem to polarize the genders, openly challenging the viewer to take sides.

This kind of forum is illustrated by a conversation held in *CS*'s local grocery shop between Deirdre, Audrey, and Emily regarding Gail's divorce from Brian following her affair with Ian. The talk is fairly intimate even though the participants are not special friends but simply female members of the community. Drawing on their own experiences as a divorcee, a single parent, and a victim of a bigamous marriage, they first analyze the triangle between Gail, Brian, and Ian. An American encounter might end at this point, but the British conversation moves on to a discussion of divorce in general. Deirdre comments on the emotions involved from the woman's viewpoint, Emily offers a moral perspective, and Audrey adds a political note.[13] Her comment is then undermined as Emily and Deirdre swap tales of male victims of divorce, whose ex-wives, as Deirdre says, are "taking women's lib a bit too far."

In the American soap opera, women and their dilemmas are also central but there is little discussion of gender differences because, ironically, the modernity of the unisex position adopted does not acknowledge these differences.[14] Each issue is represented only on the personal level of events that befall or are initiated by particular characters. Although textual analyses may reveal general trends or gender differences within the American soap operas, these generalities are not an issue for discussions among the characters. Characters are simply themselves; they do not exemplify their gender or generation; they do not attempt to "organize." For example, the women are always searching for the next romance, but never comment on this. In the situation mentioned above in *ATWT* when Meg discovers that her husband Tom is having an affair with her best friend, Emily, she does not stop to discuss problems of marriage and loyalties but immediately gets involved in an affair herself. The viewer is not prompted by the dialogue to comment upon or become critically aware of the lives of the characters or of the alternative ways that they could live.

Viewers' involvement differs in the two types of soap opera: In the American, we can sympathize or identify with a woman because she is attractive or suffering; in the British, we are also aware of the moral or social issues that provide the context for her actions and over which characters may disagree. The notion of television as a "cultural forum" (Newcomb & Hirsch, 1984) seems to fit the British soap operas better than it does their American counterparts. To take sides in a British soap opera is not only to side with a favorite character but also to take sides on a contemporary moral issue. At least in terms of openness and pluralism, the British soap operas allow more potential for the oppositional in addition to hegemonic responses. It is, of course, possible to show that social issues are frequently treated in a paternalistic, pedagogic manner, especially in characters' encounters with professional and authority figures (D. Segal, 1988). But, as Newcomb and Hirsch (1984) argue, even if the solution is conservative, it is important that the issues are raised for viewers and that oppositional readings are possible.

Despite the differences in political awareness and the differential salience of the forum, both kinds of soap opera contribute to feminist awareness by making visible what was previously invisible. Both forms attempt to overcome the cultural invisibility of women's relations with each other, particularly the mother-daughter relationship. Each may conceive of this relationship differently and as posing different problems to women, but still the problems of women in relation to their roles of mother, lover, and career person are made public. Beyond getting the mother "out of the closet," the within-gender relationships are made visible (Meyrowitz, 1985). Thus in relation to gender, the viewer sees three distinct discourses: the feminine, the masculine, and that of the interactions between men and women. This makes for textual openness as, for example, one may compare the feminine "how to get a man" discourse with the interaction discourse, in which the woman and man actually talk to each other.

Can the soap opera be regarded as feminist in the sense of coping with the dilemma of the modern woman? To this question our answer must be negative, as each type of soap opera privileges only one horn of the dilemma without facing the dilemma per se, certainly without resolving it. Whereas the American soap opera opts for social mobility and romance over motherhood, the British soap opera gives priority to motherhood. This follows from (or dictates) the choice of the different class settings. The British soaps center on a traditional working-class community, which may include a few middle-class characters; moreover, audience research shows that the characters are more working class than the viewers.[15] The Americans focus on middle-class or upper-middle-class characters (Cantor & Pingree, 1983) and are somewhat above the viewers in social class background. The American case clearly displays social mobility. As the desire to better oneself involves individual effort, the unisex rather than the sisterhood conception of femininity is shown to serve women better. The British case is more problematic, as it can hardly be enjoyed as a motivating vision. Dyer et al. (1981) analyze *Coronation Street* as offering a vision of that which is *lost* through social mobility: a nostalgia for the caring, stable community of the past, a counter to alienation. One could also see it as romanticizing stability against mobility in order to keep people satisfied with their lot.[16] This need not imply, however, that all aspects of the program are hegemonic, for certain values, especially regarding a feminine ethic or a woman-centered femininity, can be retained.

One might object that we are here equating true feminism with a solution to the dilemma of motherhood, romance, and career. Perhaps feminism is better served by opting for one of the alternatives at the expense of the others, as the British and American soap operas seem to be doing. Thus one might say that the Americans are opting for unisex ideals, where women can compete with men on their own ground and learn to use their own weapons. Kaplan (1987) terms this "bourgeois feminism": the concern for equal rights and freedom with men. On the other hand, the British soap operas advocate the importance of motherhood and solidarity among women as distinctly female strengths to be generated through connection with each other and in distinction to men. Kaplan terms this "radical feminism," that which values specifically female qualities in a women-centered environment. These two feminist opposites have been described in terms of culture and nature as "anti-essentialist" and "essentialist" (or "gynocentric"), respectively. In the latest stage of this debate, feminist critics are arguing against the dichotomy, claiming that the definitions themselves may vary from one culture to another (Curti, 1988; Kuhn, 1984) and calling for a model that integrates both types of feminism.

Even if one accepts this counterargument, that each kind of soap opera paints an idealized picture of one of the feminist options, the objection arises that the simplistic representations do a disservice to feminism. First of all, they repress the causes and consequences of the preferred choice: In the American case, motherhood and babies are concealed, and in the British, there is no way up or out from home and community.

Second, the portrayal of the preferred choice itself is far from being feminist. As Radway (1984) has observed with respect to the Harlequin romance, the American soap opera heroine is not in fact as universalistic and ambitious as she first appears. Even in a professional role, she remains childlike and dependent. Although supposedly strong and intelligent, she behaves as a hopeless, emotional romantic. Despite the continual breakdown of romance and marriage, held to be evidence of the subversive nature of soap opera, the romantic ideal is kept alive. In spite of repeated evidence of failure, each character continues to seek the perfect relationship. Remaining attractive, available, and unfettered becomes essential for new romances to be possible. For her part, the British heroine may be "essentialist," but the exercise of her essentialism is restricted to the domestic realm. Her support network cannot untie her from the kitchen sink and the neighborhood launderette.

ACCOUNTING FOR CULTURAL DIFFERENCES

Three types of explanation may account for these observed differences between British and American soap operas in their treatment of motherhood and the woman's dilemma: differences in broadcasting structures in Britain and America; differences in traditions of cultural expression; and differences in sociocultural structures.

Given that the common origins of both countries' soap operas lie in American radio series before the Second World War, it is clear that differences in broadcasting and culture have operated to produce these two different forms of contemporary soap opera.[17] Whereas the American soap operas were established specifically as a commercial venture to win the daytime, housewife audience (Allen, 1985), British soap operas were produced within the public service tradition. As Melody (1988) notes, "the BBC, in the Reithian tradition, historically has interpreted its public service mandate as a paternalistic educational uplifting of the masses" (p. 268). Placing a premium on entertainment can account for the emphasis on romance, dramatic disappearances, and rapid turnover of relationships in the American soap operas. Similarly, the British tradition of social responsibility and pedagogy rather than simple entertainment value may explain the messages that undermine romance, revealing the everyday drudgery of motherhood and including antismoking or pro-elderly concerns. The more politicized commentary with which the British characters reflect on their circumstances also fits the "social realist," pedagogic tradition.[18]

Different traditions of cultural expression, in which the soap opera genre is integrated with other cultural forms (especially films and literature), can also help account for the differences in topic, narrative style, and underlying messages in British and American soap operas. Although the British soap operas derive in part from the influence from America, they also draw importantly upon the social realism of British television and film in the late 1950s, when the major soap operas began. This tradition involves a heavy emphasis upon social class, everyday mundane reality, the so-called "kitchen sink" drama, and an ideal of earthy authenticity. In contrast, the American soap opera draws on the cinematic genre of melodrama (Allen, 1985) and on the Harlequin romance novel (Modleski, 1982; Radway, 1984). These involve emotional drama, dramatic upheaval, tragedy, rags to riches, motherless infants, romantic solutions, and the search for love (hence the continued importance of mothers in adulthood). The one offers an idealized form of the realistic and warm community. The other offers a fantasy version of individual wish fulfillment.

Finally, we must ask how much the differences in the two types of programs reflect widespread socio-cultural differences between Britain and America. As Silj (1988) notes after comparing soap operas throughout Europe, "our research has shown how the production of European fiction presents strong national characteristics which reflect the cultural and social identity of the country, its history and its traditions" (p. 208). These characteristics may provide an explanation of the fact that national soap operas are more popular than imported ones (Katz & Wedell, 1977; Tracey, 1985). Our kinship mapping reflects such differences in contents and concerns as well as the difference in style suggested by Silj. Certainly, both deal with the conflict between motherhood and romance, but there are differences in treatment (for example, reflective and didactic in the British versus pleasurable and uncritical in the American programs), in the kinds of resolutions offered to this dilemma (for example, in favor of motherhood versus subordinating motherhood to romance), and, as a consequence, in the narrative (for example, who mothers whom and why versus who is the real mother).

There are, of course, many socio-structural differences between Britain and America that may account for the different worlds portrayed in their soap operas. First, there is a difference in the salience of the social class issue. In America, middle-class aspirations are more commonly held. In Britain, however, there is a strong sense of a valued working-class traditional culture to be lost by individual self-betterment, and this is celebrated within the soap operas (Dyer et al., 1981). The representation of relationships as dyadic and exchange-based versus communal and systemic also reflects these cultural differences in individualism and competition. Second, there is a difference in the progress of feminism, which has been more successful in America. In particular, the "unisex" position, which is reflected in American soap operas, is premised on the greater viability of professional aspirations for American women. With far fewer professional opportunities for women in Britain, the soap operas offer instead an ambivalent vision of community warmth and low-paid drudgery.

Finally, an American anxiety about aging may account for the shrunken generation gap in American soap operas. American television seems concerned with the denial of aging and death by emphasizing continued availability, concern for romance, and the ever-present possibility of turning over a new leaf. Thus on the key dimensions of gender, class, age, and indeed race, cultural differences between America and Britain result in different treatments of the personal, private lives of soap opera characters, in different messages being presented about their roles and relationships, and, finally, in different world views.

Anthropologists employ cultural representations of the distinction between biological and sociological kinship that reveal the moral rules and priorities of a culture, with implications for the public/private distinction and for individuality and identity (Leach, 1982). We could say, then, that the British soap operas explore this problematic area by opposing the biological and sociological kinship relations through small but ubiquitous events. For example, a biological mother repeatedly fails to help her daughter over minor, daily troubles, and a series of mother-substitutes step in and help. Connectedness with community members and the importance of everyday problems, central to social realism, are thus emphasized. Implicit here is also a difference in what Leach terms "kinship range." Sociological kinship may be restricted to the biological or it may cover a broader range of relationships. In the British programs, the role of "mother" is spread further than the biological mother, and in fact a nonbiological mother-substitute is often sought in preference by the daughter in trouble. Possibly it is the absence of biological and marital connections in the British programs, together with a recognition of the fallibility of such kinships, that leads to an emphasis on sociological kinships to resolve problems and to integrate the community.

Interestingly, the range of sociological kinship is narrower in American soap operas, given the higher degree of biological and marital connectedness among the characters. In the American soap operas, biological and sociological motherhood are infrequently but dramatically and traumatically clashed: Typically the biological mother does indeed do the mothering, but occasionally she disappears, or is discovered not to be the "real" mother at all. The demands of an entertainment genre are thus met.[19]

Whatever the cultural and broadcasting differences, it is the popular presentation of these different world views to their audiences that is our ultimate concern. The predominantly female audience is likely to be battling with the conflict between the roles of mother, lover, and career woman. The messages in the programs may direct the viewer's conceptions of their situations in either feminist or hegemonic directions. This comparative analysis of program form and content now invites, therefore, a comparative analysis of audience reception.

NOTES

1. As is the case with other television genres, for example the news (Gurevitch, 1989).

2. The four episodes of each soap opera that were studied in detail are from 1987-1988 (January 1987 for the British programs; June 1988 for the American programs). The American soap operas are shown daily on CBS during the daytime, while the British soap operas are shown bi-weekly in the early evening. We will also draw some links between the American daytime and prime-time soap operas (for example, *Dallas* and *Dynasty*).

3. "Ironically" because "organic solidarity," according to Durkheim (Bellah, 1959), characterizes modern society, while "mechanical solidarity" marks traditional society. As we shall show, the American soaps portray a modern, achievement-oriented culture, but its solidarity is of a more "mechanical," interchangeable nature, while the British represent a more traditional community where solidarity, based on a division of labor, is organic.

4. Modleski (1982) argues that American soap operas provide the isolated viewer with a sense of community that she constructs from the series of dyadic interactions portrayed among a large cast. This contrasts markedly with the British soap operas that portray the community directly: characters regularly meet in neighborhood locales, are concerned in community affairs, and have an existence as a community outside the viewer's construction.

5. The centrality of off-screen babies in American family drama was noted by viewers of *Dallas* (Liebes & Katz, 1990). In discussing "Why all the fuss about babies?", an American viewer remarked, "Kids don't play an important part. The only time when you ever see them is when the maid is carrying the baby off," and another responded, "The babies play important roles only because of what revolves around them."

6. These details often have didactic overtones. For example, when in *CS* Gail gives birth while her mother waits outside, attention is given to the "no smoking" sign, a poster giving information on welfare benefits is visible in the background, and the details of the nurses' activities serve to establish their helpfulness and efficiency.

7. For example, when Gail in *CS* gives birth to her daughter, she cares little for the paternity fight between her husband, lover, mother, and mother-in-law. She is not interested in either of the men: "I've got all I want right now."

8. Fiske (1987, p. 182) argues that, as the incest taboo is an agent of patriarchy, the presence of incest in the soap opera permits women to interrogate the boundaries of sexual desire and family relationships that it presumes.

9. This subordination of motherhood to romance in American soap operas also involves the sacrificing of female solidarity, as romance cuts across women's friendships and leads them to betray loyalties.

10. Michelle's mothering her mother becomes salient when Pauline's husband, Arthur, who is unemployed, suffers a breakdown and Michelle takes over, convinces her father, of the need to be hospitalized, and negotiates with the doctor.

11. See also Brunsdon (1983), Curti (1988), Kuhn (1984), Radway (1984).

12. For example, in *CS* as Susan waits for her father in the office, she comments to his secretary, Janet, "Women spend a lot of time waiting around for men, don't they?" Janet's response is in accord with this note of female solidarity: "Especially as they come back from the pub."

13. Thus Deirdre says: "The worst thing for me was feeling rejected, your husband's rejected you, your crazy little family's blown up in your face, you can't sleep, you even start feeling guilty, an outcast." Emily adds: " . . . which makes you think people should try harder to get back together again. Perhaps divorce is too easy these days." And Audrey comments: "Men, they always come out best, don't they?"

14. The "unisex" position of the American soap opera mirrors the arguments for androgyny advocated by psychology in the 1970s and taken up as a feminist ideal (see Kuhn, 1987). For this position, discussion of gender differences is taken as a reproduction of those differences, and men and women are thus treated equivalently.

15. Although the soap opera audience in Britain contains more working-class than middle-class viewers, there is more spread across the classes than among the soap opera characters. This is even more true for *EE* than for *CS*. (BARB data cited in Livingstone, 1990.)

16. Often conveyed metonymically by the offer, at times of crisis, to "make a nice cup of tea."

17. Silj (1988) notes that the British soap operas in particular are unique among the European and American ones.

18. Silj (1988) argues further that these differences arise from the different relations between the developing television genres and the elite classes in different countries. Thus the greater concern of the intelligentsia in Britain results in a more educational and reflective "narrative style and packaging" compared to other countries. Melody (1988) discusses how the public service tradition itself has been differently interpreted within Europe, with not all countries following the British model.

19. Almost as if the Americans have rediscovered the secret of the success of Charles Dickens in the nineteenth century equivalent to the soap opera. In Dickens' melodrama, appearing in installments in popular magazines, real and unreal mothers disappear and reappear, terrible family secrets are revealed, and characters go through drastic transitions from misfortune to fortune and vice versa. Unlike the American soap operas, how-

ever, class plays an important role, while unlike British soap operas, Dickens's characters commute between the top and bottom of the social ladder.

REFERENCES

Alexander, J. (Ed.). 1988. *Durkheimian sociology: Cultural studies.* Cambridge, UK: Cambridge University Press.

Allen, R. C. (1985). *Speaking of soap operas.* Chapel Hill: University of North Carolina Press.

Ang, I. (1984). *Watching "Dallas": Soap opera and the melodramatic imagination.* London: Methuen.

Bellah, R. N. (1959). Durkheim and history. *American Sociological Review, 24,* 447-461.

Brown, M. E. (1987). The politics of soaps: Pleasure and feminine empowerment. *Australian Journal of Cultural Studies, 4,* 1-25.

Brunsdon, C. (1983). Crossroads: Notes on soap opera. In E. A. Kaplan (Ed.), *Regarding television: Critical approaches—An anthology* (pp. 76-83). Los Angeles: American Film Institute.

Cantor, M. G., & Pingree, S. (1983). *The soap opera.* Beverly Hills, CA: Sage.

Cavell, S. (1981). *Pursuits of happiness: The Hollywood comedy of remarriage.* Cambridge, MA: Harvard University Press.

Chodorow, N. (1978). *The reproduction of mothering.* Berkeley: University of California Press.

Curti, L. (1988). Genre and gender. *Cultural Studies, 2*(2), 152-167.

Dyer, R., Geraghty, C., Jordan, M., Lovell, T., Paterson, R., & Stewart, J. (1981). *Coronation street.* London: British Film Institute.

Fiske, J. (1987). *Television culture.* London, New York: Methuen.

Gurevitch, M. (1989). Comparative research on television news: Problems and challenges. *American Behavioral Scientist, 33,* 221-229.

Hirsch, M. (1981). Mothers and daughters. *Signs: Journal of Women in Culture and Society, 7,* 200-222.

Kaplan, E. A. (1987). Feminist criticism and television. In R. C. Allen (Ed.), *Channels of discourse: Television and contemporary criticism* (pp. 211-253). London: Methuen.

Katz, E. (1988). Personal Communication, Jeruselem.

Katz, E., & Wedell, G. (1977). *Broadcasting in the third world.* London: Macmillan.

Katzman, N. (1972). Television soap operas: What's been going on, anyway? *Public Opinion Quarterly, 36,* 200-212.

Kuhn, A. (1984). Women's genres. *Screen, 25,* 18-29.

Kuhn, A. (1987). Feminist criticism and television. In R. C. Allen (Ed.), *Channels of discourse.* Chapel Hill: University of North Carolina Press.

Leach, E. (1982). *Social anthropology.* Glasgow: Fontana.

Liebes, T., & Katz, E. (1990). *The export of meaning: Cross cultural readings of "Dallas."* New York: Oxford University Press.

Livingstone, S. M. (1988). Why people watch soap opera: An analysis of the explanations of British viewers. *European Journal of Communication, 3*(1), 55-80.

Livingstone, S. M. (1989). Interpretive viewers and structured programs: The implicit representation of soap opera characters. *Communication Research, 16,* 25-27.

Livingstone, S. M. (1990). *Making sense of television: The psychology of audience interpretation.* Oxford: Pergamon.

Melody, W. H. (1988). Pan-European television: Commercial and cultural implications of European satellites. In P. Drummond & R. Paterson (Eds.), *Television and its audience: International research perspectives* (pp. 267-281). London: British Film Institute.

Meyrowitz, J. (1985). *No sense of place.* New York: Oxford University Press.

Modleski, T. (1982). *Loving with a vengeance: Mass produced fantasies for women.* New York, London: Methuen.

Newcomb, H. M., & Hirsch, P. M. (1984). Television as a cultural forum: Implications for research. In W. Rowland & B. Watkins (Eds.), *Interpreting television: Current research perspectives* (pp. 58-73). Beverly Hills, CA: Sage.

Radway, J. (1984). *Reading the romance: Feminism and the representation of women in popular culture.* Chapel Hill: University of North Carolina Press.

Segal, D. (1988). Personal Communication.

Seiter, E., Borchers, H., Kreutzner, G., & Worth, E. M. (1989). Don't treat us like we're so stupid and naive: Towards an ethnography of soap opera viewers. In E. Seiter et al. (Eds.), *Remote control: Television audiences and cultural power.* London: Routledge & Kegan Paul.

Silj, A. (1988). *East of Dallas: The European challenge to American television.* London: British Film Institute.

Swanson, G. (1982). Dallas. *Framework, 5.*

Tracey, M. (1985). The poisoned chalice: International television and the idea of dominance. *Daedalus, 114*(4), 17-56.

Tuchman, G. (1979). Women's depiction in the mass media. *Signs: Journal of Women in Culture and Society, 4,* 528-542.

Warner, W. L., & Henry, W. E. (1948). The radio daytime serial: A symbolic analysis. *Genetic Psychology Monographs, 37,* 3-71.

Chapter 7

THE SUMMIT AS MEDIA EVENT: THE REAGAN/GORBACHEV MEETINGS ON U.S., ITALIAN, AND SOVIET TELEVISION

Daniel C. Hallin and Paolo Mancini

DURING THE COLD WAR, U.S./Soviet summits were seen above all as symbolic events. Beyond any concrete agreements reached during their closed-door meetings, they were typically evaluated by the "spirit" they created, by the sense of common commitment transcending political antagonism and presumably leading to further political accomplishment, which a successful summit was expected to produce.

In this sense, U.S./Soviet summits seem to fit fairly closely the model of "media events" put forward by Elihu Katz and Daniel Dayan (Dayan & Katz, 1988; Katz & Dayan, 1985; Katz, Dayan, & Motyl, 1980, 1981). Katz and Dayan define *media events* as planned, symbolic performances staged for a media audience. Besides summits, this definition would include such events as inaugurations and coronations, public commemorations of historical events, and launchings and landings of space missions; it excludes unplanned events covered by the media: An assassination is not a media event in this sense; the state funeral following it is.[1] Adapting the Durkheimian view of the social function of ritual, Katz and Dayan have argued that media events tend to integrate societies: They dissolve or deemphasize social divisions, and bring the members of a community together around shared values and a shared sense of identity. At the funeral of a statesman like Kennedy or Berlinguer, for example, references to partisan divisions are considered inappropriate (Mancini, 1987; Verba, 1965). The experience, shared primarily through television, is for "everyone." The event is as much a celebration of the common identity of the audience—as Americans, or Italians, or simply as human beings—as it is a tribute to the individuals who stand for the community.

All of these, of course, are primarily national media events. They may be covered by the media of the entire world, but the ceremonies involved are addressed primarily toward national audiences. A summit, on the other hand, is truly an international media event, part of a small category of such events addressed directly toward global audiences. It would follow from Katz and Dayan's analysis—and also fit with the common understanding of the symbolic effects of summitry—that summits should push toward international integration, toward a sense of common identity that transcended the nation state. This is the hypothesis we would like to take up here, using the example of the three major summits between Reagan and Gorbachev, at Geneva in 1985, Washington in 1987, and Moscow in 1988.

What makes the U.S./Soviet summits particularly interesting, as we shall see, is that they involve a particularly problematic definition of community: Who is the "we" journalists address as their audience, the community they take as a frame of reference—the nation, the bloc, or humanity as a whole? This issue, we shall argue, creates difficulties for the Durkheimian framework and suggests that in order to understand media events more fully, we need to think more systematically about different ways of conceptualizing community. We shall explore, in particular, the distinction between the Durkheimian conception of civil religion and the very different notion of the *public sphere*.

METHODOLOGY

Because the summit is in essence a global media event, it makes sense to consider its presentation in a number of different national media. The discussion that follows is based on an analysis of television coverage in three countries, two of them direct participants in the summit, the United States and the Soviet Union, and one, Italy, a spectator. In making this sort of analysis, many problems of cross-system comparison obviously arise. There is no need to summarize here the many particular problems that arise, for instance, in defining comparable variables for content analysis across systems. (The methodology, as well as much of the empirical evidence, is discussed in greater detail in Hallin & Mancini, 1990. A longer version of the theoretical argument can be found in Hallin & Mancini, 1991.) But some more general considerations are worth spelling out.

In making cross-system comparisons of media content, it is important to take into account two kinds of factors that affect the behavior of the media. The first are media system factors, the second, factors of political context. The media system and the role of television within that system is of course different in each country. American TV news, for example, is highly mediated, in the sense that the reporting is both interpretive and dramatized; the journalist is extremely active in giving ideological and narrative structure to the news. The Italian TV journalist, for reasons we have discussed elsewhere (Hallin & Mancini, 1984), normally plays a much less active role, although as we shall see the Geneva summit did provide an occasion for more interpretive commentary and more active dramatization than is usually the case in Italian news. As this example suggests, news content needs to be interpreted against the proper norm. And what is interesting is often the *direction of movement* that a particular kind of story produces: The summit as a media event pushes the Italian journalist toward a more active interpretive mode. If we merely compared the Italian content with the American, which is always more interpretive, we would miss this dynamic.

Because we are concerned in this chapter with the relation of the media to social and political consensus, it is useful to think of the distinctions among the different media systems in these terms. The American journalist claims to represent a social consensus shared by all the *individuals* of the society. The Soviet journalist has traditionally represented the vanguard party, which in turn claimed to represent the interests of Soviet society as a whole. The Italian journalist, who has neither the political autonomy of the American nor the connection to a single dominant party, could be said to have a weaker basis of legitimacy. The most important political consensus in Italy is that all the diverse parties in the country have a right to be heard, and the Italian journalist neutrally presents their views. These journalistic identities, each connected with a basis of journalistic legitimacy, are rooted in the political economy and cultural history of television in each society. Certain conventions of news presentation are associated with each of them and these are reflected, though sometimes in modified form, in summit coverage.

The news content we observe is a joint product of these kinds of journalistic factors, interacting with factors of political context. Italy, for example, is part of the Western alliance, yet at the same time is essentially a spectator to the confrontation between the United States and the Soviets. It should come as no surprise, therefore, that Italian television gave somewhat more attention to the U.S. position at Geneva, but was at the same time less partisan than either U.S. or Soviet television. If we then look at the American coverage we find that it was far more partisan than the Italian, particularly at the Geneva summit, which occurred at the peak of the Reagan era and the "Second Cold War." We also find something that appears at first glance anomalous: American television, unlike its Italian counterpart, gave more attention to Gorbachev than to Reagan at Geneva. To understand what this means, we need to know that American and Italian television allocate time differently, Italian television using more directly political criteria, American television more narrative ones. Gorbachev was a *better story* than Reagan. This overrode what might seem like the normal political response of the American media (though it also provoked considerable anxiety among American journalists about their political role and much commentary about the danger that Gorbachev would manipulate Western public opinion). The static content of the news is not meaningful by itself, and simply to describe it leads us nowhere theoretically. What is important are the patterns of interaction between journalistic conventions and political context that produce this content, and that we uncover by looking at the behavior of the media both across systems and across contexts. One reason comparative research on the news media remains difficult and a bit primitive is that we are just beginning to build up a large enough body of case studies to begin thinking about how to understand these interactions.

One final point about methodology. It is not our intention to draw any conclusion about the long-term effect of the summit as a media event on political discourse or political policy. Our purpose is to address the narrower question of the way they affect the discourse of news while they are in progress.

THE SUMMIT AS AN "INTEGRATING" EVENT

There is, in fact, a good case to be made that the summit, as a media event, pushes in certain ways in the direction of some form of global integration. Three specific effects of the summit—all of them closely interrelated—seem to us particularly important: first, expansion of the global communication flow; second, the symbolic constitution of a global community; and third, a tendency to humanize the Other.

EXPANSION OF GLOBAL COMMUNICATION FLOW

The most obvious effect of summits as media events is that they change the structure of the world communication flow, increasing the flow of communication through international—as opposed to national—channels. This has always been true of East/West summits, but it is particularly so in the Gorbachev era, as the Soviets have sought both to communicate more effectively outside their borders and to open up their own communication system (Lyne, 1987). A summit offers an extraordinary opportunity for the states involved to override normal limitations on communication, taking the spotlight worldwide and even opening direct channels of communication with the population of other states, something that was, at the height of the Cold War, normally impossible across its major line of division.

What makes this really significant, however, is that in order to take advantage of this opportunity, a state must allow itself to be drawn into a process that it cannot completely control; it must accept the rules of the international game it seeks to play. At Geneva, for instance, the Soviets held far more press conferences than they had at previous summits. But when they did, they had to be prepared to answer numerous questions about human rights, posed both by journalists and by demonstrators who had themselves come to Geneva to seek a place on the world stage. Gorbachev could seize the headlines in Washington by meeting with political leaders outside the administration and by stopping his limousine to "press the flesh." But he in turn had to grant Reagan the right to meet with religious dissidents in Moscow and to proselytize the Soviet public, when the two leaders exchanged televised New Year's greetings at the beginning of 1988, about elections, religion, and the American "standard of living." The Reagan/Gorbachev summits opened up an unusual global process of communication, and anyone who wished to participate had to be prepared to hear and to answer voices that were not normally present in national political discourse.

The implications have been particularly great for the Soviets, since the international communication process tends to be dominated by

Western conventions. In a society in which divisions among the political elite were until recently excluded from public communication, the sight of Mikhail Gorbachev responding in a televised press conference to the comments of demoted party leader Boris Yeltsin, who granted interviews during the Moscow summit to CBS and the BBC was a truly dramatic break from the past.

The role of the media in this process is a relatively active one. The media are active, first of all, in building up a global audience for the event. Their promotion and dramatization, though these take different forms in different countries, are in each country essential to the constitution of the event as something that exists for everyone; without it the sense of the "whole world watching" that surrounds the event would not exist. The media are active also in shaping the conversation that emerges in the summit, through their role as interrogators and interpreters of the summit participants. If the international communication process has certain rules that participants must follow, the journalists are among the most important arbiters of those rules.

Events like the Reagan/Gorbachev summits thus raise the issue of whether the media might be developing into a genuinely international institution—not merely conduits linking each national audience with the central event of the summit, but an actual transnational institution, with common norms and routines, capable of playing an autonomous role in world politics. Certainly, the extent of transnational institutionalization of the media should not be exaggerated. In fact, as we shall see, the summits show dramatically how nationally centered journalists still are, both in their political views and in their professional culture. Until there are international institutions around which journalists congregate on a regular and not a sporadic basis, internationalization of the press corps cannot be expected to develop beyond a limited extent (it is most developed today in the case of the world financial press, the *Financial Times* and *The Wall Street Journal,* for example, which of course are tied to increasingly internationalized economic institutions [Sparks, 1989]). But the internationalization of journalism is a process that is at least under way, and the increased intensity of interaction among national media that takes place during summits—even to the point of producing joint news broadcasts, as the United States and the Soviets did during the Washington summit—seems likely to accelerate it.[2] The consequences for world politics might in the long run be quite significant.

SYMBOLIC CONSTITUTION
OF A GLOBAL COMMUNITY

It is a common hypothesis that electronic communication tends to break down the barriers of established social groups. There are both utopian and anti-utopian versions of this argument, ranging from McLuhan's vision of the "Global Village" on one side to theories of mass society and cultural imperialism on the other. Katz and Dayan's theory of media events of course is utopian; extending it to superpower summitry, it could be argued that the power of television to override social boundaries should combine with the integrative effect of ritual to produce, at least temporarily, a global sense of community.

And in fact something like this did happen with the Reagan/Gorbachev summits. Because it takes place on a world stage, the summit constitutes international society for a brief period as a tangible, salient community. All the actors involved are acutely aware that they stand before a worldwide audience, and this has substantial impact on political discourse, shifting it away from the standard national frame of reference, toward a global frame. Journalists, for example, will frequently use the term *we* to refer not to the inhabitants of a particular nation state, but to all humanity (or in some cases to the people of both superpowers). *We* comes to mean not the particular national audience the journalists normally address, but the international audience that a summit brings temporarily into being (cf. Urban, 1988, and Wertsch, 1987). The anchor of the main Italian news broadcast summed up Geneva by saying,

> Thus the first Russian/American summit in over six years has come to a close. . . . Grounds for divergence do persist, and they are deeply rooted, but an important page has been turned. The hope of all mankind is that this day shall remain in history, that it truly marked the beginning of a process for which we all long—that is to say: May the arsenals indeed be emptied, and the granaries be filled. Of this the world undoubtedly has great need.

Once global society has been invoked, values considered appropriate to that society tend at least partly to displace more particularistic values of ideology and national sovereignty; as these examples suggest, the value of peace clearly takes center stage during a summit. The celebration of international harmony, in fact, was not confined to news during the Reagan/Gorbachev summits, but spilled into other parts of mass culture as well. Coca-Cola ran a commercial showing children of all races singing together and embracing one another: "As the leaders of the world come together, we offer this message of hope." And Parker Pen offered the image of Reagan and Gorbachev signing the INF treaty, with the slogan, "The pen is mightier than the sword."

The role of the media in the symbolic constitution of global community is complex: They are not only the channels through which a world audience is created, but also themselves represent global community. The global audience itself is invisible during the summit, for the most part, aside from few occasions when journalists interview citizens or other observers. But the *muro di giornalisti*, as the Italians put it, the wall of journalists, about 6,000 strong (up from about 1,000 during the superpower summits of the early 1960s), are extremely visible; they are one of the key visual images of the summit as a televised media event. Their role in summit coverage is double in an interesting way: They are both the narrators of the drama and a character in it. They appear as a stand-in for the world community, witnessing and interrogating the two leaders on its behalf.

Even if the institutionalization of the world press corps remains limited, their symbolic role is certainly powerful during a summit. It is parallel in an interesting way to the chorus in another kind of civic ritual—Greek tragedy.[3] The structure of tragedy, according to Vernant and Vidal-Naquet (1981), involved

> [a] tension between the two elements that occupy the tragic stage. One is the chorus, the collective and anonymous presence embodied by an official college of citizens. Its role is to express through its fears, hopes, questions and judgements, the feelings of the spectators who make up the civic community. The other, played by a professional actor, is the individualized character whose actions form the core of the drama and who appears as a hero from an age gone by, always more or less estranged from the ordinary condition of the citizen. (p. 10)

Like the chorus, the media at the summit represent world community. It is above all in the "wall of journalists" and the interaction of world leaders with them that the world community seems no longer abstract but physically present and undeniably real—an imagined community, in the words of Benedict Anderson (1983).

HUMANIZATION OF THE OTHER

This leads us to consider the role of the other symbolic element of the summit as media event, the "individualized characters" of Reagan and Gorbachev. Consider the "tea summit" (or "style wars") of Nancy and Raisa, or the sight of Gorbachev shaking hands with stunned Americans on a Washington street; these events suggest a third way in which the summit, as a media event, tends toward international integration. As Katz and Dayan (1985) have argued, media events are planned and presented as *narratives,* centering around certain characters understood as the heroes of the story. During a media event, television moves away from the usual modes of political reporting and toward a dramatic mode. The dramatic mode does two things simultaneously. First, it celebrates the event as something standing above the routine of political life. In the Italian coverage, this is manifested in a shift of journalistic roles from neutral announcing to a more active interpretation of the significance of the event, as in the comment about granaries and armories quoted above. In the American coverage, where the normal mode is analysis focused on policy conflicts, the elevation of the event above routine politics is symbolized in part in the fact that the journalists "stand back" at certain moments to put the event itself rather than their own analysis in the foreground, pausing to let the image and sound of the event fill the screen without words from the journalist to define their meaning, something very unusual in American TV news. The visual is often privileged in this sort of coverage. So, for example, the morning the Geneva summit began, the host of NBC's morning program *Today* opened the broadcast by repeating the image of the two leaders shaking hands: "The moment was so special," he said, "it bears repeating. This is the picture you will see again and again." And one of the things that is presented as special in this dramatic presentation— here we come to the second characteristic of the dramatic mode—is a personal meeting of two human beings. As a dramatic ritual, the event is both elevated above routine politics and "brought down" to human scale.[4]

The consequences of dramatization are also twofold. First, again following Katz and Dayan, it opens up a sense of possibility: "Media events testify that *voluntarism* is still alive, that the deeds of human beings—especially great ones—still make a difference and are worth recording" (Katz, Dayan, & Motyl, 1981, p. 53). Both the sense of occasion of a media event and the fact that it centers around particular human individuals rather than anonymous social institutions contribute to an impression that the laws of politics are suspended and the future is open—a naive view, certainly, but one that may at the same time encourage people to think about what *could be.* Normally political news is rigidly focused on what *is*; media events change the ontology of news. Summits are traditionally occasions when, for a brief period at least, the Cold War no longer seems natural, and we are allowed to speculate about the possibility of a different international order: "May the arsenals be emptied and the granaries be filled."

Second, because of the personal focus of the dramatic mode, the person who represents the Other also comes before each audience not as a political abstraction but as a human being. Personalization obviously can have many uses and consequences; Khrushchev functioned in a highly personalized way as a negative symbol of the Other in an earlier era. When the political context permits, however, personalization can push strongly the other way. Thus in Washington we saw Gorbachev and his wife singing along with great emotion as the pianist Van Cliburn played "Moscow Nights" at the White House, while the Reagans smiled warmly next to them. Demon images of the enemy are obviously eroded by this sort of thing.[5]

MEDIA AS NATIONAL INSTITUTIONS

In certain ways, then, it makes sense to think of summits as media events pushing toward some form of international integration. But this is only part of the story. The standard criticism of the Durkheimian approach to ritual is of course that it abstracts from structures of power and processes of change and conflict, assuming that civic ritual produces an unproblematic sense of community that stands above politics (Chaney, 1983; Kertzer, 1988; Lukes, 1975; Shils & Young, 1953). The summit is a good illustration of the limitations of this perspective. The primary political identities of each of the countries in this study are, after all, national identities strongly connected to the structure of conflict known as the Cold War. The global sense of community invoked by the summits threatened to disrupt integration at the national and bloc level. We need not discuss the content at greater length here; it will have to suffice to say that the media in each country, tied as they are to national political institutions, simultaneously celebrated global community *and* played the role of reinforcing patterns of understanding and commitment rooted in the Cold War. This was particularly true of the U.S. media, where journalistic independence had the ironic consequence of making the journalists feel a heightened sense of responsibility to uphold the dominant political consensus. For the American media the summits provided an occasion for an exceptional emphasis on the ideological division between East and West.

AN INTERNATIONAL PUBLIC SPHERE?

Clearly considerable difficulties arise in applying the concepts of ritual and of integration to the divided and conflictual global "community" of the Cold War world. It makes sense, therefore, to relate the media event to another, different conception of common social space: that of the public sphere. The concept of *the public sphere* refers to the arena of civic discourse, in which citizens enter into an ongoing dialogue about the common concerns of the society (Garnham, 1986; Habermas, 1989). It involves a conception of community centered around *participation in a common conversation* rather than *sharing of common values*. As we focus on this different conception of community, a new set of questions arises.

Does it make sense to say that the Reagan/Gorbachev summits, as media events, opened up an international public sphere? Just as when we asked whether the summit could be seen as leading to international integration, the answer is both yes and no. Certainly in some ways the summits opened a semblance of an international public sphere. The two superpowers entered into a conversation with one another before the "court" of world public opinion; they entered into a conversation with the world press; journalists from the two superpowers entered into conversation with one another. Dialogue on a global scale was the order of the day. At the same time, however, the nature of the civic discourse surrounding the summit was extremely restricted in the television coverage by each of the countries examined here.

In order to make this case in more detail, we need to begin to break down the notion of a "global dialogue" into more specific components. In particular, we need to distinguish between two different conceptions of international society. International society is most commonly conceived as a kind of second-order society, the "citizens" of which are states. If we focus on this level, the most important thing to say about the public sphere opened by the summit is that participation in it was extremely uneven, with the voice of the two superpowers overwhelmingly dominant. The notion of a world audience was invoked, of course. But the views of other members of the world community were little represented. On American television, for example, less than 5% of

Geneva coverage was devoted to the reactions of the nation's West European allies; virtually none to the views of the rest of the world. Italian television did devote significant attention—a little more than 11% of its coverage—to the reactions of Italian political parties and other West European countries; but these actors appeared in the passive role of hoping for superpower reconciliation and were rarely shown expressing independent political views. Soviet television gave the most attention to views outside the superpowers. Indeed about a third of Soviet coverage was devoted to reactions of West Europeans and the Third World, as well as nongovernment voices in the United States (an issue we will take up in a moment). But these voices functioned in the Soviet coverage mainly to praise Soviet policy, or, as in the Italian coverage, to praise summitry itself. In this sense, the summit as a media event would seem to reinforce what Fred Halliday (1988) has called hegemonic internationalism: "the belief that the integration of the world is taking place but on asymmetrical, unequal terms, and that this is the only possible and desirable way for such an integration to take place" (p. 193).

International society can also be seen, however, as composed of individuals and organizations constituted by them. Among the provisions of the Helsinki Final Act, for example, is the directive that the Final Act be publicly disseminated in each signatory state. Implicit in this provision is the idea that although the Final Act resulted from an agreement among states, the matters it deals with, particularly human rights, are the concern not just of states, but of *people*, and it is hoped that public opinion will play some role in achieving the goals of the final act. This is not the dominant conception of international society, certainly. But it seems likely to become increasingly important, at least if the trend toward public transnational institutions like the European Parliament continues. This issue is significant in the context of the Reagan/Gorbachev summits because this was a period when there was considerable tension between the points of view of government leaders and those of citizens, with, for example, a major surge of citizen activism in opposition to the regime of nuclear deterrence within NATO countries.

The media, of course, even if they have close formal or informal ties to the state, are oriented toward the ordinary citizens who make up their audience. It might be thought, therefore, that the summit, as media event, would tend at least temporarily to promote the notion of public opinion as an important basis for world order, and to shift attention from a "statist" to the "civil" point of view (Manoff, 1983). Certainly to some extent this is true. Because it invokes the standpoint of humanity as a whole, for example, and because it humanizes political leadership, the summit as media event can be seen as pushing toward a civil voice and a civil vision of the world. And yet in each country there are strong journalistic forces pushing the other way.

We can begin here with the U.S. coverage, which on this point is probably the most complex. It might be tempting to conclude simply that the American summit coverage privileged a state-centered point of view. Certainly foreign policy coverage in the U.S. media was largely dominated by the official sources on whom journalists rely (Hallin, Manoff, & Weddle, 1990; Sigal, 1973), and much of the summit coverage reflected, as one journalist put it during the Moscow summit, an "inside baseball, professional arms negotiator point of view." But if American journalists see themselves as "insiders," they at the same time see themselves as representative of the point of view of the ordinary citizen; indeed it is often stressed in coverage of U.S./Soviet relations that while the East exalts the State, the West exalts the Individual. How are the two points of view reconciled?

Here it will be useful to consider a particular text, a commentary by Bill Moyers of CBS during the Geneva summit. The commentary began with Moyers in the room where Reagan and Gorbachev had met earlier in the day.

> They were alone in those two chairs with only interpreters in the room. But if some magic camera could have flashed here, a multitude of faces would have been revealed looking on . . . [Here Moyers mentioned domestic factions in the two countries, East and West Europeans, and public opinion.]
>
> Public opinion is fickle. "My hope is for peace in the world," a voter said to a pollster. "But if not that, the complete destruction of Russia and China." It is a thought to justify a summit.
>
> You may wince, as I do, to realize that in a world of such diversity and talent, the destinies of so many ride into a single room with just two men. But as a friend of mine said this morning, "People don't want to be blown up, and these are the two guys who can do something about it." We were all in that room.

Here we see again the "magic" of the media event. Because all the world is looking toward Geneva, Geneva becomes a place from which we can "see" humanity (Dan Rather, in introducing Moyers, described the room as "a special room with a view, a *world* view"). It is "humanity," above all in the form of the invisible audience of ordinary people, that is the addressee of the commentary. Moyers identifies himself with and purports to present the perspective of the "little guy" who doesn't "want to be blown up," the "we" who were "in that room." At the same time, Moyers was "in the room" in a different sense than "we" were: When the commentary begins he is physically present in the room where the two leaders met; later he comes out into the street to speak directly to "us." We are "present" in the room vicariously, both through our leaders and through Moyers, who represents himself as a bridge between the powerful and the powerless. The journalist mediates between state and society, leader and citizen. But he clearly mediates in such a way that the dominant position of the state is affirmed: "Public opinion is fickle. . . . These are the two guys who can do something about it."

Public opinion, although it was in a sense presented by American journalists as extremely potent—there was great preoccupation in American summit coverage with the possibility that Gorbachev would win a propaganda victory—was also seen either as an essentially passive force, subject to manipulation by the two sides, or as a disturbance interfering with the rational conduct of international affairs. The journalists granted it little positive role, actual or potential, in the establishment of international political order. It was normally excluded, for instance, when journalists explained the process by which the United States and the Soviets came together to conclude the INF treaty. At the same time, the American coverage was generally very hostile toward more active manifestations of public opinion—or, to be more precise, toward such manifestations within the West; human rights activists from the East were given favorable and extensive coverage.

For the Soviet journalist, at the time of the Reagan/Gorbachev summits, the theory of the vanguard party eliminated any feeling of tension between the statist and civil perspectives. The vanguard party made state and society one, and the Soviet journalist had no problem speaking explicitly for the state. Looking at the side of domestic politics, Soviet summit coverage was strictly state-centered: The problem of peace was presented as one that the Soviet government would resolve; the citizen had no independent role or perspective. This assumption was powerfully present in the Soviet coverage of Geneva in many ways; no ordinary Soviet citizen, for instance, appeared in the news. Beyond Soviet borders the picture was more complicated; in the international arena a lively public sphere of peace movements and active citizens sprang into being, along with a wide community of nations clamoring for peace. Soviet, like American, television, payed homage to the value of citizen activism by celebrating its role in the *other* bloc. The West European peace movement, especially, was given far more attention by Soviet than by American television, accounting in fact for almost a third of the people appearing in the reporting of *Vremya,* the main Soviet news broadcast. These were not, however, independent voices: Their function in the news broadcast was to praise Soviet policy.

In Italy, television journalism normally is centered around what could be called the institutionalized public sphere of organized political forces like parties. The summit introduced a significant change, with the journalist adopting the point of view of the "man in the street": "Let us wish for them [the leaders] and for ourselves that they will make it [i.e., agreement]." "We" here means the ordinary citizen, whatever his or her political affiliation, and the whole story of the summit is told around this ordinary citizen's hope for peace: Will it be realized or not? A few ordinary people even appear in the Italian summit coverage—something very unusual for Italian television—though these are Soviets and not Italians. In a sense, the Italian coverage is the most civil-centered of the three countries. Yet the public sphere of the Italian coverage remains passive and largely devoid of content. The very word *hope*—which could be considered the key theme of the Italian coverage—sums up the nature of the community that is invoked: It is a community of *spectators*, who have no ability to influence the outcome of the process they are watching. And as we have seen, although Italian television gave considerable time to Italian and West European views of the summit, few had anything to say except to express hope.

CONCLUSION

The Reagan/Gorbachev summits, as televised media events, were politically ambivalent. They were a mixture of internationalism and nationalism, of *communitas* and structure, of openness and exclusion. How can this ambivalence be summed up? One way might be to see the summits, following Murray Edelman (1967, 1988), as rituals of pacification. Elaborate "lip service" is given to international reconciliation, but in a way that gives it only the most vague and general content. People were reassured that something was being done about the threat of nuclear war by established political authorities and structures, loyalty to which was simultaneously reaffirmed. Popular activism was discouraged, and in its place is found the "quasi-democracy of intimate access" to political leaders (Chaney, 1986, p. 121). There did in fact seem to be a pattern of demobilization of peace movements and consolidation of the Cold War following limited but symbolically celebrated moves toward détente. The disarmament movement of the early 1960s died out after the Test Ban Treaty. And there is some evidence of a similar process following the INF treaty. There was, for instance, much less coverage of Western peace activists in the American coverage of the Washington summit than at the Geneva summit. Events in the Soviet Union and Eastern Europe, of course, subsequently pushed the discussion of East/West relations far beyond what most thought possible as late as the Moscow summit. But even if we put aside this history, and ask what might have happened if the Soviet bloc had not crumbled from within, the pacification view of the summits is probably too simple. It seems to us that the contradictory character of these summits as media events is real and irreducible, expressing a genuine tension in human consciousness in this era between what is and what could be, and probably functioning—though as we have said, we cannot address the long-term effects of the summit directly—both to limit and pacify an alternative discourse looking beyond the Cold War and simultaneously to keep that discourse alive.

EPILOGUE:
SUMMITRY AND INTERNATIONAL JOURNALISM
AFTER THE COLD WAR

With the end of the Cold War, U.S./Soviet summits are increasingly treated as ordinary political news rather than as media events: They no longer have the drama of a handshake across hostile worlds that used to raise them above the routine of political life. The question of global society, in both its faces—the Durkheimian sense of a shared sense of membership and the Habermasian sense of participation in dialogue—has become less subjunctive and more practical, less a hope and more a political task. The problems of international journalism are increasingly the problems of political journalism in general. When Bush met Gorbachev in Washington in the spring of 1990, for example, American journalists moved away from the moralizing mode that characterizes media event coverage: They neither celebrated global understanding, nor did they denounce the Soviets as enemies of the West, as they had in previous summits. They covered the event as a normal, if fairly important, political meeting. Real dialogue was probably more extensive than in previous summits, with Gorbachev's words covered extensively and far more objectively than they had been in the past. And perhaps, for all the drama of the media event, this normalization of political dialogue went even further in building a sense of belonging to a community. At the same time, post-Cold War summits manifest the limitations of the normal public sphere. The range of voices represented is extremely limited, heavily centered on U.S. and Soviet officials. And the range of issues considered is correspondingly narrow, North/South issues, for example, being absent from summit coverage until the Iraqi invasion of Kuwait forced them onto the agenda of the (former?) superpowers. No doubt we are on the threshold of a period of slow change in national media institutions, as standard conventions of journalism prove inadequate to the challenge of an increasingly multilateral and interdependent world.

NOTES

1. The phrase *media event* has of course also been applied to nonplanned events covered by the media; media events in this other sense can share some of the characteristics of media events in the Katz and Dayan sense (Rosengren, Arvidson, & Sturesson, 1975).

2. Obviously there is much more to the question of the internationalization of the media than we can deal with here. There is, for example, a trend toward internationalization of *ownership* of the media in the West, as well as continuing development of the international market in news and cultural products, represented by CNN's international operations.

3. The parallel with the chorus in Greek tragedy was pointed out to us by Eric Vollmer.

4. In humanizing political leaders, the summit would seem to involve at least to a limited extent the leveling Victor Turner (1969) discusses in connection with liminality.

5. A *Newsweek* poll (December 21, 1987, p. 22) after the Washington summit showed 32% of Americans saying their opinion of Gorbachev was better than before the summit, 1% that it was worse, and 64% that it was the same; this came on top of an already greatly improved public image of the Soviet leader.

REFERENCES

Anderson, B. (1983). *Imagined communities: Reflections on the origin and spread of nationalism.* New York: Verso.

Chaney, D. (1983). A symbolic mirror of ourselves: Civic ritual in mass society. *Media, Culture and Society, 5,* 119-135.

138   *The Summit as Media Event*

Chaney, D. (1986). The symbolic form of ritual in mass communication. In P. Golding, G. Murdock, & P. Schlesinger (Eds.), *Communicating politics: Mass communication and the political process* (pp. 115-132). New York: Holmes & Meier.

Dayan, D., & Katz, E. (1988). Articulating consensus: The ritual and rhetoric of media events. In J. C. Alexander (Ed.), *Durkheimian sociology: Cultural studies* (pp. 161-186). Cambridge, UK: Cambridge University Press.

Edelman, M. (1967). *The symbolic uses of politics.* Urbana: University of Illinois Press.

Edelman, M. (1988). *Constructing the political spectacle.* Chicago: University of Chicago Press.

Garnham, N. (1986). The media and the public sphere. In P. Golding, G. Murdock, & P. Schlesinger (Eds.), *Communicating politics: Mass communication and the political process* (pp. 37-53). New York: Holmes & Meier.

Habermas, J. (1989). *The structural transformation of the public sphere: An inquiry into a category of bourgeois society.* Cambridge: MIT Press.

Halliday, F. (1988). Three concepts of internationalism. *International Affairs, 64,* 187-198.

Hallin, D. C., & Mancini, P. (1984). Speaking of the president: Political structure and representational form in the U.S. and Italian television news. *Theory and Society, 13,* 829-850.

Hallin, D. C., & Mancini, P. (1990). *Friendly enemies: The Reagan-Gorbachev summits on U.S., Italian and Soviet television.* Perugia: Provincia di Perugia.

Hallin, D. C., & Mancini, P. (1991). Summits and the constitution of an international public sphere: The Reagan/Gorbachev meetings as televised media events. *Communication, 12,* 249-265.

Hallin, D. C., Manoff, R. K., & Weddle, J. K. (1990). *Sourcing patterns of national security reporters.* Paper presented at the annual meeting of the American Political Science Association, San Francisco.

Katz, E., & Dayan, D. (1985). Media events: On the experience of not being there. *Religion, 15,* 305-314.

Katz, E., with Dayan, D., & Motyl, P. (1980). *Television diplomacy: Sadat in Jerusalem.* Paper presented at the Conference on World Communication: Decisions for the Eighties, Annenberg School of Communication, University of Pennsylvania.

Katz, E., with Dayan, D., & Motyl, P. (1981). In defense of media events. In R. W. Haigh, G. Gerbner, & R. Byrne (Eds.), *Communications in the twenty-first century* (pp. 43-59). New York: John Wiley.

Kertzer, D. I. (1988). *Ritual, politics and power.* New Haven, CT: Yale University Press.

Lukes, S. (1975). Political ritual and social integration. *Sociology, 9,* 289-308.

Lyne, R. (1987). Making waves: Mr. Gorbachev's public diplomacy, 1985-6. *International Affairs, 63,* 205-224.

Mancini, P. (1987). Rito, leader e mass media: Enrico Berlinguer. In AAVV, *Leadership e democrazia.* Padova: Cedam.

Manoff, R. K. (1983). Covering the bomb: The nuclear story and the news. *Working Papers,* Summer, 20-21.

Rosengren, K. E., Arvidson, P., & Sturesson, D. (1975). The Baresback "panic": A radio program as a negative summary event. *Acta Sociologica, 18,* 303-321.

Shils, E., & Young, M. (1953). The meaning of coronation. *Sociological Review, 1,* 63-81.

Sigal, L. V. (1973). *Reporters and officials.* Lexington, MA: D. C. Heath.

Sparks, C. (1989). *Goodbye, Hildy Johnson.* Paper presented at the 1989 Research in Journalism Seminar, "Journalism in the Public Sphere in the News Media Age," Dubrovnik.

Turner, V. (1969). *The ritual process: Structure and anti-structure.* Ithaca, NY: Cornell University Press.

Urban, G. (1988). The pronomial pragmatics of nuclear war discourse. *Multilingua, 7,* 67-93.

Verba, S. (1965). The Kennedy assasination and the nature of political committment. In B.S. Greenberg, & E.B. Parker, (Eds.), *The Kennedy assasination and the American public: Social communication in crisis.* Stanford: Stanford University Press.

Vernant, J.-P., & Vidal-Naquet, P. (1981). *Tragedy and myth in ancient Greece.* Atlantic Highlands, NJ: Humanities Press.

Wertsch, J. V. (1987). Modes of discourse in the nuclear arms debate. *Current research on peace and violence.* Tampere Peace Research Institute.

Chapter 8

THE STRUCTURAL INVARIANCE OF CHANGE: COMPARATIVE STUDIES OF MEDIA USE (SOME RESULTS FROM A SWEDISH RESEARCH PROGRAM)[1]

Karl Erik Rosengren

DISCUSSING IN 1955 television effects on children and adolescents, Paul F. Lazarsfeld rightly maintained that the real problem in the area concerned "the cumulative effects of television": Effects that make themselves felt "six years, not six minutes later" (Lazarsfeld, 1955). Today, 35 years later, a number of longitudinal projects have provided some knowledge about such effects. What we still do not know, however, is how invariant such long-term effects are—over geographical and social space, and over time. Will long-term causal patterns show long-term invariance? Will the differences in media use and effects hitherto observed between different social categories prove invariant over time? Are there invariant patterns of change? In short: To what extent are our theories valid over time and social space? In order to answer that question we must use a comparative approach.

This chapter presents an overview of an ongoing Swedish research program, the Media Panel Program (MPP), that is being carried out by a research group at the Department of Sociology, University of Lund,

AUTHOR'S NOTE: The author wishes to thank all members of the Media Panel Group, and especially Ingrid Höjerback, Gunilla Jarlbro, Ulla Johnsson-Smaragdi, Thomas Lööv, Fredrik Miegel, and Inga Sonesson, for valuable help and assistance in writing this chapter. This is a revised version of a chapter previously published in *Communication Yearbook* (Rosengren, 1991).

Sweden. One aim of this program is—by means of comparisons over time and space—to provide answers to some of the questions just posed. The MPP concerns children's and adolescents' use of television and other mass media. It consists of a number of panel and cross-sectional studies that since 1975 have been conducted on altogether some 3,000 children and adolescents (in most cases also their parents and teachers), living in the towns of Malmö and Växjö in the counties of Skåne and Småland in southern Sweden (some 230,000 and 60,000 inhabitants, respectively).

The program has produced a number of publications.[2] The most comprehensive presentation of the program and its results so far is by Rosengren and Windahl (1989). The basic epistemology and methodology behind the program is discussed in Rosengren (1989b; cf. Jarlbro, 1986). Some research projects presently growing out of the program are presented in Rosengren (1988, 1989a). Results from the program have been discussed and criticized by, for instance, Feilitzen (1991) and Murray (1991).[3]

MPP is not the first study in its area (cf. Wartella & Reeves, 1987). Two excellent recent overviews of research on children and TV are Comstock and Pail (1987) and Liebert and Sprafkin (1988). There are thousands of cross-sectional studies and dozens of longitudinal studies.[4] The combination of cross-sectional studies and long-term panel studies used in the MPP is, however, rare.

The overall design of the program is visualized in Figure 8.1. In the rest of this chapter, panels will be denoted by letters and figures referring to town and year of birth, respectively; for instance, panel "V69" is the Växjö panel born in 1969.

The panels are built on representative samples of the populations under study (or, in some cases, virtually the entire population). Usual tests of representativeness, reliability, and so on, have been undertaken (Rosengren & Windahl, 1989). Panel attrition is a problem, of course, but efforts have been made to limit it, and even in the latest panel wave so far, tests show that the remaining groups of individuals do not significantly deviate with respect to basic demographic data from the composition of the original samples (Jarlbro, Lööv, & Miegel, 1989). Because most of the panels stem from two rather different towns, and some from different communities in the countryside (the "Skåne" panel), we have some confidence in having caught—in addition to the temporal variation inherent in the design—a substantial part of existant geographical variation in Swedish adolescents' mass media use.

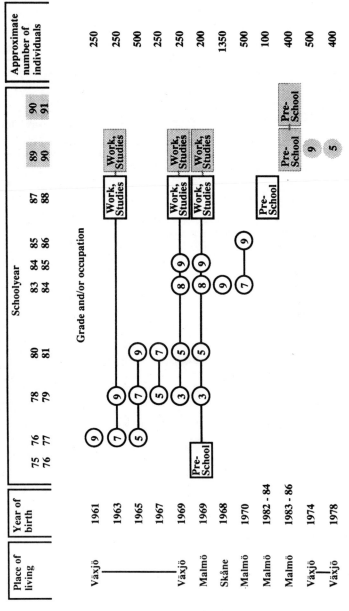

Figure 8.1. Overall Design of the Program

The mixed cross-sectional and longitudinal design has been applied because it is so efficient when looking for answers to questions about change and invariance, about invariance in change. Actually, the many waves and panels open up the possibility of carrying out small-scale "meta-analyses" (Glass, 1976; Hunter & Schmidt, 1990) based on more comparable sets of data and more intimate knowledge of those data than is usually the case. This is quite advantageous, especially when dealing with constancy and change.

Change is time-related difference. There are three types of causes of time-related differences at the individual level: maturational, situational, and generational. *Maturational change* is due to age-related processes (e.g., those occurring during adolescence). *Situational differences* are the effects of specific environmental conditions prevailing at the moment of observation (e.g., a specific media structure). *Generational (or cohort) differences* are the results of powerful circumstances making lasting imprints on a given generation (e.g., the "1968 events").

The Media Panel design admits three types of analysis that provide information about the three types of difference and change. *Cross-sectional analyses* demonstrate differences and similarities between different age-groups at the same time. These differences and similarities may be due to maturational or generational effects. *Panel analyses* demonstrate differences and similarities between the same cohort of individuals as they move through time. Such differences and similarities may be due to either maturational or situational effects. *Diagonal analyses* demonstrate differences and similarities between individuals of the same age at different periods of time. Such differences and similarities may be due to situational or generational effects. By shifting between cross-sectional, panel, and diagonal analyses, we can gain insights into the subtle interplay between maturational, generational, and situational influences.

A basic characteristic of the MPP is that it is not limited to a given theoretical or methodological perspective, nor is it dedicated to research on one substantive mass communication problem. On the contrary: It deals with a number of different aspects of media use and effects as behavioral, attitudinal, and structural causes and consequences of media use. Its main focus is television (broadcast, cable, and VCR variants), but it does heed other media as well, including the "medium" of music. Methodologically, it could be described as a combination of quantitative and qualitative studies carried out within a combined "uses-and-effects" approach (cf. Bryant & Zillmann, 1986; Rosengren, Wenner, & Palmgreen, 1985). Theoretically, three main perspectives have been applied: a development perspective, a class perspective, and a socialization perspective.

The broad theoretical and methodological approach of the MPP is manifest in the design of the program, and also in the basic conceptual scheme used to give some overall structure to the empirical studies. The scheme is visualized in Figure 8.2. Its broad character offers opportunities for studies within the various theoretical and methodological approaches mentioned above. (It should be noted that the scheme rendered in Figure 8.2 is "timeless." In longitudinal studies, of course, relevant parts of the scheme have to be repeated diachronically, often more than once.)

The main variables contained in the boxes of Figure 8.2 are listed in Rosengren and Windahl (1989, p. 10). The total number of variables is very large. The variables referred to in this chapter will be presented in necessary detail when appearing in the text.

One important task of the MPP is to chart the development of the mass media use of Swedish children and adolescents as the Swedish media scene is being reshaped by the so-called new media and the development they bring about in media structure, program fare, and so on. Simple as such a descriptive task may appear, it actually raises quite intriguing methodological and theoretical problems. Some such problems—all of which have to do, directly and indirectly, with the notions of invariance and change and therefore with comparative analysis—will be discussed in the next section of the chapter. The basic theoretical perspective behind that section is development theory. The two sections following thereafter will offer some specific results gained within the other two theoretical perspectives applied in the MPP: class and socialization. These two sections will also focus on the general theme of the chapter, which is invariance in change as revealed by means of comparative analysis.

In the final section of the chapter some general problems will be discussed, primarily the possibilities of drawing general and lasting conclusions from results such as the ones presented.

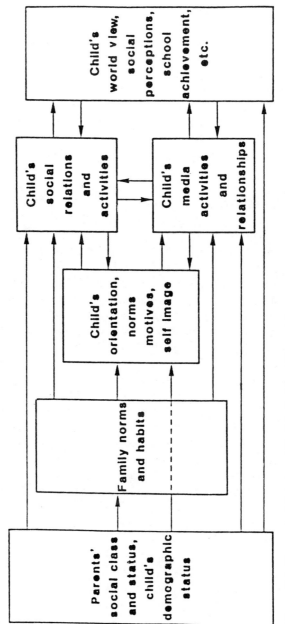

Figure 8.2. Conceptual Scheme of the Media Panel Program

The boxes in the figure contain the following text:

- Child's world view, social perceptions, school achievement, etc.
- Child's social relations and activities
- Child's media activities and relationships
- Child's orientation, norms motives, self image
- Family norms and habits
- Parents' social class and status, child's demographic status

STABILITY IN TURMOIL:
THE STRUCTURAL INVARIANCE OF CHANGE

In this section of the chapter some different types of stability and change will first be discussed. We then turn to stability and change as found in the amount of media use observed among children and adolescents. The data presented will offer some opportunities to further illuminate different methodological and theoretical problems in the area.

THE NOTIONS OF STABILITY AND CHANGE

The notion of stability may refer to a welter of phenomena. It may be applied, for instance,

in absolute or relative terms,
at the level of individual cases or aggregates,
with respect to strength (size, intensity, etc.), rank, or structure,
over cases or characteristics.

Technically, these distinctions would result in a typology of 24 cells, but some of these might be empty.

In their discussion of change and continuity (and continuity in change), Mortimer, Finch, and Kumka (1982, pp. 266-270; cf. Johnsson-Smaragdi, 1983) remain content to list four types of continuity. The list established by Mortimer et al. is no full-fledged typology, but in most cases it will suffice for our purposes, and where it does not, it will be developed slightly. In Mortimer et al.'s terminology, *level stability* is stability in the magnitude or quantity of a given phenomenon, at the individual and/or aggregate level (e.g., in the amount of TV watched). *Normative stability* is stability in individuals' ranks or differences with respect to a given phenomenon (e.g., with respect to school achievements over time). *Ipsative stability* is stability in the ordering of attributes of an individual over time (e.g., with respect to the hierarchy of interests). *Structural invariance*, finally, is continuity in the structure of the phenomenon under study. An interesting aspect of structural invariance is that it may apply to processes of change.

It is not impossible to get a hint of the actual prevalence of some of these types of stability by means of cross-sectional data. Longitudinal data are better, however, and a combined cross-sectional/longitudinal

Minutes/day

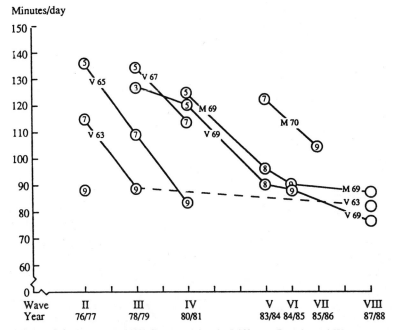

Figure 8.3. Amount of TV Consumption in Different Panels and Waves

design such as the one used in the MP program is best. In this section we will look at some phenomena of change and invariance (and invariance in change), as manifesting themselves in children's and adolescents' media use.

AGE, GENERATION, SITUATION—AND METHOD

Figure 8.3 presents the amount of TV viewing by children, adolescents, and young adults in six panels within the MPP, covering the period 1976-1988 and ages 10/11 to 24/25. Figure 8.4 presents the amount of listening to popular music during the same period of time, by the same panels (except panel M70). Both TV viewing and listening to music are measured by batteries of questions tapping media use in terms of habits rather than actual viewing during a given day or week. Note that the units of measurement in the two figures are very different: for TV, minutes per day; for music, days per week. (For further

Days/week

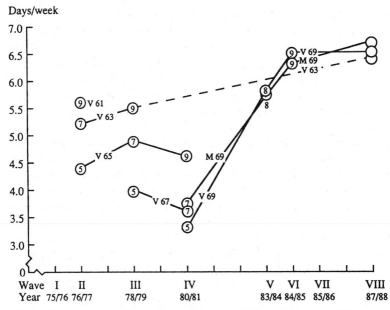

Figure 8.4. Amount of Listening to Music in Different Panels and Waves

technical details, see Rosengren, 1991a; Rosengren & Windahl, 1989, pp. 19, 105; and below.)

What do the two figures tell us? The first impression striking the eye is the high amount of variation. Take the age span 10-15, for instance (roughly corresponding to Grades 3-9 of the figures). We see that during these years the habit of TV viewing is reduced from more than two hours a day to less than an hour and a half (panels V65, V69, and M69). The change in listening to music is even stronger, although in a different direction. The amount of listening to popular music is roughly doubled from Grade 5 to Grade 9 (panels V69 and M69). This large variation showing up within age spans, which in current media statistics are often indiscriminately lumped together, does provide some food for thought.

Methodologically, the variation may be understood as effects of age (maturation), generation, and situation (cf. above). In this case, age effects should be theoretically interpreted primarily in terms of development theory, which is able to provide a quite convincing interpretation of the fact than in early adolescence children move away from family-oriented television to peer-oriented music (cf. below). Generation effects should not be expected to be very strong within the relatively short time period under study (some 12 years so far). Closer analysis does reveal, however, that within such short periods, there may already be discernible differences between "generations" (Rosengren & Windahl, 1989, p. 26). According to the same analysis, on the other hand, situation effects may be quite strong, although not as strong as age effects.

A situational effect is clearly visible in Figure 8.4. For some reason, overall listening to music is much lower in 1980/1981 than in earlier and later waves. This affects the development within all four panels measured in that wave, so that they differ from the overall pattern of continually increasing listening during adolescence, a pattern most clearly discernible, perhaps, in cross-sectional analysis (cf. Rosengren & Windahl, 1989, p. 106). Thus panel V65 gets an A-shaped development, and the increase from Grade 5 to Grade 8 is much more dramatic for panels V69 and M69 than is otherwise the case. Without our combined panel/cross-sectional design, this situation effect might have been erroneously interpreted as a maturational phenomenon.

Speculating on the causes of this strong situational effect, one may think of changes in media structure and/or music fashions (cf. Peterson & Berger, 1975). Burnett (1990) shows that around 1980 there was a strong increase in concentration in the international music industry and an extreme low in diversity of musical taste as measured by the Top Ten Hits. At the same time, a downfall of the popularity of punk was reportedly taking place in Sweden. The relationship between media structure, media fads and fashions, and individual media use is not very well known. No doubt it represents a promising area for continued study.

The overall methodological lesson to be drawn from Figures 8.3 and 8.4 is that when analyzing descriptive data about media use, it is to be preferred to have access to both narrow age categories and a combined cross-sectional/longitudinal design. Broad categories and either cross-sectional or panel data alone may result in quite misleading results. In addition, keep in mind that empirical data about the absolute level of consumption are heavily dependent on both the conceptualization and the operationalization of media use (habit versus actual consumption, type of question, etc.). Some of the data in Figure 8.3 offer a striking illustration of the latter truth.

It will be seen that the M70 panel in Figure 8.3 deviates considerably from the rest of the panels. Its values for TV consumption are some 10-20% or more above comparable values. Why is that so? Part of the difference may be ascribed to the difference in media habits between the city of Malmö and the town of Växjö. A quick comparison between panels V69 and M69, however, shows that difference to be in the order of 5-10%, whereas panel M70 differs much more from the rest of the panels. The difference between Malmö and Växjö, then, does not suffice as an explanation. Actually, the main reason for the difference is of quite a different character. It is methodological: For technical reasons, the number of questions in the battery tapping TV viewing was increased from six to eight. This gave us better validity with respect to changing leisure habits in Sweden (cf. Rosengren, 1991), but it also resulted in an apparent increase in the level of consumption.

The short and the long of all this is a caveat with respect to figures about actual level of media consumption based on survey questions (cf. Comstock & Pail, 1987, p. 13). To a considerable extent, such figures are dependent on the formulation of the question and/or the construction of the index. In comparative studies of media habits in different countries, the risk of meeting with such artifactual differences should be even higher. For instance, U.S. kids are reported to have a viewing time double that of Norwegian kids, with Swedes coming somewhere in between (Rosengren & Windahl, 1989, p. 21). But only very careful comparisons could reveal how much of those differences is a methodological artifact, and how much is due to differences in media structure and general societal structure—for instance, the difference between the commercial U.S. system of radio and TV on the one hand, and the Scandinavian public-service type of system (cf. Pingree, Hawkins, Johnsson-Smaragdi, Rosengren, & Reynolds, in press).

The fact that the absolute level of media consumption is a tricky thing to measure does not mean that relative levels cannot be measured, of course. In Figures 8.3 and 8.4 the really important thing to observe is not the absolute levels but the strong dynamics observable in relative terms: the enormous increase in the importance of music during adolescence, and the corresponding reduction in the importance of television viewing. With respect to these two media, then, adolescence is really— as with respect to so many other phenomena—a period of dramatic upheavals. It deserves pointing out, though, that in the midst of upheaval, there is considerable stability. Stability in consumption, however, is perhaps an even more tricky concept to conceptualize and operationalize than is consumption itself. The concepts of level stability, normative stability, and structural invariance presented above will help us do just that.

INVARIANT CHANGE

Looking at each one of the several MP panels, we have already noted that the level of television use is substantially lowered during adolescence, whereas that of music is even more substantially heightened. Strong level *instability*, that is. Controlling for age by means of comparing *between* instead of *within* panels, however, we find instead strong level *stability*, for level differences are almost negligible within grades (excepting, of course, differences between the Malmö and Växjö panels, as well as, for reasons mentioned above, panel M70). Thus overall level stability is low; age-specific level stability, high.

One interesting aspect of structural invariance in the phenomena under study is visualized by the fact that in the age span between Grades 5 and 9, the rate of level change in TV consumption is almost linear, the slope being almost identical for the six panels (Figure 8.3). In this connection, panel M70 is especially valuable. In spite of its somewhat different index of consumption (which gives it a higher absolute level of consumption; cf. above), the slope is much the same as for the five other panels. It is also interesting to note that the use of Grade 8 instead of Grade 7 in panels M69 and V69 only seemingly disturbs the linearity.

With respect to pop music listening, the results would have been much the same were it not for the strong situation effect observed in 1980/1981. This effect, of course, has nothing to do with structural invariance per se, and it could have been controlled away had I chosen to use the well-established control techniques developed in cohort studies for that very purpose (cf. Glenn, 1973). It does not seem unwarranted, therefore, to conclude that for both TV viewing and music listening, our combined cross-sectional and panel design has been able to reveal considerable structural invariance, in spite of the low overall level stability observed for the same activities.

What phenomena lie behind this structural invariance, one may ask. In order to provide an answer to that question we should try to find the best expression possible of the general tendency of the case of structural invariance at hand.

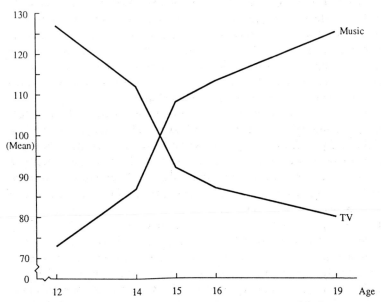

Figure 8.5. Development of TV Viewing and Listening to Music
NOTE: Standardized TV viewing and listening to music. 100= Mean during age period.

BEHIND STRUCTURAL INVARIANCE

A glimpse of the general tendency hidden behind the sometimes accidental variations of Figures 8.3 and 8.4 may be had from Figure 8.5, presenting an overall picture of the dramatic changes in television viewing and listening to music that take place during teenage (in this case, age 12-19). The data of the figure synthesize the data visualized in Figures 8.3 and 8.4 above, unweighted means being calculated first for Malmö and Växjö separately, then for the two towns together. In this way, cohort, situational, and geographical effects are controlled for, letting age (developmental) effects stand out as clearly as possible. The deviating values of panel M70 were not included in the calculations. (Note that the levels of the two curves are dependent on the standardization of the data. The units are no longer minutes per day and days per week, as in Figures 8.3 and 8.4, respectively. In order to facilitate comparison, the unweighted mean for each of the two curves has been set at 100.)

By means of the averaging and standardizing procedures, the two curves have become quite smooth, calling to mind classical S-curves of growth and decline, a type of curve followed by many basic developmental phenomena. The steep part of the curves in both cases falls between ages 14 and 15—that is, toward the end of the physical growth spurt phase that is such a visible sign of biological development in the puberty period (Tanner, 1962). Biological development is accompanied and followed by cognitive and social development.

A basic observation of Brown, Cramond, and Wilde (1974) is that, because of biological, cognitive, and social development during late childhood and early adolescence, the need structure changes in that a set of intermittently felt needs ("spasmodic" needs in the expressive terminology of Brown et al.) are added to a set of more or less constant needs. These new, spasmodic needs naturally call for increased control of the adolescents' environment.

In terms of media use, all this means that mere access to a given medium is no longer enough. Adolescents feel they need to control media use themselves. Consequently, they increasingly try to escape the relatively tight control of the family, turning instead to the peer group, which provides better opportunities for satisfaction of this new set of needs. At the same time they turn from the family medium of television to the peer medium of music, which comes to them by way of more easily controllable media (primarily radio, recordplayer, taperecorder, and VCR).

What actually takes place is a thorough-going functional reorganization of adolescent media use (Brown et al., 1974). This functional reorganization is neatly illustrated by the curves of Figure 8.5. In the combined cross-sectional/longitudinal MPP data we find it again and again, manifesting itself as low overall level stability, high age-specific level stability, and structural invariance in the changes of media use during childhood and adolescence. Behind this structural invariance lies biological, cognitive, and social development.

NORMATIVE STABILITY

So far we have been discussing level stability and structural invariance. What about the two other types of stability mentioned above, ipsative and normative stability? To demonstrate the degree of ipsative stability (the ordering of attributes of an individual over time) would demand quite a different organization of our data than the present one. Our design does provide good information about the normative stability of the phenomena under study, however. (Normative stability, it will be remembered, is stability in individuals' ranks or differences with respect to a given phenomenon.)

Measurement of normative stability demands longitudinal analysis at the individual level: some type of correlational analysis of panel data, showing the extent to which individuals high on a given phenomena at time T1 tend to be high also at T2 (regardless of the amount of level stability of the phenomenon). Sometimes the correlational analysis is developed into more or less advanced, multivariate analysis, for instance LISREL analysis (Jöreskog & Sörbom, 1989). LISREL analyses of this type have indeed shown that the degree of normative stability of TV viewing seems to be invariant over at least short periods of time: two to four years or so (cf. Johnsson-Smaragdi 1983, in press; Rosengren, 1991). Continuing analyses of different Media Panel cohorts will hopefully add to our knowledge about what—applying a novel combination of the terms used by Mortimer et al. (1982)—might be called the "structural invariance of normative stability."

In this section we have been looking at invariance and change in the media use by some Swedish children and adolescents, as they grew from children to adolescents, at the same as the surrounding media structure was undergoing considerable change. In the next section we will first look at class-related differences in children's and adolescents' mass media use. By asking to what extent such class differences are stable over time we will then gradually return to our continuing theme of invariance and change.

A CLASS PERSPECTIVE

Society is stratified along a number of basic dimensions; age, gender, and social class are the three most important ones. Two values on each of these dimensions create 8 different social worlds; three values on age and class, 18. That is more worlds than most students of mass media use care to include in their analyses. The problem is further complicated by the fact that social class is no unidimensional concept, the distinction between a Marxian notion of class and a Weberian notion of status being the first one to come to mind. In addition, a temporal distinction should be made between class of origin, class of context, and class of destination: where do you come from, where do you stand, and where are you going (cf. Rosengren & Windahl, 1989, p. 114). (*Mutatis mutandis,* this distinction, of course, might be equally well applied to status.)

The notions of social class and status are relevant to communications studies for the simple reason that social class exerts an almost ubiquitous influence on a number of communication processes—for instance, on mass media use. Regardless of what conceptualization and operationalization of the notions of class and status one happens to prefer, two basic problems turn up when relating class or status to media use:

What type of relationship do we find?
How stable is that relationship?

The latter question, of course, has a bearing on the general theme of this chapter: change and invariance as revealed by comparative analysis. When looking at the stability of a given relationship between two variables, we are looking at what Mortimer et al. (1982) call "structural invariance" (cf. above).

The Media Panel Program offers rich opportunities to approach these problems in empirical terms (Rosengren & Windahl, 1989, pp. 111-157). We start with a section providing some information about our way of operationalizing the central concepts of the problematic at hand. Then we turn to the type of relationship existing between, on the one hand, class and status, on the other, mass media use. In a later section we ask whether that influence is stable during childhood and adolescence. Finally, we approach the question of whether the relationship between class and media use may be affected by ongoing changes in the media structure.

CLASS AND STATUS MEASURED

In the MPP, class of origin has been measured as a composite index of parents' occupation (based on the semiofficial classification systems used in Sweden; cf. Rosengren & Windahl, 1989, p. 23, 125). Class of destination has been measured as the occupational expectations of the children and adolescents under study (cf. Flodin, 1986); class of context, as the proportion of children of working- or middle-class origin in a given school class.

Status has been measured by means of a composite index of parents' education, roughly corresponding to the number of years of schooling. (Education has sometimes been used also as an indicator of "cultural capital," a metaphorical concept of some heuristic value; cf. Bourdieu, 1984; Rosengren & Windahl, 1989, p. 113d; Rosengren, 1991b).

In terms of the conceptual scheme of Figure 8.2 above, status and class of origin are located in the leftmost box of the figure; class of context, in the box labeled "Child's social relations," and class of destination, in the rightmost box of the figure.

CLASS AND MEDIA USE:
WHAT TYPE OF RELATIONSHIP

Although some dissenting voices have been heard (for instance, Morley, 1980; Piepe, Crouch, & Emerson, 1975), one usually assumes and finds a linear relationship between, say, amount of TV viewing and social class or status. Looking closer at the relationship, however, we find that curvilinear class relationships do turn up again and again in the MPP data. Status relationships, on the other hand, tend to be linear at the level of zero-order correlations (Höjerback, 1986; Roe, 1983; Rosengren & Windahl, 1989, p. 129).

In addition, we found intricate interaction effects between class (occupation) and status (education), effects that in the last analysis result in very strong differences in TV viewing between various class/status categories. For instance, even in the same grade, kids having high class/low status background watched an hour or more of television a day than did kids having high class/high status background (cf. Rosengren & Windahl, 1989, p. 130). Combining, however, not class and status, but two different types of social class—namely, class of origin and class of context—one finds a somewhat more regular pattern.

According to prevailing ideology, Swedish schools should be socially integrated. It is well known, though, that there is still considerable school segregation in Sweden (Arnman & Jönsson, 1983). But no schools are completely segregated. Consequently, many children belong to school classes dominated by children from a social class different from their own. This makes it possible to study the joint and separate influence of class of origin and class of context on the amount of adolescents' TV viewing. Both types of class were found to have a curvilinear influence, and the combined result of the two curvilinearities sometimes stands out rather strikingly (cf. Rosengren & Windahl, 1989, p. 144; see also Rosengren, 1991a). The combination of an origin in the middle strata of society and a class of context dominated by the middle strata thus constitutes the heartland of television viewing.

Interesting as the curvilinearity may be in itself, it also presents a technical problem, because many types of conventional statistical analysis assume linear relationships. When suspecting curvilinearity, it is wise, therefore, to apply more than one type of statistical analysis to the same problem. In the MPP we have combined, for instance, MCA-analysis (giving information about curvilinearity) with techniques building on the assumption of linearity, such as, say, LISREL (cf. Rosengren & Windahl, 1989, p. 131).

SOCIAL CLASS AND TELEVISION USE: DIMINISHING INFLUENCE?

So far we have been discussing the first of the two basic problems about social class and media use mentioned above: What type of relationship do we find? Let us now turn to the second question: How stable is that relationship? In this case we are dealing with the stability of a relationship between at least two variables—that is, in the terms of Mortimer et al. (1982) referred to above, structural invariance.

More precisely, there are two main ways in which the relationship between social class and media use may be said to be invariant or stable over time: within and between cohorts. In addition, we may be talking about stability measured cross-sectionally and longitudinally. Finally, we have the two basic distinctions between (on the one hand) class and status and (on the other) class of origin, context, and destination. Space permits only some illustrations of the many combinations available.

It seems to be a reasonable assumption that in the lives of children and adolescents, the influence from class of origin should diminish over time, that of class of context be stable, and that of class of destination should increase. The simplest way to look empirically at the problem of stable, diminishing, or increasing influence from social class on the use of mass media is to produce some cross-sectional coefficients of association between, say, class of origin and TV consumption among different age categories. Analyzing a number of cross-sectional beta-coefficients from five of our panels, covering ages 10 to 25, we found no linear tendency of increasing or decreasing strength within panels. Within the period covered (about a dozen years) there was no discernible trend of weakening relationship between class and media use as measured over different cohorts (cf. Rosengren, 1991a).

Turning instead to longitudinal data within one and the same panel, we did find in some LISREL analyses signs of decreasing influence from class of origin. It cannot be ruled out, though, that this result may be a methodological artifact (cf. Johnsson-Smaragdi, 1983, p. 143). Using MCA analysis, however, we did measure for panel V69 in Grade 9 the influence of class on TV use, controlling for class as measured in Grade 5 (Rosengren & Windahl, 1989, p. 134). The unique influence in Grade 9 was 0.17, as compared to the total influence of 0.26 in Grade 5. (At the first point of measurement—in this case, Grade 5—we cannot, of course, distinguish between direct and indirect influence.) Part of the total influence manifesting itself in Grade 5 of the model must in reality have been exerted at a much earlier point in time. We thus draw the tentative conclusion that what reduction there may be during adolescence in the unique influence of class of origin on amount of TV viewing probably is not all that great. (In addition, it should be borne in mind that we have not yet touched on the question of whether in its turn the reduction, be it weak or strong, is invariant over cohorts; cf. below.)

CLASS, GENDER, AND MEDIA USE: STRUCTURAL CHANGE

So far, we have been dealing primarily with the relationship between class and amount of TV consumption. Turning now to the relationship between class and use of other media as well, we start by mentioning that at least for our much analyzed panel V65 it has been found repeatedly that the influence of class of origin on various aspects of media use (and also activities related to media use) is much stronger for girls than for boys. That is, class of origin and gender interact so that class has differential effects on media use among the two genders (Rosengren & Windahl, 1989, p. 127; cf. Flodin, 1986; Johnsson-Smaragdi, 1983; Roe, 1983). Similarly but conversely, mass media use has also been found to have differential effects among different social classes (Rosengren & Windahl, 1989, p. 154). The detailed character of such structural relationships, as well as their potential invariance over time, remains to be studied, however. There is some reason to expect that the entrance upon the Swedish media scene of the so-called new media—particularly, perhaps, the VCR—should have affected the invariance of such complex relationships.

A first indication of these relationships is found in simple comparisons of the zero-order correlations (cross-sectional and longitudinal) between amount of use of a number of different mass media for boys and girls from different social classes. A number of such correlations for working-class boys and middle-class girls in Grades 5, 7, and 9 of panel V65 are graphically presented in Figures 8.6a and 8.6b. All positive correlations greater than 0.30 were included, along with all three negative correlations found (cf. Rosengren & Windahl, 1989, p. 123). The contrast between the two categories is striking (middle-class boys and working-class girls fell in between).

The conclusion to be drawn is that the media habits of working-class boys and middle-class girls are very differentially structured. At least that was the case in our panel V65. Later MPP panels provide an opportunity to take a look at the invariance of this differential degree of structuring. Figures 8.7a and 8.7b offer parallel data from panel M69, representing a cohort that is four years younger and from another town.

On the face of it, it would seem that the contrast between the two categories showing up in panel V65 is totally lacking in panel M69: The number of significant correlations is exactly the same (10) for working-class boys and middle-class girls. (The number of significant correlations should be expected to be lower in Figure 8.7 than in Figure 8.6, because n is much lower: some 50 individuals rather than some 100; cf. Figure 8.1 above.) Looking closer at Figures 8.7a and 8.7b, however, we do find a difference between the two categories. For working-class boys, 7 of the 10 arrows have to do with VCRs; for middle-class girls, only 4. Without VCRs, then, middle-class girls would have double the number of positive correlations than working-class boys. Similar results have been found for panel M70, and also—although admittedly less clear-cut ones—for panel V69. (It should be mentioned that at the site of that panel (Växjö), the VCR penetration was much less than in Malmö.)

Now, how could we explain this difference between later and earlier cohorts? And what does the original difference found for panel V65 between working-class boys and middle-class girls really mean?

Direct parental control of adolescents' media use seems to be rather weak, especially for boys (Rosengren & Windahl, 1989, p. 43). At the

160

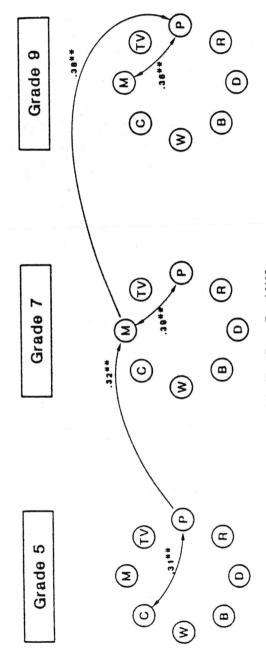

Figure 8.6a Pattern of Media Use, Working-Middle Class Boys, Panel V65
NOTE: M: movies; TV: TV viewing; P: Pop; R: Radio; D: Dailies; B: Books; W: Weeklies; C: Comics

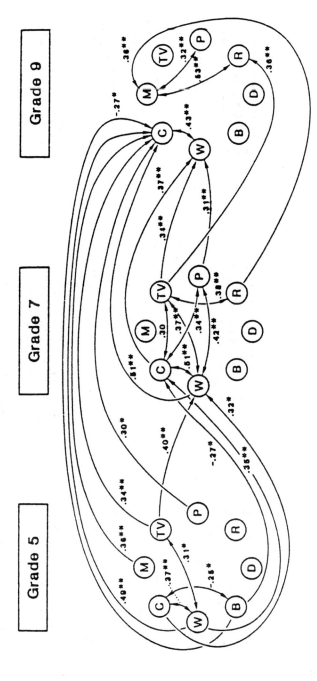

Figure 8.6b Pattern of Media Use, Middle-Class Girls, Panel V65

NOTE: M: movies; TV: TV viewing; P: Pop; R: Radio; D: Dailies; B: Books; W: Weeklies; C: Comics

161

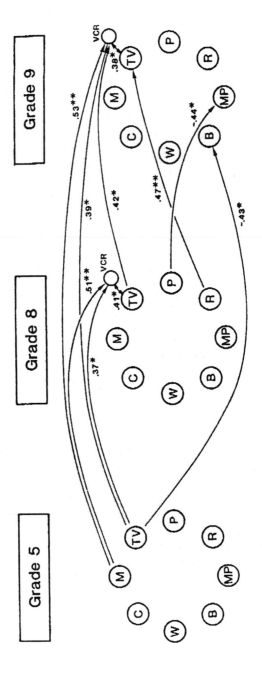

Figure 8.7a Pattern of Media Use, Working-Class Boys, Panel M69

NOTE: M: movies; TV: TV viewing; P: Pop; R: Radio; D: Dailies; B: Books; W: Weeklies; C: Comics

162

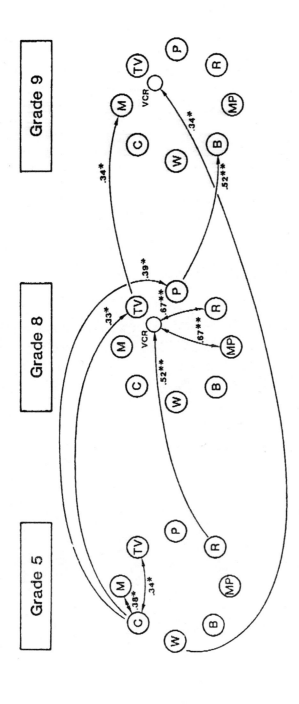

Figure 8.7b Pattern of Media Use, Working-Class Girls, Panel M69

NOTE: M: movies; TV: TV viewing; P: Pop; R: Radio; D: Dailies; B: Books; W: Weeklies; C: Comics

163

same time, a number of MPP results rather convincingly demonstrate that parents' attitudes toward TV do influence the media behavior of their children (cf. Jönsson, 1986; Sonesson 1979, 1989). Presumably, then, there is such a control, and it seems to be indirect rather than direct.

Against this background, a reasonable interpretation of the original difference might be that, all in all, working-class boys probably are under less tight parental control with respect to their overall media use than are middle-class girls. Consequently, their media habits should become much less structured. At least, that was the case for panel V65. For somewhat later cohorts—for instance, M69, V69, and M70—something seems to have happened that gradually started to alter this structural difference. What happened?

NEW MEDIUM:
EMERGING FUNCTIONAL REORGANIZATION?

One thing that did happen was that VCR entered the Swedish scene in the early 1980s. In 1980, 3% of the households had access to VCR; in 1985, 23%, and in 1988, 41% (Alvarado, 1988; Feilitzen, Filipson, Rydin, & Schyller, 1989; Gahlin & Nordström, 1988; Levy, 1990; Roe, 1988; cf. Rosengren & Windahl, 1989, p. 5). There is considerable social and geographical variation behind these overall figures, however. In 1988, for instance, the figure was 60% among 14-year-olds.

The rapid and uneven diffusion process of VCR actually released something of a moral panic in Sweden, characterized by genuine concern for children and adolescents, and, of course, also by strong group and party interests (Roe, 1985). Several governmental committees were looking into the new medium, which in some circles was considered a threat to the public service monopoly of Swedish Radio and Television. At the time of writing, however, it may be said that by and large this moral panic over VCR has abated. In Sweden, just as in many other countries, video viewing has found its niche somewhere between cinema and traditional television.

We first measured VCR use among our panels in 1980/1981 (cf. Rosengren & Windahl, 1989, p. 49). In 1984/1985, VCR viewing had become so widespread that it was meaningful to use the same type of index as the one used for TV viewing (regarded as habit; cf. above). In Grade 9, average viewing time was then 2.3 hrs/week in the town of

Växjö, 3.1 in the city of Malmö. Three years later, it was 3.8 and 5.0 hrs/week for the same individual (who had then become 19 years old). In an older panel, V63 (whose members were by then 25), it was considerably lower in the same wave: 2.0 hrs/week (Jarlbro et al., 1989; Sonesson & Höjerback, 1989).

The VCR is a medium easy to control for those who are sometimes left to take care of themselves—for instance, working-class boys. They seem to have seized the opportunity, and as a consequence, their media habits may now be in a process of getting the structure they were formerly lacking. In qualitative terms (structure in media habits) they may thus be approaching middle-class girls. (For quantitative comparisons of VCR use, see Höjerback, 1986; Johnsson-Smaragdi & Roe, 1986; Sonesson & Höjerback, 1989.)

To conclude: In a previous section we saw that the introduction of the VCR did not substantially affect the level of TV viewing (or, for that matter, age-related changes in that level). Level stability was left unchanged, and so was its structural invariance. The introduction of the VCR may have had other and more subtle effects, however. Figures 8.7a and 8.7b, and 8.8a and 8.8b seem to provide a snapshot of an ongoing functional reorganization of adolescent media habits, a reorganization caused not by biological, cognitive, and social development (cf. above) but possibly by changes in the media structure, interacting with an already existing class/gender structure. *The structural invariance of the relationship between class, gender, and media use may not have withstood the introduction of the VCR.* In the long run, one might speculate, such a reorganization may even have some reverberations on that class/gender/media-use structure itself, for mass media are powerful— although sometimes rather haphazard—agents of socialization.

A SOCIALIZATION PERSPECTIVE

Socialization is the process by which societal culture is communicated between generations. It is also the process by which the delicate balance between continuity and change is upheld in society. In its turn, this process of socialization itself shows both continuity and change, and also continuity in change: structural invariance. In this section we shall take a look at the process of socialization from the perspective of structural invariance. Before doing so, however, we must discuss some basic concepts related to socialization and socialization research.

AGENTS OF SOCIALIZATION

In modern societies, there are eight main types of socializing agents: the family, peer groups, and work groups; schools, churches, and judicatures; various formal organizations; and the mass media. The process of socialization always implies close interaction, not only between these agents of socialization and the individual socialized, but also between the agents of socialization themselves.

The socialization agents vary considerably with respect to both form and content of the socialization process in which they engage. Some focus on abstract, formal culture; others on lived culture. Some proceed quite systematically and purposively; others act almost without knowing it themselves (something that does not necessarily make them less important as agents of socialization, of course). As agents of socialization the mass media deal with both abstract, formal culture, and with lived culture. They sometimes act quite purposely as agents of socialization, and sometimes without any socializing purpose at all. For more than a century, and especially during the last few decades, their importance as agents of socialization has been constantly on the increase.

PERSPECTIVES IN SOCIALIZATION RESEARCH

In socialization research, two main societal perspectives and two main perspectives on the human individual have been prevalent. Society has been regarded from a perspective of consensus or conflict; the human individual, as an active subject or a passive object. The four combinations of these twin pairs of perspectives result in four main traditions of socialization research, neatly corresponding to a well-known typology for schools of sociology originally presented by Burrell and Morgan (1979) and related to mass communication research by Rosengren (1983, 1989a,b).

In the Media Panel Program, we believe that all societies are characterized by both consensus and conflict, and also that all individuals are both subjects and objects. Indeed, some of the most interesting problems in connection with socialization by means of mass communication arise only when the different perspectives are combined. How is consensus arrived at in spite of conflict? How is conflict made palpable in spite of superficial consensus? How may seemingly passive objects of vile oppression turn into willing and acting subjects? Obviously, such grand questions cannot all be answered within one single research program. But that is no reason not to try to keep the questions alive also when dealing with less grandiose phenomena related to socialization. That is what we have tried to do in the MPP.

There is always interaction between all eight main types of socialization agents. Sometimes this interaction turns into relatively conscious and open competition (for instance, between school and family, school and mass media). Parents sometimes denounce teachers on more or less specific points. Teachers sometimes denounce mass media content across the board, trying to substitute their own messages for those of the mass media. In such cases, agents of socialization (or their representatives) sometimes regard the individuals socialized as passive recipients, vessels to be filled to the brim with this or that type of knowledge, this or that skill, this or that view of society and the world at large. But children and adolescents certainly are not passive vessels. On the contrary. Especially in cases of competition between different agents of socialization about the domination over the supposedly passive objects of socialization, they are most adept at turning one agent against the other, to their own advantage—at least in the short run. In the long run, of course, the end result may be quite different.

Within the MPP, the relations between the individual socialized and the four socializing agents of family, school, peer group, and the mass media have time and again been studied in detail by means of a great number of MCA analyses, LISREL, and PLS models. Such analyses sometimes offer graphic illustrations of the abstract argumentation of socialization theory summarized above. The structural models, especially, offer good opportunities to combine the deterministic, causal perspective naturally prevalent when the individual is regarded as a passive object of strong internal and external forces, with the voluntaristic, finalistic perspective naturally prevalent when she is regarded as a willing and acting subject. In terms of mass communication research they offer opportunities to combine the two sometimes antagonistic research traditions of effects research and uses and gratifications research (Bryant & Zillmann, 1986; Rosengren et al., 1985).

STABILITY IN
FAMILY COMMUNICATION PATTERNS

Logically, before asking questions about the ways and means by which mass media act as agents of socialization for our children and adolescents, one should ask how children and adolescents come to use the media, and how that use is shaped by other agents of socialization. An obvious answer to questions such as these is that—in this case as in so many others—the family, that primordial agent of socialization, acts as the prime mover.

In an oft-quoted chapter, McLeod and Brown (1976) discuss three modes in which socialization may take place: modeling, reinforcement, and interaction. As socializing agents, all families draw on all of these three modes. Yet we know that the pattern of socialization may be radically different in different families. The explanation most often used for this differentiation, of course, is social class. Another reason is that—over and above class differences—differentiation in the general family communication pattern is quite considerable. This fact, in its turn, has important consequences for the role played by other agents of socialization, not least for the role of TV.

In the first waves of the MPP we measured the parents of our children and adolescents by means of the well-known scale for family communication patterns developed by Chaffee, McLeod and their associates (Chaffee, McLeod, & Atkin, 1971; Ritchie, 1990; Tims & Masland, 1985). In a number of quantitative analyses, Jarlbro (1988) showed the importance of family communication patterns for the use and effects of television, demonstrating that under certain conditions the family communication pattern may actually neutralize the influence from social class. She thus provided some information about the structural invariance over space (USA-Sweden) of the relationship between family communication patterns and mass media use.

Jarlbro (1988) did more than that, however. Combining in an innovative panel study the quantitative approach of traditional family communication pattern measurements with qualitative in-depth interviews with children of parents measured five years before, she was able in a double blind test without any error to locate 16 out of 16 young adults into the correct cell of the fourfold family communication pattern typology (the cell to which their family had been shown to belong five years earlier, by means of the formalized quantitative Likert scale responded to by the parents in a mail survey). In the terms of Mortimer et al. (1982), Jarlbro convincingly demonstrated normative stability with respect to a two-dimensional typology. Formalized, quantitative techniques, and informal, qualitative techniques thus proved able to bridge a gap stretching over five years and between two generations.

This is a result that has some general methodological implications with respect to the old debate between proponents of quantitative and qualitative methods. The methodological debate, in its turn, is closely related to the theoretical debate between the four main schools of socialization and communication research previously mentioned in this section of the chapter. Both debates have actually been characterized as a pseudodebate, and results such as those produced by Jarlbro offer strong support for that contention (cf. Rosengren, 1989b).

It should be added, though, that although Jarlbro's results are impressive, they call for further theoretical elaboration and specifications by means of more powerful techniques of analysis, such as structural modeling. It will be an important task in the continued work within the MPP to explicate these and other results in terms of structural models. In this way we will be able to provide more explicit theories and more precise assessments of the degree of stability of that important phenomenon, the family communication climate, and its effects on mass media use. We will then know whether the relations between family communication patterns and mass media use—so important for the general socialization of children and adolescents—are structurally invariant not only over space, but also over time.

THE INVARIANCE OF CAUSAL STRUCTURES

At present we do not have available any longitudinal structural models of the role played by the family communication climate in the socialization process. (For a tentative cross-sectional model, however, see Hedinsson, 1981.) Suppose we had. What then?

The logical next step would then be to look into the stability of such models between different panels and cohorts. The important question will thus become: How stable is a longitudinal LISREL model? To reformulate the question in the terms used by Mortimer et al. (1982): What is the structural invariance of longitudinal causal structures as mapped by means of a LISREL model? In yet other words: How generally valid are our theories?

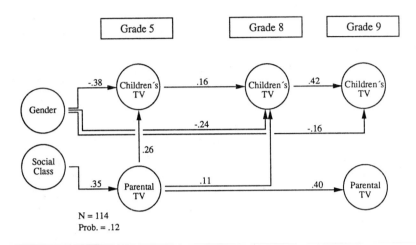

Figure 8.8a A LISREL Model of Children's and Parent's TV Viewing, Panel V69
NOTE: N=114; Prob. =.12

In some disciplines and research traditions—for instance, in the sociology of work and class—series of increasingly better structural models are accumulating as researchers build upon and gradually refine
each others' models, as well as improve the conceptualizations and
operationalizations behind them. Because of the cost in time and
money, however, only a few models have been replicated within precisely the same theoretical, methodological, and empirical surround-
ings. Actually, we have been able to find only one such replication with
at least some relation to substantive problems dealt with in the MPP:
two cross-sectional LISREL models of schooling in the first grade, 10
years apart (Entwisle & Alexander, 1986).

Structural models built on panel data are more rare than cross-sectional models. A number of longitudinal models have been presented in
different communication studies, two well-known examples being
Milavsky, Kessler, Stipp, and Rubens (1982) and Huesman and Eron
(1986). As to replications of longitudinal models, so far we have been
unable to find any. The Media Panel Program, however, with its store
of longitudinal models already built and under construction, offers a
rich potential for such replications (cf. Johnsson-Smaragdi, 1983; Roe,
1983; Rosengren & Windahl, 1989). As a matter of fact, two such rep-
licative longitudinal models have already been presented in a recent

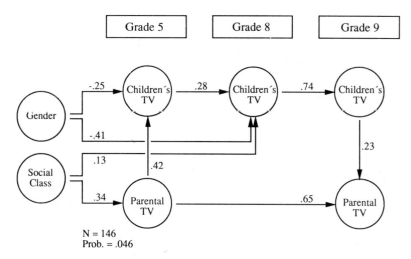

Figure 8.8b. A LISREL Model of Children's and Parent's TV Viewing, Panel M69
NOTE: N=146; Prob.=.046

report from the program (Johnsson-Smaragdi & Höjerback, 1989), and more are on their way (Johnsson-Smaragdi, in press).

Figures 8.8a and 8.8b show two different LISREL models of the interplay between the individual socialized and two agents of socialization, family and television, within the structural framework established by gender and social class (the latter variable in both cases being measured—for technical reasons—by maternal occupation; Johnsson-Smaragdi & Höjerback, 1989). More specifically, for two Malmö and Växjö panels (M69 and V69) the two models show how and to what extent the amount of children's and parents' TV consumption mutually influence each other.

The two models are replications of a model presented in Johnsson-Smaragdi (1983, p. 161), building on data from panel M65. The interested reader may compare the original model with the two replications, finding basic structural similarities. For the sake of simplicity, however, we restrict our discussion to the two models presented here.

The models offer the structural parts of two large LISREL models. The coefficients attached to the arrows are standardized beta coefficients, expressing the unique influence of one variable on another after control for all relevant variables in the model. (For further information about the LISREL technique, see, e.g., Cuttance & Ecob, 1987; Jöreskog & Sörbom, 1989; Saris & Stronkhorst, 1984.)

The structures of the two models are by no means identical, but there are considerable similarities. Both similarities and dissimilarities have their interest.

In both models, gender exerts a considerable influence on children's viewing, and so does social class—on children's and parents' TV viewing alike. In panel V69, there is a direct, unique influence from gender in all three waves, whereas in M69 that influence is found only in the first two waves. In panel V69, the influence from social class on children's TV viewing is only indirect (relayed by the parental TV habits), but in M69 there is also a direct influence. In addition to such qualitative differences, there are also quantitative differences in the size of coefficients expressing the strength of the causal influence.

The main difference between the two models, however, lies in the relationships between children's and parents' viewing in Grade 9. In both panels, there is considerable influence from parental viewing to children's viewing in Grades 5 and 8 (although in the Malmö panel, that influence is direct only in Grade 5). In the Malmö panel, however, there is also a significant causal influence on parental viewing from children's viewing in Grade 9. In the Växjö panel there is no such thing.

Parental influence on children's viewing has been much discussed (cf. above). Influence in the other direction has been less discussed, but the very interesting possibility of "reversed modeling" has been recognized, and the phenomenon has been empirically observed (Johnsson-Smaragdi, 1983, pp. 154 ff; Rosengren & Windahl, 1989, p. 194). Figure 8.8b graphically visualizes this possibility. The phenomenon would no doubt deserve a discussion of its own (Johnsson-Smaragdi, in press). Interesting as the substantive interpretations of specific similarities and dissimilarities between the two models may be, however, our concern here and now is more with the general formal similarity and/or difference between the models.

In the most general terms, what Figures 8.8a and 8.8b visualize is the fact that structural invariance is a matter of degree. Actually it is so in at least two ways. In the first place, even if most arrows are identical in the two models, the coefficients attached to the arrows are by no means identical. As a rule the difference is small, but sometimes it may be considerable. That is a quantitative difference. Second, the structures themselves, the two patterns of arrows between latent variables, although similar, are far from identical. As we have seen, some arrows may be found only in one of the figures. That is a qualitative difference. There are at least two types of structural invariance, then: quantitative and qualitative. Intuitively, the latter stands out as more important than the former.

Figures 8.8a and 8.8b show some lack of both quantitative and qualitative invariance. This is so in spite of the fact that we are dealing with two equal-age samples measured three times in exactly the same way at about the same time, differing only in the *place of living*.

Part of the differences may be due to the heavy and uneven reduction in *N* caused by missing answers on one or more of the many variables of the models. Missing answers are dealt with by either listwise or pairwise deletion. In this case, we used listwise deletion, which has its advantages but eliminates more cases than the other technique. Systematic comparisons based on the two techniques may shed some light on the problem. Building on previous experiments of that type (Flodin, 1986; Rosengren & Windahl, 1989, p. 266), we are fairly convinced, however, that this is no serious cause of difference between the two models.

Continued work with replication of longitudinal structural models will show the extent of quantitative and qualitative structural invariance to be expected in cases like these. As mentioned, work in this direction is on its way within the MPP. Because the relevance of all research rests on the assumption of structural invariance (or reliable knowledge about the lack of such invariance), the outcome of such studies must be considered to be of some interest.

What outcome may we expect? Personally, I expect the amount of both quantitative and qualitative structural invariance to be less than has implicitly been taken for granted. If that is so, it may have some consequences—in communication research as well as in the general debate. Cases of lack of structural invariance will point to the need for renewed theoretical and methodological efforts. Cases of structural invariance will provide strong support for existing theory and methodology.

CONCLUDING DISCUSSION

The Media Panel Program was inaugurated with a view to

(a) describe the mass media use of children and adolescents, and
(b) arrive at some reasonably safe conclusions about its causes and effects.

To the extent that we did not know it beforehand, it did not take us very long to realize that our descriptive data were completely dependent on two contingencies: the state of the media structure at the time of the measurement, and the conceptualizations and operationalizations used. Neither of these dependencies, of course, represents any strong argument against the production of descriptive data about media use.

On the contrary. Because the media structure is gradually and continuously changing (the rate of change—as well as the media structure itself—differing considerably from time to time, and from society to society), the dependency of descriptive data on the surrounding media structure is a very strong argument for the continuous collection of such data. The fact that—like all data—these data are contingent on the conceptualizations and operationalizations behind them, could be regarded as trivial. It is, however, probably best looked upon as a challenge, a demand for methodological development, in its turn calling for basic theoretical research about various aspects of media use and its relationship to social structure in general and to media structure in particular.

As work within the MPP continued, it was not long until we realized that not only descriptive results, but also results about the causes and effects of media use, might be bound to specific situations and structures. We soon found out, for instance, that whereas among Anglo-American children of the early 1950s high TV viewing seems to have been related to low social interaction, that was not so among Swedish children of the late 1970s and early 1980s. (Actually, it was the other way round.) Causes and effects of the use of a relatively new medium in one society, we concluded, were not necessarily the same as causes and effects of the use of a well-established medium in another society—even if, superficially, that medium was one and the same in the two cases (Rosengren & Windahl, 1989, p. 189; cf. Johnsson-Smaragdi, 1983; Sonesson, 1979, 1989).

This may be a rather trivial insight, too. But it does point to the fact that now that a number of American and European longitudinal studies have provided some answers to Lazarsfeld's 30-year-old question about the long-term effects of TV use (as quoted in the introduction of this chapter), we may generalize his question. Which—if any—causes and effects of social phenomena are independent of the surrounding social structure? More specifically: Is the structural invariance of individual media use (including causes and effects of that use) strong enough to survive the change of the media structure presently going on in Sweden and many other European countries?

Looking around for specific answers to questions such as these forms an important part of the activities going on right now within the Media Panel Program. Some preliminary attempts in that direction have been presented in this chapter. Others will hopefully follow. The "specified lack of knowledge" is certainly large. We do not know what the answers will be. But we do believe that some of them will be rather unexpected. After all, that is what makes the game worthwhile.

NOTES

1. The program has for many years enjoyed generous support from the Swedish Social Science Council, the Bank of Sweden Tercentenary Foundation, and the Swedish National Board of Education.

2. A number of detailed reports have been published, including seven doctoral theses appearing as books (Flodin, 1986; Hedinsson, 1981; Jarlbro, 1988; Johnsson-Smaragdi, 1983; Jönsson, 1985; Roe, 1983; Sonesson, 1979). Presentations of different waves, panels, and approaches of the program may be found, for instance, in Höjerback (1986); Jarlbro, Lööv, and Miegel (1989); Johnsson-Smaragdi and Höjerback (1989); Johnsson-Smaragdi and Roe (1986); Lööv and Miegel (1989a, 1989b); Rosengren (1986); Sonesson (1989); Sonesson and Höjerback (1989).

3. Unfortunately, due to time restraints, it was not possible to comment upon some interesting points made in these two articles.

4. Including classics such as Himmelweit, Oppenheim, and Vince (1958) and Schramm, Lyle, and Parker (1961); the oft-quoted panel study by Lefkovitz, Eron, Walder, and Huesman (1972), and more recent panel and/or cohort studies by Huesman and Eron (1986); Milavsky, Kessler, Stipp, and Rubens (1982); Singer, Singer, and Rapaczynski (1984); Werner (1989); Wiegman, Kuttschreuter, and Baarda (1986); Williams (1986).

REFERENCES

Alvarado, M. (Ed.). (1988). *Video world-wide: An international study.* Paris: UNESCO (John Libbey).

Arnman, G., & Jönsson, I. (1983). *Segregation och svensk skola.* Lund: Studentlitteratur. (With a summary in English)

Bourdieu, P. (1984). *Distinction.* London: Routledge & Kegan Paul.

Brown, J. R., Cramond, J. K., & Wilde, R. J. (1974). Displacement effects of television and the child's functional orientation to media. In J. Blumler & E. Katz (Eds.), *The uses of mass communications* (pp. 93-112). Beverly Hills, CA: Sage.

Bryant, J., & Zillmann, D. (Eds.). (1986). *Perspectives on media effects.* Hillsdale, NJ: Lawrence Erlbaum.

Burnett, R. (1990). *Concentration and diversity in the international phonogram industry.* Gothenburg, Sweden: University of Gothenburg, Department of Journalism and Mass Communication.

Burrell, G., & Morgan, G. (1979). *Sociological paradigms and organisational analysis.* London: Heineman.

Chaffee, S. H., McLeod, J. M., & Atkin, C. K. (1971). Parental influences on adolescent media use. *American Behavioral Scientist, 14,* 323-340.

Comstock, G., & Pail, H. J. (1987). *Television and children: A review of recent research.* Syracuse, NY: ERIC.

Cuttance, P., & Ecob, R. (Eds.). (1987). *Structural modeling by example.* Cambridge, UK: Cambridge University Press.

Entwisle, D., & Alexander, K. (1986). The schooling process in first grade: Two samples a decade apart. *American Educational Research, 23,* 587-613.

Feilitzen, C. von. (1991). Children's and adolescents' media use: Some methodological reflections. In J. A. Anderson (Ed.), *Communication yearbook 11* (pp. 91-101). Newbury Park, CA: Sage

Feilitzen, C. von, Filipson, L., Rydin, I., & Schyller, I. (1989). *Barn och unga i medieåldern.* Stockholm: Rabén & Sjögren.

Flodin, B. (1986). *TV och yrkesförväntan: En longitudinell studie av ungdomars yrkessocialisation.* Lund: Studentlitteratur. (With a summary in English)

Gahlin, A., & Nordström, B. (1988). *Video i Sverige.* Stockholm: Sveriges Radio/PUB.

Glass, G. V. (1976). Primary, secondary and meta-analysis of research. *Educational Researcher, 5,* 3-8.

Glenn, N. D. (1973). *Cohort analysis.* Beverly Hills, CA: Sage.

Hedinsson, E. (1981). *TV, family and society: The social origins and effects of adolescents' TV use.* Stockholm: Almqvist & Wiksell International.

Himmelweit, H., Oppenheim, A. N., & Vince, P. (1958). *Television and the child.* London: Oxford University Press.

Höjerback, I. (1986). Video i Malmö. *Lund Research Papers in the Sociology of Communication, 3.*

Huesman, L. R., & Eron, L. D. (1986). *Television and the aggressive child: A cross-national comparison.* Hillsdale, NJ: Lawrence Erlbaum.

Hunter, J. E., & Schmidt, D. L. (1990). *Methods of meta-analysis.* Newbury Park, CA: Sage.

Jarlbro, G. (1986). Family communication patterns revisited: Reliability and validity. *Lund Research Papers in the Sociology of Communication, 4.*

Jarlbro, G. (1988). *Familj, massmedier och politik.* Stockholm: Almqvist & Wiksell International. (With a summary in English)

Jarlbro, G., Lööv, T., & Miegel, F. (1989). Livsstil och massmedieanvändning: En deskriptiv rapport. *Lund Research Papers in the Sociology of Communication, 14.*

Johnsson-Smaragdi, U. (1983). *TV use and social interaction in adolescence: A longitudinal study.* Stockholm: Almqvist & Wiksell International.

Johnsson-Smaragdi, U. (in press). *Structural invariance in media use: Some longitudinal LISREL models replicated.* Lund: University of Lund, Department of Sociology.

Johnsson-Smaragdi, U., & Höjerback, I. (1989). Replikation av en LISREL-modell på ett nytt urval: Likheter i barns och föräldrars TV-konsumtion. *Lund Research Papers in the Sociology of Communication,* 13.

Johnsson-Smaragdi, U., & Roe, K. (1986). Teenagers in the new media world. *Lund Research Papers in the Sociology of Communication,* 2.

Jönsson, A. (1985). *TV ett hot eller en resurs för barn?* Lund: CWK Gleerup. (With a summary in English)

Jönsson, A. (1986). TV: A threat or a complement to school? *Journal of Educational Television, 12*(1), 29-38.

Jöreskog, K. G., & Sörbom, D. (1989). *LISREL 7: A guide to the program and applications* (2nd ed.). Chicago: SPSS Publications.

Lazarsfeld, P. F. (1955). Why is so little known about the effects of television on children, and what can be done? *Public Opinion Quarterly, 19,* 243-251.

Lefkovitz, M. M., Eron, L. D., Walder, L. O., & Huesman, L. R. (1972). Television violence and child aggression: A follow-up study. In G. A. Comstock & E. A. Rubinstein (Eds.), *Television and social behavior,* III (pp. 35-135). Washington, DC: Government Printing Office.

Levy, M. R. (Ed.). (1990). *The VCR age: Home video and mass communication.* Newbury Park, CA: Sage.

Liebert, R. M., & Sprafkin, J. (1988). *The early window* (3rd ed.). New York: Pergamon.

Lööv, T., & Miegel, F. (1989a). The notion of lifestyle. *Lund Research Papers in the Sociology of Communication,* 15.

Lööv, T., & Miegel, F. (1989b). Vardagsliv, livsstilar och massmedieanvändning: En studie av 12 malmöungdomar. *Lund Research Papers in the Sociology of Communication,* 16.

McLeod, J., & Brown, J. D. (1976). The family environment and adolescent television use. In R. Brown (Ed.), *Children and television* (pp. 199-234). London: Collier Macmillan.

Milavsky, J. R., Kessler, R. C., Stipp, H. H., & Rubens, W. S. (1982). *Television and aggression: A panel study.* New York: Academic Press.

Morley, D. (1980). *Reconceptualizing the media audience.* Birmingham, UK: Centre for Contemporary Cultural Studies.

Mortimer, J. T., Finch, M. D., & Kumka, K. (1982). Persistence and change in development: The multidimensional self-concept. In P. B. Baltes & O. G. Brim (Eds.), *Life-span development and behavior* (Vol. 4, pp. 264-315). New York: Academic Press.

Murray, J. P. (1991). Nothing lasts forever: Instability in longitudinal studies of media and society. In J. A. Anderson (Ed.), *Communication yearbook 11* (pp. 102-110). Newbury Park, CA: Sage.

Peterson, R. A., & Berger, D. G. (1975). Cycles in symbol production: The case of popular music. *American Sociological Review, 40,* 158-173.

Piepe, A., Crouch, S., & Emerson, M. (1975). *Television and the working class.* Farnborough, UK: Saxon House.

Pingree, S., Hawkins, R., Johnsson-Smaragdi, U., Rosengren, K. E., & Reynolds, N. (in press). Patterns of television viewing behavior: A Swedish-American comparison. *European Journal of Communication.*

Ritchie, L. D. (1990, June). *The family communication patterns instrument: Epistemic explorations.* Paper presented at the meeting of the International Communication Association, Dublin.

Roe, K. (1983). *Mass media and adolescent schooling: Conflict or co-existence?* Stockholm: Almqvist & Wiksell International.

Roe, K. (1985). The Swedish moral panic over video 1980-1984. *The Nordicom Review of Mass Communication Research,* June, 20-25.

Roe, K. (1988). *Adolescents' VCR use: How and why?* Gothenburg: University of Gothenburg, Unit of Mass Communication.

Rosengren, K. E. (1983). Communication research: One paradigm or four? *Journal of Communication, 33*(3), 185-207.

Rosengren, K. E. (Ed.). (1986). *På gott och ont: TV och video, barn och ungdom.* Stockholm: Liber.

Rosengren, K. E. (1988). The study of media culture: Ideas, actions and artifacts. *Lund Research Papers in the Sociology of Communication,* 10.

Rosengren, K. E. (1989a). Medienkultur: Forschungsansatz und Ergebnisse eines schwedischen Langzeitprojekts. *Media Perspektiven, 6,* 356-372.

Rosengren, K. E. (1989b). Paradigms lost and regained. In B. Dervin, L. Grossberg, B. O'Keefe, & E. Wartella (Eds.), *Paradigm dialogues: Theories and issues* (pp. 21-39). Newbury Park, CA: Sage.

Rosengren, K. E. (1991a). Media use in childhood and adolescence: Invariant change? In J.A. Anderson (Ed.), *Communication yearbook 14* (pp. 48-91). Newbury Park, CA: Sage.

Rosengren, K. E. (1991b). Combinations, comparisons and confrontations: Towards a comprehensive theory of audience research. *Lund Research Papers in Media and Communication Studies, 1.* Lund: Media and Communication Studies.

Rosengren, K. E., Wenner, L. A., & Palmgreen, P. (Eds.). (1985). *Media gratifications research: Current perspectives.* Beverly Hills, CA: Sage.

Rosengren, K. E., & Windahl, S. (1989). *Media matter: TV use in childhood and adolescence.* Norwood, NJ: Ablex.

Saris, W., & Stronkhorst, H. (1984). *Causal modelling in non-experimental research.* Amsterdam: Sociometric Research Foundation.

Schramm, W., Lyle, J., & Parker, E. B. (1961). *Television in the lives of our children.* Stanford, CA: Stanford University Press.

Singer, J. L., Singer, D. G., & Rapaczynski, W. (1984). Family patterns and television viewing as predictors of children's beliefs and aggression. *Journal of Communication, 34*(2), 73-89.

Sonesson, I. (1979). *Förskolebarn och TV.* Stockholm: Esselte Studium.

Sonesson, I. (1989). *Vem fostrar våra barn? Videon eller vi?* Stockholm: Esselte.

Sonesson, I., & Höjerback, I. (1989). Skolungdomars medievanor före och efter videon. *Lund Research Papers in the Sociology of Communication,* 12.

Tanner, I. M. (1962). *Growth at adolescence.* Oxford: Blackwell Scientific Publications.

Tims, A. R., & Masland, J. L. (1985). Measurement of family communication patterns. *Communication Research, 12,* 35-57.

Wartella, E., & Reeves, B. (1987). Communication and children. In C. R. Berger & S. H. Chaffee (Eds.), *Handbook of communication science* (pp. 619-650). Newbury Park, CA: Sage.

Werner, A. (1989). Television and age-related differences. *European Journal of Communication, 4,* 33-50.

Wiegman, O., Kuttschreuter, W., & Baarda, B. (1986). *Television viewing related to aggressive and prosocial behaviour.* The Hague: SVO/THT.

Williams, T. M. (Ed.). (1986). *The impact of television: A natural experiment.* Orlando, FL: Academic Press.

Chapter 9

MAGAZINE ADVERTISING CONTENT IN SWEDEN AND THE UNITED STATES: STABLE PATTERNS OF CHANGE, VARIABLE LEVELS OF STABILITY

Kjell Nowak

IN A BASIC SENSE all scientific work is "comparative." Research is a question of finding differences that are theoretically meaningful (or lack of them), and that necessarily involves comparisons of one sort or another. "Comparative research," however, seems to be used primarily to denote comparisons between different sociocultural contexts and between different points in time. In some cases such research is used descriptively, to study the degree of generality (across cultures) or stability (across time) of a particular phenomenon. Theoretically more rewardingly, however, temporal and/or spatial analyses may be seen instead as a form of quasi-experimental approach. Time and space variables typically are of no theoretical interest in and of themselves, but they indicate variation in factors assumed to affect the phenomenon under study. In other words, comparative and temporal research may involve causal models predicting specificity as well as generality, and variability as well as stability.

The present chapter is based primarily on results from a longitudinal study of magazine advertising in Sweden, covering the period 1935-1980.[1] The purpose of the study was to describe, by means of content analysis, ideological and rhetorical aspects of advertising, and to relate the results to developments in the Swedish society during the period. The general interpretive frame of reference was to regard magazine advertising as a specific cultural system that is affected by the wider economic, social, and cultural context prevailing at a particular time in a particular society. To some extent it is possible to compare some of the Swedish data with results from North America, thus permitting spatial as well as temporal comparisons. The chapter first reviews the empirical material available, and then summarizes the results in an attempt at systematizing various types of comparisons.

THE STUDIES

The material on Sweden covers advertising in popular magazines during the period 1935-1980, and it is composed of stratified random samples of 90 advertisements for each year. Through balancing summer and winter seasons and applying a three-stage procedure that included weighting of sampling probabilities on the basis of circulation figures,[2] the magazines in the samples are represented in proportion to their annual circulation. Three ads were randomly chosen for each magazine issue in the samples.

The statistical population consists of all advertisements in the total yearly circulation of popular magazines. The term *popular magazine* was defined in accordance with the classification used by the semi-official agency controlling circulation figures (*Tidningsstatistik*). The samples include a variety of publications, ranging from large-circulation magazines published by cooperative and other consumer organizations, over traditional family magazines to those more specifically oriented toward female or male readers.

The content analysis covers a large number of variables, only a few of which are mentioned here. Ideological aspects of the advertisements particularly refer to images of persons portrayed (age, gender, class, activities, relations, etc.), whereas the rhetorical aspects concern the amount and kind of information given and the techniques of persuasion applied. Several coders were used, and the variables presented in this context all have intercoder reliability greater than 0.80 (Scott's Pi).

Data on magazine advertising in the United States have been reported by Richard Pollay in several articles (Belk & Pollay, 1985; Pollay, 1984, 1985, 1986). His material consists of 2,000 advertisements drawn from the 10 largest selling magazines for each of the eight decades during the period 1900-1980. The magazine issues were randomly sampled from the years 3 to 7 of each decade, and the results are reported as mid-decade averages (Pollay, 1985). In a few cases comparisons can be made also with a Canadian study (Leiss, Kline, & Jhally, 1986), which analyzed advertisements in two major magazines, one female-oriented and one male-oriented, both in operation since the beginning of this century.

Because the three studies were initiated independently of each other and were not intended to be "comparative," the data do not permit statistical comparisons. Overall patterns of change and stability can be visually inspected, however, and subjected to tentative interpretations. The Swedish and the U.S. material may be roughly compared with respect to the composition of product categories, and in spite of somewhat different classification schemes they show considerable similarity (Nowak, 1989, table 1; Pollay, 1985, table 1). In both cases the largest product category is "personal care" (19% and 27%, respectively), and the next largest is "food and drink" (17% and 20%). Also, in both cases "personal care" represents a shrinking proportion, whereas "food and drink" remains at the same level throughout the period under study. The major difference is that "consumer durables" is a larger category in U.S. advertising (17% versus 7% in Sweden).

RHETORICAL FORMS

MODES OF PERSUASION

One of the truly classical issues in the theory and practice of rhetoric is the question of rational versus nonrational communication, and it has been a recurrent discussion theme among practitioners and critics of advertising. From the practitioner's point of view the question is which approach is more effective in persuading and influencing the consumer, and the choice between the two necessarily implies hypotheses about processes governing human behavior. As manifested in the leading U.S. advertising trade journal, the prevailing attitude during the last 50-60 years seems to have been a belief in emotional appeals (Curti, 1967). Particularly in the 1950s there was a growing interest among marketers in using "motivation research" as a basis for advertising, and concepts like "brand image," "profiling," "positioning," and "life-styles" have become standard elements in advertising textbooks.

There is of course no clear division between a rational and a nonrational or emotional approach in creating advertising messages. The terms are notoriously ambiguous, and what is rational may depend on circumstances in the particular situation. Certain kinds of content of an ad, however, may be said to be generally more the one than the other, and Pollay's study of U.S. magazine advertising gives some indication of the development during this century (Pollay, 1985). He classified the ads with respect to "rhetorical focus" in three categories, Logos, Pathos and Ethos, and the first two roughly correspond to the rational-emotional distinction. The rational focus was found in more than half of the ads over the whole period, but its relative dominance is highest before 1930 (about 60%). The emotional or associative approach was characteristic among more than one third of the ads, but the pattern is curvilinear, increasing to 50% in the 1940s. From the 1930s and onward the variation is not very large, however, and emotional appeals do not seem to have been a dominant characteristic of U.S. magazine advertising.

Data about the rhetoric in the sample of Swedish magazine ads were collected and analyzed by Andrén (1988). He identified seven techniques of "nonrational persuasion" (for example, assertions about the popularity or newness of the product, or about the goodwill of the advertiser; associations to various values; humor, flattery, etc.), and found that the average number of such "nonfactual" techniques used varied between 1.1 and 1.5 across the whole period (see Table 9.1). On the average, one fourth of the ads employ none of the seven techniques. It is interesting to note that the level of nonrational persuasion is lowest between 1970 and 1975, which was a period when advertising and consumer policy were subject to a lively public and political debate, and when legislative restrictions on marketing were introduced. If this had an effect, however, it was short-lived, all but disappearing in the latter half of the 1970s.

The level of nonrational persuasion has thus been consistently low, according to the definition used in the Swedish study. A secondary analysis of Andrén's data, using a more differentiated index covering 12 indicators of nonfactual techniques, does not change this impression—only 16% of the ads contain more than two techniques, and the average number ranges between 1.2 and 1.6.

LEVEL OF INFORMATION

Closely related to the rational versus nonrational issue is the question of the informativeness of advertising. Rationality and informativeness may be independent in principle, at least to some extent, but they would be expected to correlate in practice. A noninformative ad may be rational or nonrational, but because rational appeals usually include assertions that are relevant and useful for the buying decision, they would tend to increase informativeness. The definitions of *informative* vary, of course, and in the context of content analysis the term *potential information* has often been used, in order to accommodate the fact that many dimensions of content may be more or less informative depending on the situation and the particular consumer (several studies are reviewed in Pollay, 1984). Typically all assertions about the product are accepted as "potential information," and this approach also was taken by Pollay, who identified 16 information dimensions in his analysis of U.S. magazines. On the average, 4 dimensions were present in the ads, and, although there was a slight declining trend, the level is remarkably stable (Pollay, 1985).

Andrén (1988) employed a normative analysis in order to determine categories of facts that constitute informative aspects of an ad. Six such categories were used to form an index of information level, and the ads in Swedish magazines on the average contain 1.6-1.8 such aspects. In the United States there has thus been little variation in the level of information. There is a temporary increase toward the end of the 1970s, which coincides with a new Marketing Act that came into effect in 1976. One purpose of the Act was to improve the amount and kind of information provided to the consumer in advertising, but if the Act had any effect it was temporary, at least in magazine advertising.

In order to increase comparability with the U.S. data reported by Pollay (1985), a secondary analysis of the Swedish data was carried out, using a 10-point index based on a more liberal definition of *informativeness*. The pattern does not change, however: More than one half of the ads contain less than three information units, and the index is very stable, varying between 2.3 and 2.6. The curve is slightly U-shaped, reaching a low point at the end of the 1960s, when two thirds of the ads carried less than three units of information (Table 9.1).

In summary, these data about Sweden and the United States clearly do not substantiate the claim that emotional or nonrational techniques of persuasion are common elements in magazine advertising as a totality. Even with a wide definition of such techniques they are totally absent in one Swedish ad out of four, and only 16% employ more than two techniques. On the other hand, the ads are not very informative either. It is much more common, however, that the ads contain some

TABLE 9.1   Distribution of All Ads on Some Major Variables

A. Aspects of rhetoric (in percentages unless otherwise indicated). n = all ads

Period	1935-38	—	—	50/54	55/59
n	150	—	—	444	449

Information level

Mean of index (max 6)	1.93	—	—	1.64	1.79
> 2 units of info	33	—	—	21	24

Nonrational techniques

Mean of index (max 7)	1.31	—	—	1.30	1.33
No technique	20	—	—	26	26
> 2 techniques	11	—	—	16	15

Testimonials	27	28	28	27	21

B. Demographic representation (in percentages). n = all ads.

Period	1935/39	40/44	45/49	50/54	55/59
n	416	421	429	444	449

The ad contains:

Male person(s)	50	57	61	59	51
Female person(s)	60	57	69	72	68
Young person(s)[a]	64	69	68	61	62
Mature person(s)[a]	53	49	59	40	43
Old person(s)	5	5	2	1	1
Person(s) whose social class is identifiable	35	38	45	35	27
Upper-class person(s)	9	9	10	8	5
Working-class person(s)	4	6	7	7	5

NOTE: a. The content analysis was done in two stages, first the period 1950-1975 and a few years later the
the stages, but with respect to the coding of age it seems that a change in coder instructions has affected the
be compared only among themselves and not with other numbers. As a consequence no total is reported for

60/64	65/69	70/75	76/80	Total
450	*439*	*530*	*182*	*2,644*
1.61	1.56	1.61	1.86	1.66
22	18	21	30	23
1.41	1.30	1.08	1.48	1.29
20	23	33	21	25
16	12	8	20	14
20	14	13	15	21

60/64	65/69	70/74	75/80	Total
450	*439*	*445*	*535*	*4,028*
50	37	36	42	49
64	57	46	47	59
60	56	55	*54*	—
38	37	32	*49*	—
1	2	4	7	3
22	17	18	20	28
4	4	2	4	6
3	2	2	3	6

periods 1935-1949 and 1976-1980 (italic figures in the table). Intercoder reliability was checked between results differentially for women and men portrayed in the ads. Italic numbers in the table should therefore these variables.

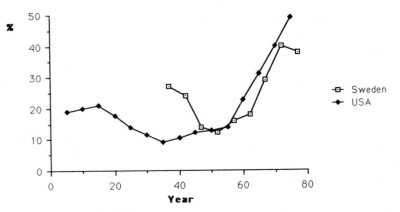

Figure 9.1. Ads Without Person
NOTE: Swedish data are 5-year averages for 1935-1939, 1940-1944, etc.; U.S. data are from Pollay (1985) who reports mid-decade averages. These have been extrapolated in the figure.

information than that they contain nonrational persuasion. Between 40% and 50% carry at least three units of information, and 10-20% employ three or more nonrational techniques; and whereas 5% of the ads are nonrational only (no information, but at least one nonrational technique), 16% contain some information but no nonrational persuasion. These results from Sweden are in line with Pollay's conclusion that U.S. magazine advertising in this century has consistently promoted practical product attributes more than other qualities (Pollay, 1985).

TESTIMONIALS

At least since Aristotle it has been known that audience perceptions of the communicator may strongly affect responses to the message, and long before empirical research on this aspect of persuasion took place (for instance, Hovland, Lumsdaine, & Sheffield, 1949), advertising utilized well-known, attractive, well-liked, knowledgeable people to testify as to the product's qualities. In U.S. and Canadian magazine advertising, the testimonial technique reached a peak during the 1930s; this is true also of Sweden (see Figure 9.1). According to Pollay (1985) this was a period of increasing competition, with a proliferation of techniques and tactics in advertising. Leiss et al. (1986) instead argue that testimonials were part of a close connection between advertising and the star system of the entertainment industry. These arguments may not be valid in the Swedish context, but a more general explanation may be that the testimonial technique is simply "worn out." It invites the reader to rely not on the advertiser's claims but rather on the judgment of others, allegedly knowledgeable or otherwise trustworthy persons. Such straightforward attempts to avoid the reader's assumed predisposition to disregard the advertising message may have been successful in the early phases of the consumption society, but it is not surprising that they are less frequent as everyday life has become permeated with sales-promoting messages. Most likely, more sophisticated techniques to the same end have been developed.

IMAGES OF PEOPLE

PRESENCE OF PERSONS

One of the most common bases for criticism of advertising (and of capitalist society generally, of course) is its role in promoting materialist attitudes and life-styles and in reinforcing a reification process where goals and feelings are displaced from people to objects (cf. Pollay, 1986). Advertising may contribute to such a development in many and complex ways, but a simple indicator of the human-nonhuman balance may be the absence of persons in the advertisements. Across the whole period, about one fourth of the Swedish ads contain no persons, but the proportion shows a clear curvilinear pattern. The proportion of nonperson ads reach their lowest point in the early 1950s but rise sharply after 1960 to about 40% (Figure 9.1).

A very similar curvilinear pattern is present also in the U.S. study. In both countries, advertisements without persons are relatively common in the early phase of the periods studied, that is, before 1920 in the United States and before 1950 in Sweden. The lowest point is about 20 years earlier in the United States, but the period of most rapid growth occurs simultaneously, starting in the 1950s, and the U.S. curve reaches a higher level at the end of the period (Figure 9.1). Data on Canadian magazine advertising during this century shows a corresponding U-shape pattern, with a rapid increase from 1950 onward (Leiss et al., 1986).

The relative absence of persons in the early and late periods most likely has different explanations, but the postwar trend does lend some support to the criticism referred to above. It may indicate a significant change in the value system of a society when human beings become symbolically less prominent and are subordinated in favor of products and other material phenomena, particularly because the pattern coincides with economic and social developments such as rising consumption expenditures and consumption-oriented ways of life.

DEMOGRAPHIC REPRESENTATION

The idea of representation or reflection underlies a large number of content analytic studies of mass media during the last half-century (cf. Feilitzen, Strand, Nowak, & Andrén, 1989; Nowak, Strand, Andrén, Ross, & Feilitzen, 1989). One of the most consistent results seems to be that the representation of social and demographic groups by the mass media tend to be biased in a way that corresponds with hierarchical patterns in society. A particularly common finding is that over- and underrepresentation of demographic, ethnic, and socioeconomic groups is correlated with their social position—women, old people, children, working-class people, and ethnic minorities are consistently underrepresented (McQuail, 1987; Nowak et al., 1989).

A similar pattern might be expected in advertising, but its purpose to persuade and promote sales makes it more likely that the representation of population categories may be related to their purchasing power, that is, to their position as buyers and consumers rather than to their social position generally (power, prestige, etc.). The fact that advertising is markedly oriented to particular audiences may also increase the probability that these groups become represented in the content (cf. Martel & McCall, 1964).

Gender

The latter consideration would primarily affect the presence of women in the ads, because they are and have long been the target of the majority of magazine advertising (both as buyers and as buying decision makers; cf. Schudson, 1984). The results show a consistent but slight overrepresentation of women among the persons depicted in magazine advertising (Figure 9.1). This is clearly different from most other media content, where women are typically about half as common as men (cf. Andrén, 1989; Tuchman, Daniels, & Benet, 1978). Interestingly enough, however, men were in fact a majority in the ads during the period 1940-1944. Thus although Sweden was not engaged in actual warfare, it seems that the male sphere gained in symbolic power during the war. It should be mentioned that the overrepresentation of women refers only to adult persons in the ads: Among all children depicted during the period, boys are a majority (54%).

Age

It would be reasonable to expect the representation of age groups to be affected by the rising purchasing power of the younger generation in the postwar period and to the development of a commercially based youth culture. This has not been the case, however. There is in the advertisements a high and stable level of young persons, which indicates that the changing pattern of purchasing power is overridden by the universally applicable persuasive strategy to associate with positively evaluated phenomena.

Youth, of course, is a highly evaluated characteristic in Western society. It is worth noting, however, that although the youth ideal seems to have become particularly salient during the last 10-15 years, that is not reflected in the content data. On the other hand, a strong increase in average buying power among the elderly, coupled with an increasingly top-heavy age distribution in the Swedish society, is paralleled in the material. Toward the end of the period old persons constitute a noticeable proportion, after having been almost totally absent in the early postwar period.

PHYSICAL PROPERTIES
OF THE ADVERTISEMENTS

Although it represents a relatively small part of total advertising expenditure,[3] magazine advertising as a whole reaches a large majority of the population. Sweden does not allow advertising on television or radio, and so weekly magazines have for a long time been an important medium in brand advertising on a national scale. Their relative role has

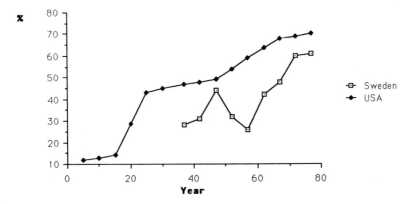

Figure 9.2. Full Page Ads
NOTE: Swedish data are 5-year averages for 1935-1939, 1940-1944, etc.; U.S. data are from Pollay (1985) who reports mid-decade averages. These have been extropolated in the figure.

declined during the last two decades, but their advertising volume has grown in an absolute sense. Full data on the developments in total magazine circulation, in the number of ads per issue, and the average size of ads are not available, but total circulation of the kind of magazines sampled in the study has increased from about 2 million in 1935 to more than 5 million in 1975. Total circulation has been slowly declining since the mid-1950s, but in the same period the average number of pages per issue has increased by about 50%. In 1940, advertisements accounted for about 15% of total space in an average magazine, and after an increase to 25% in the 1950s and 1960s the figure was about 20% at the end of the 1970s (Bernow & Österman, 1979).

Very roughly, these figures show an increase in total circulation by a factor of 2.5, while the number of pages has increased by a factor of 1.5 and the proportion of advertising space by a factor of 1.33. The figures stem from different statistical estimates and are not quite comparable, but taken together they indicate a growth of magazine advertising volume by a factor of 4-6 during the period studied.

The growth pattern described above depends in part on the increasing size of the advertisements: During the last two decades of the period the proportion of full-page advertisements doubled (see Figure 9.2). Over the whole period practically all advertisements contain pictures and, although no data about the size of pictures were collected, a general impression is that the relative role of artwork has increased. A

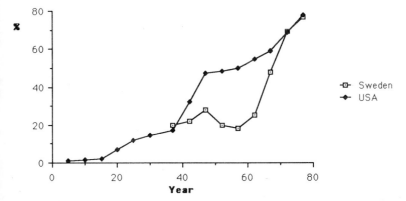

Figure 9.3. Color Ads
NOTE: The Swedish data are 5-year averages for 1935-1939, 1940-1944, etc.; U.S. data are from Pollay (1985) who reports mid-decade averages. These have been extrapolated in the figure.

growing majority of the pictures are photographic, and since the end of the 1960s most of them have been in color.

These trends are, of course, related to technological developments with respect to reproduction methods, printing techniques, and paper quality. But they also reflect how advertising has become an increasingly important tool in the fight over market shares in a growing market for consumer goods characterized by oligopolistic competition. In the United States, the process toward a mass market consumption society started earlier and, as would be expected, there is a clear tendency for periods of dramatic change to occur earlier in the United States than in Sweden. The increase in advertisement size (Figure 9.2) is already particularly strong in the United States around 1920, whereas in Sweden a similar jump takes place after 1955. There was, however, also a peak in the 1940s; due to lack of data from before 1935 we cannot exclude the possibility that in Sweden there was also an earlier period of increase (but still later than that in the United States). A lagged relationship between the two countries is also seen in the use of color (see Figure 9.3), which increases sharply between 1935 and 1945 in the United States, whereas a corresponding change takes place in Sweden during the 1960s.

The use of photographic depictions has been more or less parallel in U.S. and Swedish advertising (see Figure 9.4). It should be noted that differences in coding principles may account for the relatively high

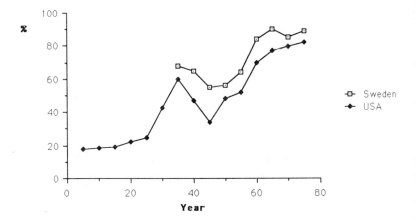

Figure 9.4. Ads with Photogaph
NOTE: The Swedish data are 5-year averages for 1935-1939, 1940-1944, etc.; U.S. data are from Pollay (1985) who reports mid-decade averages. These have been extrapolated in the figure.

level in the Swedish data (photo-like paintings or drawings have been coded as photographs). The two curves show a very similar pattern, however, and in both countries there is decline in the use of photographic images during the 1940s. Possible reasons for this remain to be explored.

ENCODING PRACTICES AND SOCIETAL CHANGE

The developments of advertising content reported so far have all been related to changing structural conditions that are generally common to Sweden and the United States. There are, however, also patterns of change or stability that depend on the interplay between, on the one hand, stable patterns of behavior among those who are responsible for the form and content of advertisements and, on the other hand, particular societal developments. At this point no comparisons across societies can be made, partly because no data are available, and partly because the societal processes involved are specific to Sweden.

ADVERTISING ENCODING

Little systematic research has been carried out that throws light on the professions and practices involved in advertising production (Dyer,

1982; Leiss et al., 1986; Schudson, 1984; Sinclair, 1987). One may assume, however, that there are considerable similarities with other professional, organized encoding practices such as news production. Like news journalists, one would think, advertising professionals are guided by their particular educational training and by a strong socializing effect of daily work routines and a long tradition of unwritten rules and norms. One would also guess that their main reference group is their peers, that audience response is sometimes but not frequently an important issue to them, and that they often feel that those who control their work do not understand or appreciate their new ideas or initiatives. Further, like journalists, they operate within organizations that have more or less concrete linkages to major power structures (economic and/or political), and that depend for their existence on other organizations (clients, sources) as well as on their ability to attract the attention of large audiences.

The analogy between news and advertising serves to show that there are strong forces toward stability in the content of any form of mass communication. Short-term changes most likely occur primarily as a consequence of—or in response to—developments in relevant parts of the surrounding "reality." In news reporting, the most important "reality" is the sources and the events they are associated with; in advertising, it is the clients and their products. As politicians start to talk more about, say, pollution, that will affect the content of news, and when products are constructed to be less polluting or poisonous, that will affect advertising content. Another basic mechanism of external influence, of course, is that professional communicators respond to assumed changes in interests among target audiences. When journalists believe there is an interest in pollution problems among the public, they are apt to interpret and report a variety of events in that perspective, just as a campaign planner or copywriter might try to associate various products with nonpollution. The need to "feel" and respond to what audiences consider important and interesting exists in news journalism as well as in advertising.

Although seemingly trivial, these relationships indicate major mechanisms through which changes in the content of a particular message system may come about: There are new things to communicate about and there are, among communicators, new ideas about what people want to hear about (ideas that may be correct or incorrect). Both processes may be subsumed under the general notion of media content as "reflecting" societal phenomena, but it should be noted that their importance lies in the explanation of *change* in media content, not in explaining the ways in which media content represents phenomena in the surrounding society. That is primarily determined by basic structural factors (economic, political, organizational, professional, technological) that, as was briefly indicated above, tend to bring about stability rather than change.

The two forms of external influence may of course also involve changes in beliefs and attitudes among the professional communicators themselves. In a longer time perspective, these changes could be strengthened by cohort effects (new generations entering the profession), although these effects would themselves be weakened by a strong workplace socialization.

Given this overall frame of reference, it is obvious that advertising communicators are subject to particular restricting and determining factors. First, on a general level, advertising encoding practices are confined by their basic function to promote the sales of commodities and services and to serve the interests of industry and business. Second, a more specific restriction is the high degree of control by clients, the advertisers. They define more or less explicitly what kinds of content are desirable and acceptable, and a client's clearance of the final message is always a necessary stage in the encoding process.

A primary goal from the advertiser's point of view is to establish a sense of trust and sympathy on the part of potential consumers, and clients are apt to be very sensitive to any content that they believe might arouse negative associations with respect to their product or company. That might affect the content in a generally conservative direction; more specifically it seems likely that ideas or phenomena that are considered controversial would be banned. Advertisers would avoid making references to conflicting social interests or to other societal problems (and even individual problems, except those that can allegedly be cured by buying the product).

A third major characteristic of advertising encoding is the relatively high degree of systematic study of target groups. Although the level of sophistication in market research and the use of advanced psychological manipulation in message design is usually highly overestimated (see Schudson, 1984), there is no doubt that the design of advertising messages, more than many other forms of mass communication, is supported by empirical data in its attempts at adapting to interests and preferences among audiences. This might work to make advertising sensitive to tendencies in the cultural climate, but many advertising professionals would argue that systematic research is less valuable than the intuition and creativity among good copywriters and art directors. Part of the professional role and a measure of success in the trade is the ability to sense social and cultural trends early and accurately—to the extent that such trends may be linked to products or services so that they would be reflected in advertising. There is in fact some evidence showing that changes in the values appealed to in magazine advertising may be used as a predictor of changes in the cultural climate (Fowles, 1976).

Roughly, then, there is on the one hand a pressure on advertising encoders to avoid ideas or phenomena that are or tend to become controversial, and on the other hand there is an effort to associate with ideas or phenomena that are or tend to become widely accepted. These rather simple relationships may account for a considerable part of the patterns of change and stability observed in the present study. In the following section, two variables will serve as illustration of the assumed approach-avoidance tendency. One is gender differences, the other is presence of social class.

WOMEN'S AND MEN'S ACTIVITIES

In Sweden, as in other Western countries, the 1960s meant a reawakening of feminist movements and a heightened public awareness of the nature and consequences of various aspects of gender segregation. In varying degrees this has had consequences for the economic, social, and political position of women, but the most concrete and socially significant change that has taken place is no doubt the massive entry of women into the labor market. Between 1950 and 1975 the proportion of gainfully employed women doubled, from 30% to 60%, and the increase has continued (*World of Women and Men*, 1986). The development was particularly rapid among married women, for whom the percentage rose from 15 to about 60. Today gainful employment is almost as common among women as among men.

In spite of this radical change in working life, the role distribution in the family seems to have remained very much the same. Male gender role demands have become somewhat softened both in the home and in the public sphere, but survey research reveals that responsibility for child care and household work still rests with the woman in most families. Employed married women spend almost twice as much time on household work as do their husbands (*World of Women and*

Men, 1986). Also, a large proportion of the employed women work part-time. According to interview data the majority of them prefer not working full-time because it allows them time to care for the family and the household.

Because magazine advertising to a high extent is directed toward women, its content could be expected to reflect this contradictory development of change and stability in the life situation of many women. For each activity shown or referred to in the ad, the coder registered whether the activity was linked to a male or female person, and on the basis of labor market statistics the occupational activities were classified into "male," "female," and "other," respectively. When "female" occupations occur in the ads, they are primarily subordinate service and office jobs, whereas "male" occupations cover a wider range in social position and type of job. Further, whereas "male" occupations almost never are associated with a woman, more than one out of five "female" occupational activities are practiced by a man. The category "other," finally, consists mainly of jobs like doctor, researcher, artist, journalist, teachers in high school or at universities, and only 20% of jobs like these are associated with a woman. In magazine advertising, as in much other media content (Tuchman et al., 1978), the occupational sphere is clearly dominated by males, and women more than men are confined to particular types of work.

In the case of household activities, of course, the situation is reversed. In almost 90% of all cases where such activities are associated with a person, that person is a woman. The two predominant activities are cooking and cleaning (including other forms of maintenance of the home), which account for nearly two thirds of the household work activities coded.

The above data about the gender distribution among persons associated with different activities refer to the period as a whole. The number of activities coded is too small for a longitudinal analysis, but a more detailed analysis of patterns of change can be made by studying the probabilities of finding a woman or man linked with the respective activities in the ads. This is done by analyzing the frequency of ads in which a woman/man is associated with occupational and household activities, respectively, given that there is at least one woman/man in the ad.

In view of the radical change on the labor market, the most striking result is that the proportion of ads with a woman engaged in an occupational activity shows no clear trend and remains less than 10% over the whole period (see Figure 9.5). The pattern is curvilinear and follows

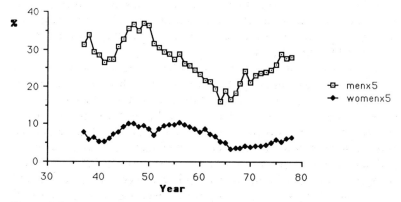

Figure 9.5. Ads with Man/Woman in Occupational Activity
NOTE: Percentages based on ads with at least one man/woman. Values are 5-year sliding averages.

rather closely the curve for ads containing men. On the whole it is about three times as likely among men in the ads to be associated with employment as it is among women. Applying a linear trend to the data shows a slightly shrinking distance between the two curves, indicating that the gender differential has diminished somewhat across the period as a whole. On the other hand, the shape of the curves indicates a growing differential toward the end of the period. In the case of household activities this differential is more pronounced, but it also declines more during the period (see Figure 9.6). This is due to the fact that men are increasingly likely to be associated with household work, whereas there is no trend in the case of ads containing women.

Summarizing, magazine advertising does not reflect the changing life situation among a large part of the female population, but there was a tendency for the different portrayals of men and women to become less pronounced during the 1970s.

As was noted earlier, the structural change on the labor market has affected the lives of women in contradictory ways. Although most employed women like to work outside the home, many evidently find themselves in a difficult situation, both in terms of conflicting role demands and in terms of available time. Female employment thus may be a conflict-charged issue associated with feelings of ambivalence, something that advertising encoders would avoid linking with their product, according to the above reasoning. Thus, employed women would be

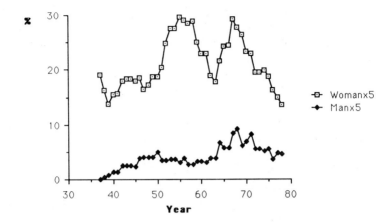

Figure 9.6. Ads with Man/Woman in Household Activity
NOTE: Percentages based on ads with one man/woman. Values are 5-year sliding averages.

unusual in magazine advertising. Further, assuming that advertising encoders are sensitive to prevailing ideas in society, one would not expect employed women to have become more frequent in the ads, because attitudes and patterns of behavior in family life indicate a fairly high degree of stability at the cultural level despite the structural change on the labor market.

The ambivalence attached to the changing female role does not seem to apply to the male role. The idea of men taking over some part of women's traditional duties is most likely less controversial, and in some social strata men in fact gain status and prestige by engaging in child care and household work. This is, therefore, a social change that advertising encoders would respond to, and, as has been shown, that has indeed been the case.

THE PRESENCE OF SOCIAL CLASS

The reduction of economic and social inequality has been a major political goal in Sweden since the early 1930s, when the Social Democratic party took power for a period of more than 40 years. Through taxation policies, social security systems, educational reforms, work environment control, and many other measures, attempts have been made to improve the lot of the less privileged and to realize the "welfare society." One basic dimension in this development, of course, is income distribution; time series data show that the process toward lower income inequality took place primarily at the beginning of the period, from 1935 to 1950.[4] After that, income dispersion has been relatively constant, although there are other signs that economic inequalities have been growing during the 1980s.

During the prosperous times of the 1950s and early 1960s, the image of Sweden as a society with small and shrinking class differences was gaining wide acceptance, even if egalitarian goals were still a matter of political controversy. During the late 1960s and well into the 1970s, however, concepts of equality were incorporated into the vocabulary of all parties, and egalitarian attitudes were expressed in practically all spheres of society.

These material and cultural trends related to social class differences are paralleled in the content of magazine ads in several ways. One is the presence in the ads of persons belonging to different classes. In the coding of the ads, the coder registered whether there was any person(s) whose social class could be identified and, if so, whether that person was clearly upper or lower (working) class. One third of the ads containing persons allowed class identification of at least one person, and in 60% to 70% of the cases those persons were middle class; among the rest, upper class was somewhat more common than lower class. This is quite similar to the pattern typically found in mass media fiction content (see Nowak, 1988; Nowak & Ross, 1989; Ross, 1988), where the large majority of persons either cannot be identified with respect to class or belong to the (upper) middle class.

The class distribution is relatively stable (see Figure 9.7), but the relative dominance of upper over lower class disappears around the year 1950. Most striking, however, is the sharply declining proportion of ads with class-identifiable person(s), starting at the end of the 1940s. This would seem to be entirely in line with the spreading image of Sweden as a "classless society." The curve is U-shaped, however, and the rising level at the end of the period precedes or parallels what is often called a "neoliberal" trend in the political climate.

The reduction of economic and social inequalities, a growing middle class, an image of Sweden as a more or less "classless" society and, later, the seemingly total rallying around general ideas about equality, would all be factors that make advertising appeals to class differences or social prestige less attractive as a persuasive approach. The assumed tendency to avoid ideas that are controversial or losing ground in the

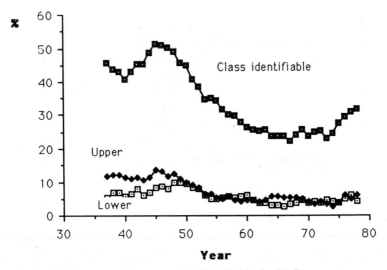

Figure 9.7. Presence of Persons with Identifiable Social Class
NOTE: Percentages based on ads with at least one man/woman. Values are 5-year sliding averages.

population would create a tendency to portray persons without particular social class characteristics.

In contrast, advertising appeals could be positively linked with another egalitarian trend, namely an increasing use of informal modes of address in public discourse. Around 1970 in Sweden, there was a strong trend toward establishing (or creating the impression of) less authoritarian relationships in workplaces, in public service institutions, in schools, and in social discourse generally. An indication of this was a seemingly rapid change in the way people addressed each other. In a few years time at the end of the 1960s, the informal pronoun *Du* replaced the formal *Ni* in most social contexts, and in 1970 a large majority (80%-90%) of the population under 35 years of age used the informal pronoun of address to unfamiliar persons with a social status different from their own (Korpi, 1978, p. 107).

The spreading of an informal manner of address in society would seem to be highly relevant for all forms of persuasive communication. A basic technique in such communication is to establish feelings of confidence and mutual trust, which is assumedly much easier when an informal and more personal approach is allowed. Advertising would

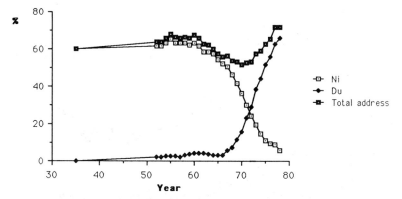

Figure 9.8. Pronoun of Address
NOTE: Percentages based on ads with at least one man/woman. Values are 5-year sliding averages.

therefore be likely to respond quickly to this development, and that was the case. The use of *Du* and *Ni* in ads exhibits the most dramatic pattern of all variables studied (see Figure 9.8). The figure shows 5-year sliding averages, but a close look at yearly data reveals that 1968 is a very marked turning point, after which the rapid change takes place. The year before, the newly appointed Director General of the Board of Social Welfare had publicly declared that the informal *Du* was to become the proper pronoun of address among all employees, including himself. The mass media paid much attention to the change, and during 1968 the use of informal address spread rapidly. Advertising obviously responded early, but it is interesting to note that the proportion of ads using a personal pronoun of address declines during the period of most rapid change from *Ni* to *Du*. This possibly reflects an uncertainty on the part of advertisers about the most acceptable mode as perceived by the audience.

STABILITY AND CHANGE,
SIMILARITY AND DIFFERENCE

Summarizing the results, we find considerable stability as well as patterns of change. To the extent that comparisons between countries have been possible, they show strong similarities between Sweden and the United States. Several patterns of similarity have emerged, illustrating various outcomes of spatial-temporal comparisons.

One pattern is represented by variables that *remain at the same level in each of the countries* across the time period studied. This is the case for the variables indicating two basic characteristics of the rhetoric: the amount of information and the presence of nonrational persuasion. The information indices, particularly, show very slight cyclical changes and no clear long-term trends. Absolute levels cannot be compared because different indices were used, but the fact that both measures exhibit the same pattern over time is an indication of similar underlying causal processes. The levels of information may be compared in a relative sense, though, and it turns out that the average number of information units is in both cases about one fourth of the maximum number possible (see Pollay, 1985).

In the case of nonrational persuasion, qualitatively different measures were used in the two studies, one based on overall judgments of the general character of the ad (Pollay, 1985), the other derived from a detailed analysis of statements expressed or implied in the ad (Andrén, 1988). Nevertheless, from the 1930s on, both studies indicate considerable stability[5] in the level or frequency of nonrational or emotional appeals. Thus, during the period for which data are available in both countries, this aspect of rhetorical form also has remained fairly stable.

The Swedish data on information and nonrational persuasion were subjected to 3-way analyses of variance, with type of product, type of medium, and time period as independent variables. Due to large Ns, each of these factors shows highly significant main effects, but their combined explanatory value is only 5% to 10% of the variance. Inspection of the means within subsets of data reveals that even if the average level of information and nonrational persuasion varies depending on type of product and medium, there are no systematic changes over time within these sets.

These patterns of results might be explained in various ways and on different levels of analysis, but generally speaking, the cross-cultural similarity indicates that the same set of determining factors have been in operation in both countries, and the temporal stability indicates that these determinants have remained stable during the time period studied. This suggests that levels of information and nonrational persuasion are related to basic functions of commercial advertising in a free enterprise market economy, which is on the whole characteristic of Sweden as well as of the United States. The two countries certainly differ in many political, social, and cultural aspects, but general structural conditions affecting consumer marketing and the role of advertising are no doubt quite similar. And, although such conditions may have changed in many ways during the half-century covered by the studies, the functions of consumer advertising within the economic system are not qualitatively different.

A second pattern is represented by variables that show a *stable distribution across time in both societies*. In this case only indirect evidence is available for spatial comparisons, but this kind of structural stability seems to characterize variables relating to the portrayal of persons. The Swedish data show that basic structures remain stable in terms of the rank order between frequencies with which persons with particular characteristics appear in the ads. This applies to the distribution of gender, age, and class, of activities, of combinations between gender and other variables (age, activities, being alone, facial expression, etc.). These distributions may show various patterns of variation, but the rank order of the categories does not change (women are always more frequent than men; the rank order of age groups is always young-mature-old, women are always more often young, etc.)[6]

No long-term time series data are available on U.S. magazine advertising in these respects. However, studies of, for instance, gender stereotyping in advertising during the 1960s and 1970s indicate a corresponding pattern in at least some of these variables (Belakaoui & Belakaoui, 1976; Skelly & Lundstrom, 1981; Venkatesan & Losco, 1975). Also, considering the stability and generality of demographic representation in other media content that has been found in comparisons between the United States and Sweden (Andrén, 1989; Feilitzen, 1989; Nowak & Ross, 1989; Strand, 1989), it seems likely that the similarity also applies to advertising. Typically, the representation of sociodemographic categories in the media reflects their position in the societal hierarchy (prestige, power, status). The structural stability in advertising and other media content thus would indicate that Sweden and the United States are similar and have not changed to any large extent since the 1930s with regard to basic cultural evaluations of social positions.

The similarity between magazine advertising in the two countries is also reflected in two kinds of change patterns. One is illustrated by variables that exhibit *parallel simultaneous change*. These are the gradual disappearance of testimonials from the 1930s and onward, the increasing use of photographic pictures from the 1940s, and the growing absence of persons in the ads beginning in the 1950s. Whether these parallel developments indicate cross-cultural influences (from the United States to Sweden), or if they are the effect of underlying factors that are common to both countries, is impossible to say. The other pattern is represented by variables that show *parallel but lagged change.* This is the case with advertisement size and the use of color, where in both cases, periods of rapid growth take place 20-30 years earlier in the United States than in Sweden. This time lag is congruent with differences between the countries in the feasibility of new technology and in the growth of consumer markets and brand advertising.

As pointed out in the introduction, the present study was not designed to be comparative, and the interpretations are post hoc and preliminary. However, the results show a considerable degree of similarity in the development of magazine advertising content in Sweden and the United States, and it is suggested that the various patterns are related to economic, cultural, and technological conditions that are common to both countries. The analysis also included a number of variables illustrating certain approach-avoidance processes inherent in advertising production that were assumed to result in general relationships between advertising content and the prevailing climate of opinion. At this point only data on Sweden were available, but there is no reason to disbelieve that the proposed adaptive tendencies of advertisers and advertising encoders are operative in any market economy. This does not mean that, say, the portrayal of women necessarily follows the same lines in Sweden and the United States, only that the same causal model is applicable. There are in fact studies showing that U.S. magazine advertising in the early 1970s more often than 15-20 years earlier presented women in occupational roles (Belakaoui & Belakaoui, 1976; Venkatesan & Losco, 1975). This difference between the countries could depend on the nature of the magazines studied, the types of products involved, and a host of similar "technical" factors, but it might also indicate a different climate of opinion, or different perceptions of consumer attitudes by advertising encoders. In other words, depending on the values of the various components in the underlying causal model, cross-cultural and temporal comparisons would be expected to show similarity or differences as well as stability or change.

NOTES

1. The research was conducted by Gunnar Andrén and the author, both at the University of Stockholm. The study started as part of the research program Cultural Indicators: The Swedish Symbolic Environment 1945-1975, which was initiated and coordinated by Karl Erik Rosengren, University of Lund, and it initially covered the period 1950-1975. Results from that stage were reported in Nowak and Andrén (1981) and Nowak (1984). In a second stage the data were extended to also cover 1935-1949 and 1976-1980. Time series for this longer period have been reported in Eriksson and Andrén (1987), Andrén (1988), and Nowak (1989). To a considerable extent the content analysis was designed by Gunnar Andrén, and parts of it were based on earlier studies by Andrén et al. (1970; 1978). Gunnar Andrén also had responsibility for the training of coders and for the data collection generally. Sven Ross, also at the University of Stockholm, organized the data bases for the whole material and handled computer data processing for the present article. The research was financed primarily through grants from the Bank of Sweden Tercentenary Foundation, the Swedish Council for Research in the Humanities and the Social Sciences, and the National Swedish Board for Consumer Policies.

2. In the first stage, 15 magazine names were sampled from a list of all magazines belonging to the population that particular year. Sampling probabilities were proportional to each magazine's percentage of total magazine circulation during that year, and one and the same magazine name could occur more than once in the same sample. In the second stage, two issues were sampled for each magazine name. The first issue was sampled from the summer season, the other from the winter season. In the third stage, all ads covering more than 1/3 page in an issue were numbered from 1 to *n*, and by random numbers three ads were sampled from each issue. The third stage took place at the Royal Library, Stockholm, where all print media publications are available for research purposes. The advertisements were photocopied, after registering physical properties such as color, illustrations, and size.

3. Today popular magazines account for no more than about 5% of total advertising space expenditures in the sector of "traditional media," which includes newspapers, magazines and journals, outdoor, and cinema advertising. In the early 1960s the figure was about 15%, and in the 1930s probably considerably higher (Gröndal, 1984, 1988).

4. The measure used is the percentage of total income that must be transferred from individuals with more than average income in order that all individuals have the same income (Spånt, 1979). If this measure is applied to working males over 20 years of age, the level of income dispersion has been rather stable from 1950 to the end of the period studied. Applied to the whole population, however, the measure indicates a continuously decreasing dispersion because of the growing proportion of women entering the labor market.

5. The U.S. data show a peak in the 1940s, but Table 3 in Pollay (1984, p. 29) seems to contain a miscalculation at this point. All ads were coded into one of the three forms of rhetorical focus, and the percentages for each decade—except the 1940s—sum to 100. The column for the 1940s sums to 120%, which indicates that one or more of the three percentages is too high.

6. Even if the distributions show this general kind of structural stability, there may be cyclical variation or overall trends with respect to the difference between the category frequencies. For instance, whereas men are always associated with occupational activi-

ties more often than women and the opposite applies to household activities, both these differences vary cyclically along a slightly declining trend.

REFERENCES

Andrén, G. (1988). *Reklamens retorik 1935-1984.* Stockholm: Centrum för masskommunikationsforskning vid Stockholms universitet (Mass nr. 12).

Andrén, G. (1989). Kön, kultur och samhälle. In K. Nowak, H. Strand, G. Andrén, S. Ross, & C. von Feilitzen (Eds.), *Folket i TV: Demografi och social struktur i televisionens innehåll.* Stockholm: Centrum för masskommunikationsforskning vid Stockholms universitet (Mass nr. 14).

Andrén, G., Ericsson, L. O., Hamilton, I., Hemberg, G., & Tännsjö, T. (1970). *Argumentation och värderingar i reklamen.* Lund: Studentlitteratur.

Andrén, G., Ericsson, L. O., Ohlsson, R., & Tännsjö, T. (1978). *Rhetoric and ideology in advertising.* Stockholm: Liber.

Belakaoui, A., & Belakaoui, J. (1976). A comparative analysis of the roles portrayed by women in print advertisements, 1958, 1970, 1972. *Journal of Marketing Research, 13,* 168-172.

Belk, R. W., & Pollay, R. W. (1985). Images of ourselves: The good life in twentieth century advertising. *Journal of Consumer Research, 11,* 887-897.

Bernow, R., & Österman, T. (1979). *Svensk veckopress 1920-1975.* Solna, Sweden: Forskningsgruppen för samhälls och informations studier.

Curti, M. (1967). The changing concept of human nature in the literature of American advertising. *Business History Review, 41.* Cited in Leiss, W., Kline, S., & Jhally, S. (1986). *Social communication in advertising.* Toronto: Methuen.

Dyer, G. (1982). *Advertising as communication.* London: Methuen.

Eriksson, B., & Andrén, G. (1987). *Ben -Get -Elsa och doktor Berg: Könsroller in svensk populärpressreklam 1935-1984.* Stockholm: Konsumentverket.

Feilitzen, C. von. (1989). Barn, ungdomar, vuxna och äldre i TV. In K. Nowak, H. Strand, G. Andrén, S. Ross, & C. von Feilitzen (Eds.), *Folket i TV: Demografi och social struktur i televisionens innehåll.* Stockholm: Centrum för masskommunikationsforskning vid Stockholms universitet (Mass nr. 14).

Feilitzen, C. von, Strand, H., Nowak, K., & Andrén, G. (1989). To be or not to be in the TV world: Ontological and methodological aspects of content analysis. *European Journal of Communication, 4,* 11-32.

Fowles, J. (1976). *Mass advertising as social forecast.* Westport, CT: Greenwood Press.

Gröndal, T. (1984). *Reklamstatistikens grundbegrepp.* Göteborgs universitet, företagsekonomiska institutionen, rapport 4.

Gröndal, T. (1988). *Reklammarknaden 1975-1987.* Handelshögskolan i Göteborg, Informations- och massemediegruppen, rapport 20.

Hovland, C., Lumsdaine, A., & Sheffield, F. (1949). *Experiments in mass communication.* Princeton, NJ: Princeton University Press.

Korpi, W. (1978). *The working class in welfare capitalism.* London: Routledge & Kegan Paul.

Leiss, W., Kline, S., & Jhally, S. (1986). *Social communication in advertising.* Toronto: Methuen.

Kjell Nowak   207

Martel, M. U., & McCall, G. J. (1964). Reality-orientation and the pleasure principle: A study of American mass periodical fiction 1890-1955. In L. A. Dexter & D. M. White (Eds.), *People, society and mass communication* (pp. 283-336). New York: Free Press.

McQuail, D. (1987). *Mass communication theory.* London: Sage.

Nowak, K. (1984). Cultural indicators in Swedish advertising 1950-1975. In G. Melischek, K. E. Rosengren, & J. Stappers (Eds.), *Cultural indicators: An international symposium* (pp. 218-235). Wien: Verlag der Österreichischen Akademie der Wissenschaften.

Nowak, K. (1989). *Advertising and social change: Magazine advertising in Sweden 1935-1980.* Paper presented at the ICA Convention, San Francisco.

Nowak, K., & Andrén, G. (1981). *Reklam och samhällsförändring: Variation och konstans i svenska populärpressannonser 1950-1975.* Lund: Studentlitteratur.

Nowak, K., & Ross, S. (1989). Samhällsklasserna i TV. In K. Nowak, H. Strand, G. Andrén, S. Ross, & C. von Feilitzen (Eds.), *Folket i TV: Demografi och social struktur i televisionens innehåll* (pp. 59-78). Stockholm: Centrum för masskommunikationsforskning vid Stockholms universitet (Mass nr. 14).

Nowak, K., Strand, H., Andrén, G., Ross, S., & Feilitzen, C. von. (1989). *Folket i TV: Demografi och social struktur i televisionens innehåll.* Stockholm: Centrum för masskommunikationsforskning vid Stockholms universitet (Mass nr. 14).

Pollay, R. W. (1984). The determinants of magazine advertising informativeness throughout the twentieth century. *Written Communication, 1,* 56-77.

Pollay, R. W. (1985). The subsiding sizzle: A descriptive history of print advertising, 1900-1980. *Journal of Marketing, 49,* 24-37.

Pollay, R. W. (1986). The distorted mirror: Reflections on the unintended consequences of advertising. *Journal of Marketing, 50,* 18-36.

Ross, S. (1988). *Samhällsklasser i TV-fiktion: Social position och kulturellt utrymme.* Stockholm: Centrum för masskommunikationsforskning vid Stockholms universitet (Mass nr. 13).

Schudson, M. (1984). *Advertising, the uneasy persuasion.* New York: Basic Books.

Sinclair, J. (1987). *Images incorporated: Advertising as industry and ideology.* London: Croom Helm.

Skelly, G., & Lundstrom, W. (1981). Male sex roles in magazine advertisements 1954-1970. *Journal of Communication, 31,* Autumn, 52-57.

Spånt, R. (1979). *Den svenska inkomstfördelningens utveckling 1920-1976.* Stockholm: Ekomonidepartementet, DsE 1979:4.

Strand, H. (1989). The relationship between social power and linguistic dominance on Swedish television. *Papers from the Eleventh Scandinavian Conference on Linguistics, 3,* 490-508.

Tuchman, G., Daniels, A. K., & Benet, J. (1978). *Hearth and home: Images of women in mass media.* New York: Oxford University Press.

Venkatesan, M., & Losco, J. (1975). Women in magazine ads: 1959-1971. *Journal of Advertising Research, 15,* 49-54.

World of women and men (1986). (1986). Stockholm: Statistics Sweden (Statistika Centralbyrån).

Chapter 10

COMMUNICATION AND
CULTURAL CHANGE IN CHINA

Steven H. Chaffee and Godwin Chu

CULTURAL CHANGE, the broadest kind of communication effect, may also be the most imposing subject for study in empirical social science. Not only must one define *culture* in terms of its "change" and relevant forms of "communication," but these controversial concepts must be tied to bodies of evidence that are comparable to one another. The difficulties are so immense that interpretation of cultural change is normally left to scholars who see empirical approaches as inherently inadequate to the task. Those who utilize empirical methods implicitly agree, as they turn their tools to more tractable subjects.

Our purpose in this chapter is, nonetheless, to lay a groundwork for empirical analysis of cultural change, particularly in China and other Confucian societies. We view the many barriers as a set of challenges to be addressed, not as insurmountable.

China is arguably the most imposing venue for the study of human behavior in the contemporary world. Not only is it the largest country and one of the oldest societies in the world, it has remained for the most part closed to social scientific research since the Communist revolution of 1950 (Chu & Hsu, 1979, 1983; Houn, 1961; Rosen, 1989; Wong, 1979; Yu, 1964). Before World War II, social science was in its infancy; its early flowering coincided with the closing of China to the West. Not until the mid-1980s did Communist China open its door to Western researchers (Rosen, 1989). Since then, some scholars have published survey studies of media audiences and effects (Chu & Ju, 1990; Rogers, Zhao, Pan, Chen, & Beijing Journalists Assn., 1985; X. S. Zhao, Zhu,

& Li, 1990; X. Y. Zhao, 1989), among other social science topics. But the Chinese would surely remain at the bottom of a world list of peoples ranked in terms of communication studies, especially on a per capita basis.

Culture and Cultural Change

Culture refers to what people think, without their particularly thinking about it. Only when it changes do most people become aware of their own culture. Many writers have attempted to define *culture,* and we will not add to the list. Kroeber and Kluckhohn (1952) sorted through 164 definitions, most of them quite global in nature. Here we need to be as specific as possible, to point the way toward questions that can be asked and answered in survey research. Still, culture is inherently a most global idea, and we must admit from the beginning that precise explication of the concept in the manner of, say, physics, is not in the offing.

Most definitions of culture focus on the process by which it is maintained. As many writers emphasize, it is historical, learned, and a matter of socialization, all of which is to say that it is a human product of communication. Although that is surely true, it is just as surely beside the point for us. We are interested in cultural change, and the processual nature of culture does not change. Culture is always historical, learned, and so on. We need to attend instead to the content of culture, because that is what changes. Global definitions of culture do not tell us much about content, because each culture is unique.

Not all definitions neglect the content of culture. Boas (1938), for example, noted that culture "includes the multitude of relations between man and nature." Murdock (1941) added relationships, or "interpersonal habitual responses," and ideas, including knowledge, beliefs, and "a conceptual formulation of normal behavior." Kluckhohn and Kelly (1945) extended this last conception a bit when they wrote of "designs for living" that provide "potential guides for the behavior of men [sic]," and "a set of ready-made definitions of the situation which each participant only slightly retailors in his own idiomatic way." These approaches provide us with a starting perspective, in that traditional Confucian culture clearly provides a design for living based on relational definitions of situations.

Hsu, a Chinese-American, has contributed illuminating explications of both those cultures (Hsu, 1970, 1971). A number of scholars have analyzed Chinese culture from the perspectives of history, philosophy, language, sociology, and communication. The starting procedure for our present research was a week-long conference of specialists from such disciplines, in which we sought to transform their conceptions of Chinese culture into questions that could be asked in survey interviews.[1] Without attempting here to recapitulate the entire exercise, the project began with an analysis of Confucian culture as embodying such values as these:

- The network of obligations within the family, extending in the male (father-son) lineage to both ancestors and descendants, and laterally to brothers, uncles, and so on. Family obligations include both performance, such as helping the family, and reputation, the obligation not to discredit the family name.
- An authoritarian hierarchy based upon age, with greatest deference to the senior male (Hsu, 1971). This hierarchy traditionally applied to the workplace and to politics as well as to the family.
- Veneration of learning, devotion to the scholarly tradition.
- Virtues of frugality, diligence, generosity, and loyalty.
- Women's virtues of deference, obedience, chastity, discretion, and maintenance of harmony.

Although this brief listing fails to do justice to the richness and complexity of the Confucian tradition, it does include some of the major themes we have pursued in the survey work described in this chapter. It contrasts vividly with the value systems propagated in modern China by several major agencies of change, both indigenous and western.

COMMUNICATION AND CULTURAL CHANGE

Cultural change in China has been, in various quarters, either a hope or a fear, and a great deal of communication effort has gone into either fostering or stemming it (Howking, 1982; Liu, 1981; Yu, 1971). First, there has been the general process of modernization. A second, somewhat contradictory program has been that of China's Communist government. More recently, Western mass communication has brought a third set of cultural influences into China. These three are in effect hypotheses to which changes away from traditional Confucian culture, and from one another, might be attributed.

Modernization

One inescapable theory of economic development is the expectation that Confucian culture will change gradually in all East Asian countries as part of a general worldwide pattern of modernization. This process, detailed in many studies, includes industrialization, participation in world markets, technological innovation, and an extended communication infrastructure that links people throughout a country to its central information sources. Modernization generally implies economic specialization, which in turn would lead to greater emphasis on the individual rather than the family, for example.

China's East Asian neighbors (Japan, Korea, Taiwan, Singapore) have recently achieved high levels of modernization in the virtual absence of natural resources or empire, factors that were given great historical emphasis in accounting for the earlier modernization and world dominance of Western nations. The suspicion arises that something in the culture might instead account for the rise of these Confucian nations on the world scene. Still, it is that very culture that modernization appears to erode in some respects. It is clearly worth our understanding just which respects those are, how they are changing, and why. In evaluating evidence on change in China, we will also need separate evidence of changes that have occurred due to the modernization common to many Confucian societies in recent decades.

Counterstructuring

Politically, China (by which we mean the People's Republic of China) offers the most massive field test of a hypothesis of cultural change imaginable. The Communist regime of Mao and Deng can be viewed as a decades-long effort directed toward changing traditional Chinese culture through both the restructuring of society and the ideological indoctrination of a billion people. China is not only the most populous country ever united under one government, it is an unusually homogeneous one culturally.

Beginning with the land reform of the 1950s, Mao upended landlord-peasant relationships; families were forcibly broken up, destroying day-to-day filial relationships; male-female differences were obliterated by placing women into the workforce in jobs identical to those of men. Ancestor worship was physically discouraged first by moving people from the environs of their family burial places, and later by plowing over graveyards to add to the farmland. Centralized media of mass communication were devoted to propaganda in support of these social changes. All of this unprecedented structural change was profoundly cultural, in our sense—even before the explicitly designated Cultural Revolution of 1966-1976. The very image of society available to the Chinese people in their daily lives was radically restructured, accompanied by a communication campaign to reinforce these lessons.

Because it is unique in human experience, no language (not even Chinese) has a ready term to describe what has taken place in China in the past 40 years. We have no simple way of contrasting it verbally with the modernization process. Here we call it *counterstructuring,* a term that describes the intent of the program and is thus parallel to the equally teleological notion of modernization. By counterstructuring we mean, then, this entire revolutionary program directed toward cultural change, in which social relationships of one third of the people on earth were fundamentally altered, and the population was subjected to a relentless program of ideological indoctrination to establish the new social structure as normative. Several recent studies suggest that this counterstructuring campaign has had major effects on people's values (X. S. Zhao et al., 1990; X. Y. Zhao, 1989).

The economic and political processes we are calling *modernization* and *counterstructuring* are alternative accountings of cultural change, but they are not incompatible. Some degree of economic modernization, certainly, has taken place in Communist China. That is why we treat modernization and counterstructuring here as parallel hypotheses rather than seek a singular description. A particular element of Confucian culture might undergo modification in any country for a combination of reasons. When we attempt to attribute some feature of change to one or the other process, our inference will refer to what we conclude is the preponderant causal process, not the exclusive one.

Western Media

Many students of international communication are concerned with communication from outside a developing nation, particularly with the cultural effects of Western mass communication. Critical phrases such as Cultural Imperialism, Media Imperialism, and Cultural Domination are often treated as facts (Dorfman & Mattelart, 1971; Lee, 1980;

Schiller, 1976). We will adopt the more neutral label "Western media" to refer to this third hypothesis of cultural change. Mass communication from the West reaches all Asian countries, and it brings them images of a decidedly non-Confucian culture. Western society prizes individualistic values, which stand in stark contrast to both the Communist state and the Confucian design for living. Is cultural change resulting from this media incursion?

Research on effects of mass media indicates that people draw interpretations of mass communication that are compatible with their existing value structures; they do not swallow whole the conclusions intended by the source or manifest in the content. In an early study, bigoted readers failed to see the satire in cartoons attacking bigotry (Cooper & Jahoda, 1947). More recently, Katz and Liebes (1984) have found that Asian viewers of an American television series get from it messages about familial relationships that are different from those perceived by Western viewers. Just as advertising is resisted by wary consumers, so is international propaganda by its target audiences. Because one's culture is by definition so all-encompassing, it should presumably be resistant to Western media influence.

Still, Western commercial television and films and the individualistic consumer culture they promote cannot be presumed to have no influence on Confucian values. Western media tend to accompany other features of modernization. Economic development means, in part, the availability of television, the literacy required by newspapers and magazines, and the discretionary income to buy these media as well as the products they promote. In a way, then, Western media influence is not so much a separable hypothesis as a corollary of the modernization process. It is almost parallel in its functional implications to the role ideological indoctrination—another kind of communication influence—plays in China's counterstructuring program.

We will treat the Western media hypothesis separately here for empirical reasons, more than theoretical. Modernizing countries vary in the extent to which they allow Western media to be available to their citizens, but there is some opportunity for Western media influence even in China. X. Y. Zhao (1989) has found evidence that exposure to Western media among Chinese career women encourages more individualistic value priorities. Thus it is really a third alternative explanation of cultural change in China, and one that can be distinguished empirically both from counterstructuring communication, and from other features of modernization.

Communist indoctrination, on the other hand, cannot be separated empirically from the enormous structural changes that have been undertaken as part of China's overall program of counterstructuring. Although we could in theory separate the communication program from the political overhauling of social relationships, in reality these experiences have been shared by the Chinese people. There is no satisfactory way to disconnect these two prongs in a survey of people. Those who have been subject to the one have also been subject to the other; further, these people are clearly defined in that everyone in China has experienced both, and no other people has directly experienced either. Individuals do vary within China, however, in their exposure to Western media and in their experience of economic modernization; both these experiences are, for example, more characteristic of urban than of rural Chinese. The same is true in other Confucian countries, giving us a basis for evaluating these hypotheses in both contexts.

CULTURAL CHANGE AS A COMPARATIVE RESEARCH PROBLEM

Change, being a problem of comparison over time, is inherently comparative. This does not necessarily mean historical research, though. Indeed, that scholarly avenue is often all but blocked because the time at which earlier data might have been collected has passed. Historical scholarship presumes the existence of archives as benchmark evidence. Lacking that, empirical research demands special resourcefulness and offers less than ideal research designs. Let us consider some alternative kinds of comparative studies that might aid in a study of cultural change in China. A full listing would include the following:

(a) China today versus China at some time in the past
(b) China today versus China at a future time
(c) Some population segments of China versus others
(d) Some cultural elements of China versus others
(e) China versus other countries that share Chinese culture but are at different stages of change

In this chapter we will analyze data from a large-sample survey in China, first with purpose (a) in mind; this survey is also intended as a baseline for future work in the vein of (b). Next, we will examine this same survey in further detail, following purposes (c) and (d). Finally, we build on that context to interpret results from a Taiwan survey that has the features of method (a); this is the general logic of (e).

Empirical Research

We conceive of our research quite broadly, to include all manner of evidence: personal observation and experience, texts and documents, tales and sayings that are retold to new generations, and other traditional tools of the anthropologist or historian. In this chapter, though, we focus on survey interview methods, a tool of social science we employ in several of the ways outlined above.

The essential criterion of usefulness of any kind of evidence is its comparability. Much of the evidence an anthropologist might use in studying a single culture, or that a historian might employ in analyzing a single period of change, may fail to meet this criterion. So might survey interview data. We shall need all the tools we can find, not only to provide raw evidence, but also to evaluate its comparability vis-à-vis other evidence.

An empirical scholar is a creator, as well as a user, of evidence. We find the cultural anthropologist in the field living among a people to experience the culture firsthand, and we find the social historian poring over volumes of aged records to reconstruct patterns of human action in times past. These are prototypic forms of research work; until the researcher makes the sustained data-collection effort, there is no anthropology, no history. Nor will there be until that researcher follows through with an analysis and interpretation of the evidence in discursive form.

So it is with survey interview research. Regarding data collection, the interview method shares some assumptions with participant observation. Both methods assume that the topic of one's study, in this case communication and cultural change, is sufficiently experienceable to those participating in it that they can (and will) report it. A central difference is that the survey respondent does not know in advance that she is going to be asked about her self-observations, nor have any training for the task. Against this deficiency of skill and hence of depth, the large-sample survey offers the tradeoff of breadth: Many points of view and idiosyncratic personal experiences of the culture are tapped, when many different people are asked about it. The participant observer only has one set of eyes, and one set of experiences. (To the extent that he relies on others' accounts, he is conducting an unsystematic and narrow form of survey interviewing, not participant observation.) Survey research is most helpful when it is grounded in knowledge that has been built up through other methods. It is useful for testing the generality of inferences drawn from anthropological, historical, and journalistic accounts.

METHODOLOGICAL ARTIFACTS AND COMPARABILITY

Use of survey interview data admits into the research process the danger that artifacts of the method might be mistaken for cultural change. Aging is one such confound. Individuals—either survey respondents or trained participant observers—grow older. No one is the same person twice, and each of us has had the experience of sensing that "times have changed" when it is instead ourselves that have changed. The time line for cultural change is in general a long one—a few years is rarely sufficient to see clearly the outlines of lasting changes—whereas in the life of any individual even a few years is likely to encompass considerable maturation of one's outlook and perceptions.

Other artifactual explanations are possible, too, when one relies on any single kind of data. For instance, historical comparison of official records is questionable because the method of record-keeping might have changed; definitions of what is to be recorded (e.g., what is a crime?) often change without notation, even in a stable society. In survey research we should be wary of self-reported opinions in a country like China, where people have long been in danger of punishment for expressing "wrong" political views—and where the definition of what is politically correct has sometimes shifted.

Our approach to such problems of comparability is not to throw away any single body of data, but to add to it. The "multiple operationism" approach of social science presumes that there is some validity to each kind of data, and that although each is potentially flawed they do not all have the same flaws. Validation of an inference is not achieved through literal replication, repeating approximately the same study, but through conceptual replication, testing the same inference via different methods. By adding survey research to the methods of field observation and historical analysis, we are attempting to develop a convergent approach to knowledge of cultural change. The more different kinds of tests we apply to a principle, the more confidence we might place in it.

COMPARISON WITH A RECONSTRUCTED PAST

If we could choose one single study to do, it would be a careful empirical examination of changes in China over the past 40 years of Communist counterstructuring [design (a), in our list above]. But this is the least possible of all models. The time is past, and the governments of Mao and Deng did not until fairly recently permit independent survey interviewing. What we have at this writing is no more than a handful of studies. We will draw here from our research group's 1987 survey of cultural values in the city, regional, and rural environs of Shanghai (Chu & Ju, 1990) and compare it to a reconstruction of the past that is based on quite different kinds of data.

A great deal has been written by Chinese scholars about the cultural values of China before Mao and in the early years of his regime. We cannot know how extensively these values penetrated into the total population, but by almost all accounts Confucian culture was pervasive and ubiquitous. The question of major exceptions scarcely arises. The features we have outlined above provide a flavor of the content of that culture, although they may fail to convey just how thoroughly Confucianism permeated all aspects of social conduct and thought. With all these caveats of method in mind, let us turn to the recent survey research.

Data Collection

Random sampling of individuals is more literally feasible in China than in countries where sample surveys are more common, due to strict control over people's place of residence. Residential lists, quite complete and up-to-date, were used by our research colleagues to sample individuals in districts that had been selected by multistage random sampling procedures. Residents were asked to come to a meeting place (typically an elementary school classroom) to be interviewed by personnel from Fudan University. Cooperation exceeded 90%, a much higher response rate than is common in general population surveys in other countries. Questionnaires were distributed by teams of, typically,

TABLE 10.1 Education of Respondents and Their Parents, Shanghai Region, 1987

	Respondents Men	Respondents Women	Respondents Fathers	Respondents Mothers
Illiterate	10%	10%	26%	55%
Some primary school	8	9	23	18
Primary graduate	12	13	21	13
Junior high	31	37	16	9
Senior high	27	24	9	5
College	12	7	6	2

SOURCE: Chu & Ju (1990), Table 2.10

one professor and two or three students, to groups of 15-20 respondents at a time. The questionnaire was explained by the research team and then filled out individually and in anonymity by each respondent. The total sample numbered 2,000, including 1,199 in metropolitan Shanghai, 304 in two regional cities, and 497 in 12 rural village settings.

Demographic Changes

Some explicit demographic comparisons with China of time past [method (a), above] are possible. We will begin with education and gender differentiation, two topics for which traditional Confucian values are strong and clear, and then consider some evidence on related values.

Shanghai-area respondents were asked how much education their parents had; this is compared with their own education levels, as shown in Table 10.1. Between generations, there is a clear-cut increase in the lower and middle range of the educational spectrum. Illiterates outnumbered high school graduates almost 4 to 1 in the parental generation, a ratio that is approximately reversed among today's respondents. But a college education, although more common in the current generation, is still a rarity enjoyed by less than 10% of the population. The Communist regime has not encouraged mass higher education, but it has dramatically raised the educational floor in Chinese society. (Higher education would have probably been the more Confucian thing to emphasize.)

A similarly dramatic equalization in education between the genders has taken place in this generation, as Table 10.1 also shows. More than one half of the respondents' mothers had been illiterate, compared with only about half that many among their fathers; at the other extreme, their fathers were more than three times as likely as their mothers to go beyond high school. Today, though, there is no male-female disparity at the lower educational levels. Some gender difference remains at the college level, but the male-female ratio in college attendance has declined from more than 3 to 1 in the parents' generation to less than 2 to 1 today.

These demographic changes do not necessarily represent changes in cultural values, of course. The intergenerational shifts in Table 10.1 are the result of change that has to some extent been imposed as a part of counterstructuring. Illiteracy and gender inequalities have been targeted by the Communist regime from the start, whereas severe restrictions on higher education date at least from the Cultural Revolution. Have these undeniable demographic shifts been accompanied by corresponding changes in values?

Cultural Values

We cannot discern with confidence what values characterized an earlier generation, but Confucian culture has traditionally been closely identified with a veneration of learning and education and with male dominance in gender relations. In comparisons with Western values, education and gender have seemed to most observers to be among the most salient features of Confucian value systems. The raised educational floor could be interpreted as a realization, under counterstructuring, of traditional Confucian values related to learning. The shift toward gender equality, on the other hand, is clearly a counter-Confucian social change.

Education does not at first blush loom large in the Chinese mind today, to judge from Chu and Ju's (1990) findings. Given a list of 14 desirable goals and the task of picking the 5 that were most important to them, the Shanghai respondents overwhelmingly picked those relating to family and career accomplishments. Less than 1 in 4 selected "education and knowledge" and less than 1 in 10 picked either "a college degree" or "going abroad for education" as among their life goals. By contrast, 4 out of 5 wanted "a warm and close family," and majorities also picked "successful children," "harmonious family relations," "career accomplishments," and "a comfortable life." On an open-ended question asking what the most important element of career success is, only about 1 in 8 mentioned any kind of personal qualification, a category that includes education. The dominant answer instead was "diligence," along with such idiosyncratic concepts as "drive and ambition" and "opportunity."

Education seems to fare a bit better as a value in selection of a marriage partner. Respondents were asked to pick the 3 characteristics, from a list of 11, that they thought were the most important to young people today in making a marriage decision. More than one third selected education, which ranked it fourth (behind high moral standards, emotional compatibility, and common interests). Fewer chose the more Western "looks" or "love," or the seemingly Confucian "family financial condition" or "family social position" options.

But education is very much in the mind of today's parents in China. Under the Cultural Revolution, universities were open primarily to those who could demonstrate a revolutionary class background and ideological purity (Chu & Ju, 1990). These restrictions, which partly account for the attenuated increase in higher education (Table 10.1), have been eased greatly in recent years; more than four out of five parents say they will support their child to go to college.

As for gender differentiation, Chu and Ju (1990) find practically no difference in parental willingness to support a son versus a daughter, a finding that bespeaks an absence of traditional gender discrimination in values—at least at the parent-child aspiration level. Such gender differentiation as exists is found among the more educated parents only. At the other extreme, among parents who had never attended even elementary school 16% say they would support a son through graduate school—and likewise 16% said they would support a daughter to that extent.

There are some differences in occupational aspirations for sons and daughters. The most common choice for a son is scientific and technical work, whereas for a daughter it is to be a medical doctor. (During the Cultural Revolution, many of the "barefoot doctors" had been women.) The second most common choices were for a son to be a factory worker, a daughter a school teacher.

Chu and Ju (1990) find many indicators of more egalitarian male-female relationships in China today. For example, more than 40% of families report husband-wife disputes over "character incompatibility," a topic that presumably would not have arisen in a strict Confucian home, where the wife was supposed to be subservient to her husband.

Women and men differ somewhat in their views of male-female relationships. Men are slightly more likely to tolerate the idea of a couple living together before marriage, for example. But the data bespeak gender similarities much more than differences. Only statistically nonsignificant male-female differences are found for opinions on female chastity, teenage pregnancy, equal pay for equal work, and the role of love in choosing a mate (Chu & Ju, 1990).

A traditional Chinese of 100 (or even 50) years ago might be quite shocked to find women expressing independent opinions on such matters at all. We can imagine that in pre-Communist China, many women would have had difficulty thinking how to answer. The situation of women in China may have changed in ways parallel to what Lerner (1964) encountered when he first tried to conduct public opinion surveys in traditional villages in the Middle East. When asked by an interviewer what he would do if he were the editor of a major newspaper or the president of the country, the typical villager in effect responded, "How could you ask me this question? I could never be such a person." Lerner labeled this a lack of "empathy" for alternative life situations, which he concluded was common among those in ascriptively fixed positions in a traditional society. When he returned to the same villages a few years later, after roads and mass media had reached these remote areas, he found that people had little difficulty giving opinions as to how the country should be run. We cannot know with certainty whether Chinese women of a half-century ago had the empathy to compare their own character to that of their husbands, and to argue over incompatibilities, but it certainly appears that they do today.

Gender differentiation also involves views of the younger generation. Dating remains a Western social practice that most Chinese reject, but those who accept it do not discriminate. Respondents were asked two nearly identical questions, as to whether they would permit a son/daughter to carry on with several girl/boy friends before marriage. Gender differentiation was minuscule; 20.4% of respondents said it would be all right for a daughter, 20.8% for a son.

Chastity for women was a traditional Confucian value implicitly attacked by egalitarian themes in Chinese counterstructuring media of the past 40 years. In the Shanghai survey, more respondents say it should be rejected than say they are proud of it. Rejection of chastity is more marked among the older respondents; young people still seem to have virginity on their minds, and perhaps have not yet been fully in-doctrinated in the Communist value structure. Chastity is, after all, a more abstract issue for those no longer of an age to be unchaste.

The traditional Confucian value of "a house full of sons and grand-sons" also seems to have eroded. More than half of the Shanghai re-spondents think this patriarchal notion should be discarded, and only about 1 in 5 are proud of it. A general principle of differentiation be-tween men and women is even more universally rejected. Only 1 re-spondent in 10 is proud of this tradition, which in effect sanctions discrimination against women in all walks of life. The most widely re-jected concept in the survey's entire inventory of values is the old list of "three obediences and four virtues" that women were traditionally supposed to pursue. More than 7 of 10 respondents reject this feudalis-tic concept; many of the others seem not even to know what it means (Chu & Ju, 1990). Opposition to the "obediences/virtues" tradition in China dates back to 1919 and is an example of change in women's sta-tus that was under way well before the Communist Revolution.

What we have been doing in the past few pages is comparing pres-ent-day data to what we imagine would have been found in a similar survey at an earlier time. The topics we have been examining are fairly safe ones for this purpose. It is not difficult to assume that gender dif-ferentiation and educational values are part of what we mean by "Con-fucian culture," even if they might not have shown up in a survey interview such as the one we are relying upon here. But on many topics anthropological and literary sources are not so easily interpreted. It is possible that an identical survey of Chinese in 1950 would have pro-duced results similar to those reported by Chu and Ju (1990), although that seems doubtful in the main. What we need to evaluate the validity of specific results is comparable analyses of different kinds. Let us turn to some of those and give examples of how we use them in our overall attempt to trace the path of cultural change in China.

COMPARING POPULATION SEGMENTS
AND VALUES IN CHINA

Cultural change does not take place at a constant rate for everyone within a society. We can gain some idea of social processes by compar-ing urban residents to rural, young people to old, and educated to less educated. This is the logic of method (c) in our list, above. In the main, we expect new trends to show up most commonly among the urban, the young, and the educated. But there are problematic aspects to each of these comparisons.

First, these are mostly demographic locator variables rather than functional sources of cultural change. Youth, for example, simply locates the absence of a number of prior attachments, and an urban setting is no guarantor of the kind of value influences at work on the person. There are in any large city many young adults who remain quite isolated despite a clamor of cultural influences elsewhere in town.

Further, these correlates are themselves intercorrelated, which makes it difficult to separate their effects. The impact of urbanism on cultural change could, for example, be entirely due to the greater access the city provides to educational institutions. Age and education are in China (as in most countries) negatively correlated, because the current generation is better educated (see Table 10.1). But in some respects age and education should produce the same effect, not opposite results. For instance, both are ways of sharing human experience, and so they should lead to some similar kinds of knowledge. Correlational analysis is as much art as science when dealing with such nested factors.

Third, each of these variables is associated with some specific influences apart from those involved in value change. Rural residents by definition live farther apart, and so they might relate differently to one another in a spatial sense that is not otherwise an indicator of values. Education brings to people their value heritage, even as it might open their eyes to alternatives. Its many effects could cancel one another out.

Most important, these demographic variables are at best rough predictors of change. In some instances the relationship might be, or seem in a cross-sectional survey to be, the opposite of what we assume. Younger people, for example, are more concerned with male-female relationships than are senior citizens. If we find age correlated cross-sectionally with romantic values, it may not mean that the culture is changing, but simply that some concerns look different to young adults in any society at any time in its history.

Those reservations stated, let us look in some detail at these points of comparison, to see what kinds of insights they afford us. Table 10.2 compares 10 value items in the Shanghai survey in terms of their correlations with urban residence, age, and education levels.

TABLE 10.2 Effects of Residence, Age, and Education on Value Agreement, Shanghai Region, 1987

	Base %[a]	Urbanism effect	Youth effect	Education effect
Take care of aging parents[b]	87	+++	– –	+++
Equal pay for equal work	83	+++	– –	+++
Divorce OK if no children	77	+++	0	+++
Divorce OK even with children	36	++	++	+++
Love important in marital choice	22	– –	+++	0
OK to live together before marriage	10	0	+++	++
Proud of tradition: Chastity of women[b]	33	0	– – –	–
Proud of tradition: Men-women[b]	10	0 +	0	0 +
Proud of tradition: Pleasing superiors[b]	7	++	0 –	++
Religious faith necessary	29	– – –	0	0 –

+++	Hypothesized relationship significant, monotonic, > 10%
++	Hypothesized relationship significant, monotonic
+	Hypothesized relationship significant
0 +	Hypothesized relationship monotonic, nonsignificant
0	No relationship
0 –	Counterhypothetical relationship monotonic, nonsignificant
–	Counterhypothetical relationship significant
– –	Counterhypothetical relationship significant, monotonic
– – –	Counterhypothetical relationship significant, monotonic, > 10%

SOURCE: Pan, Chaffee, Chu, & Ju (in preparation).
NOTE: a. Base % is the percentage for each item, in the total sample.
 b. Hypotheses for these traditional values were opposite to hypotheses for other values listed in this table.

Urbanism

The urban centers of any society tend to be the locus of change. Innovations are commonly created in cities, and they disseminate more rapidly where people are in close contact with one another and with communication media (Rogers, 1983).

Mass communication represents one facet. Newspaper reading, for example, is much more prevalent in urban areas. About four out of five respondents in Shanghai and nearby cities said they read a newspaper every day, compared with only about one in three among the villagers in the region (Chu & Ju, 1990). At a more interpersonal level, the survey asked if the respondent felt he could approach a neighbor to borrow 80 Yuan, which at that time represented about one month's pay for a typical worker. More than four out of five villagers felt close enough to their neighbors to make this request, but less than one half of those living in cities gave this response. At the same time, neither the borrowing nor the habit of newspaper reading is severely confined in these geographic terms. There are plenty of newspaper readers even in the villages, and even in Shanghai the percentage who would feel comfortable borrowing a large sum of money from a neighbor is dramatically larger than one should expect anywhere in the United States.

Our overall expectation is that cultural change will manifest itself first, and therefore at any time most strongly, among those who live in cities. In Table 10.2 this hypothesis is tested as the "urbanism effect." Entries in this table indicate whether that hypothesis was supported in the 1987 survey, when we compared those in Shanghai to those living in villages, with the regional cities inserted as an intermediate category.

A scoring system was used to create the entries in Table 10.2, as explained at the bottom of the table. If the Shanghai-Village difference was significant in the predicted direction, a plus (+) sign was entered. If the relationship was monotonic (i.e., if the regional cities were intermediate) we also entered a plus sign. If the difference between Shanghai and the village sample was greater than 10% we added a third plus sign. If the relationship was opposite to the prediction, minus (−)signs were entered in Table 10.2 instead.

For the first four value items in Table 10.2, we found the effect hypothesized. The more urban the people, the less likely they were to say children should take care of their aging parents, and the more likely they were to endorse the principle of equal pay for equal work and to approve of divorce. The equal pay and divorce items are the strongest evidence of overall cultural change, as they were endorsed (excepting divorce of couples with children) by large majorities.

A result opposite the urbanism hypothesis was found for mention of "love" as a criterion for young people's marital choices. We did not expect rural Chinese to endorse this value, and perhaps they do not; they do mention it more often than do city-dwellers, though, perhaps because they see it as a change in values among the young, of which they disapprove. The survey showed no relationship between residence and the distinctly minority view that it would be all right for a couple to live together before marriage.

The next three items in Table 10.2 are part of a list of traditional Confucian views. Respondents were asked if they were "proud of" these values, or if they instead thought the values should be "discarded." Each of them has shrunk to a minority position (see Base % in Table 10.2), and we expected villagers to hold on to them more than urban residents. This was not the case for the tradition of chastity for women, nor in any strong degree for male-female differentiation. Rural respondents did still express some pride in the tradition of pleasing superiors.

The final value item in Table 10.2 is the statement that it is necessary to have religious faith. This we viewed as a traditional value, and accordingly we hypothesized that it would be a more common view among villagers. The result was the opposite. Shanghai residents were the ones more likely to see a need for religious faith. But this is a prime example of the limitations of cross-sectional surveys for tracing change. Religious faith was a target of counterstructuring and seems to have been driven into a minority position; less than one in three agree with the statement. But by 1987 the government had for several years been easing its antireligion campaign. If this change in position had been picked up earliest in the cities, as we might expect, that would account for the result in Table 10.2.

Youth and Educational Effects

The remainder of Table 10.2 shows analogous correlational results testing the hypotheses that altered cultural values would manifest themselves more strongly in young people and in those with more education. This seems to be the case more often for education than for youth. More than half of the values represented in the table correlate in the expected direction with education. Age is a much less reliable correlate of these values, working in the direction opposite to expectations as often as not.

Some particular correlations of education and age in Table 10.2 are worthy of comment. The better educated are clearly more likely to endorse new feminist policies like equal pay for equal work, and divorce. They also retain some pride in the concept of pleasing superiors, perhaps because they are the likely beneficiaries to that tradition. The pre-

TABLE 10.3 Demographic and Media Use Predictors of Values, Shanghai Region, 1987

	Openness to divorce	*Openness in male-fem rel.*	*Traditional fem. stat.*	*Accept seniority*
Residence (urban)	+	0	–	– –
Age	–	–	– –	+
Education	++	0	0 –	0 –
Gender (female)	0	–	–	0
Income	0	0	0 –	0
Occupational status	0+	0	0	0
Married	0 –	0 –	0	0
News exposure	0	0	0 –	0 +
Traditional entertainment	0 –	0 –	0	0 +
Western entertainment	0 +	++	0	0
Government propaganda	0 +	0	–	0 +

0	No significant correlation or beta
0 +	Significant positive correlation, but not beta
0 –	Significant negative correlation, but not beta
+	Significant positive beta in multiple regression
–	Significant negative beta in multiple regression
	Double sign indicates strongest beta in equation

SOURCE: Based on Pan, Chaffee, Chu, & Ju (in preparation) multiple regressions.

dicted correlations with age lie more in matters of the heart; young people are more likely to say love is a factor in choosing a mate and that it is all right to live together before marriage.

In general, though, these correlations are cumbersome and do not get us very far toward our hypotheses of cultural change, which have to do with modernization, counterstructuring, and Western media. Table 10.3 is an attempt to examine these possibilities through multiple regression. As in Table 10.2, the exact numbers have been replaced by symbols that enable one to make comparisons more easily. In Table 10.3, however, the plus and minus signs indicate the direction and significance of each relationship between two variables (regardless of the hypothesis), when all other predictors are statistically controlled.

The four columns of Table 10.3 represent four different value clusters, based on factor analyses. The first two, "openness to divorce" and "openness in male-female relationships," are values on which we expect change to be occurring. The second two, "traditional female status" and "acceptance of the principle of seniority," are Confucian values that we expect to find in erosion. This does not mean that we would simply propose mirror-image hypotheses or the four value areas, though. It depends upon the predictor in question.

The first three predictors in Table 10.3 are the demographic correlates examined singly in Table 10.2, urbanism, age, and education. In regression, the effect of each with the other variables controlled can be interpreted with more confidence. All three work in the predicted direction for the divorce index. With regard to male-female openness, age works in the predicted direction (older people are less approving), but neither residence nor education has any effect. Traditional female status is negatively correlated with all three; here, we had made a prediction only for age (Pan, Chaffee, Chu, & Ju, in preparation). Finally, the seniority principle is associated in this regression analysis with age, rural residence, and slightly lesser education.

Four other demographic variables have also been entered in the regression analyses summarized in Table 10.3: gender, income, occupational status, and marital status. None of the regression coefficients is significant, except that women are less supportive of traditional status for women (which is understandable) and of openness in male-female relationships (which is not so readily understood). There are significant correlations, but not beta weights in multiple regression, between being married and rejecting both divorce (understandable) and male-female openness (not so understandable). Occupational prestige and income are, somewhat surprisingly, unrelated to acceptance of seniority principles. Overall, then, the statistical associations between these added demographic factors and the value indices in Table 10.3 are spotty at best; they do not follow any simple pattern of prediction. They do, however, increase the stringency of tests of communication effects, by serving as additional statistical controls.

The communication variables listed at the bottom of Table 10.3 include two that represent central hypotheses of cultural change: exposure to government propaganda and to Western entertainment. Also included are indices of exposure to news, and to traditional Chinese entertainment in the media. Government propaganda is a negative predictor of traditional views of the proper status of women, which is consistent with a major theme of the counterstructuring campaign. Otherwise government propaganda produces no significant regression coefficients. Western entertainment is the strongest predictor among the 11 variables in Table 10.3, for values of openness in male-female relationships. Both propaganda and Western media are correlated with approval of divorce, and traditional entertainment exposure is a negative correlate, but none of the three remains significant once the three strong demographic correlates (urbanism, age, and education) are accounted for.

Overview

We have been looking here at only a few findings from a very large and complex survey analysis, more to get the flavor of what this kind of research can add to our knowledge than to arrive at definitive conclusions. It seems clear, though, that China's decades of counterstructuring have had a major impact on that culture. We have noted several old Confucian values that are in almost total recess. Predictors of exposure to governmental communication efforts, including education and urban residence, are among the strongest correlates of new values involving gender parity and the legalization of divorce.

Western media too seem to have had some impact, although this survey is not as thoroughly dedicated to testing that proposition as, say, the corroborating work of X. Y. Zhao (1989). What we cannot address within this project is the effect that modernization might have had in the absence of China's pervasive counterstructuring effort.

Part of our research plan is to return to China after the passage of some years, to replicate the survey described above and see what changes have occurred. There are several problems in this approach, though. First, the cultural changes of greatest interest have already occurred; it is unlikely that any counterstructuring process comparable to that which began in the 1950s will be undertaken in China or any other nation in the foreseeable future. Second, counterstructuring continues. China is, as we have noted, somewhat like one huge experimental group. For a control group we would need to look elsewhere, to a Confucian society that has modernized without the imposition of China's counterstructuring. It is to such a comparison that we now turn.

COMPARISON TO A SIMILAR CULTURE:
THE REPUBLIC OF CHINA (TAIWAN)

China is not the only (nor even the most) Confucian country today. Confucian influence has spread throughout East Asia and is particularly marked in Korea, Japan, and the Republic of China (Taiwan). Our studies, projected for the next few years, include comparisons with those and other neighboring countries. Here we will report an earlier study, conducted by Chu and Chi (1984a) over a 14-year period in eight villages in rural northeast Taiwan. Our purpose in examining change in these villages during a period of modernization of the Taiwanese economy is mainly to see whether Confucian values change while more overt features of society are in rapid flux.

Chu and Chi (1984b) combined a panel design, in which the same individual villagers were interviewed in both 1964 and 1978, with a successive cross-sections design in which the 1978 sample is a new "after-only" cross-section of residents of the same village, sampled by the same methods as the original cross-section of 1964. Table 10.4 summarizes the results we will discuss here. The columns of Table 10.4 represent the 1964 sample, and then the two 1978 samples that we will compare with it, that is, the panel and the after-only groups. A major difference between the two 1978 samples is that the panel is a considerably older group, having aged 14 years from the time these same respondents represented a random cross-section of villagers (the 1964 sample). The 1978 after-only respondents, on the other hand, are of roughly the same age distribution as the original interviewees had been in 1964.

The 1964 Taiwan survey is technically comparable to the 1987 Shanghai area survey in that each is a one-wave study of cultural values. By examining the kinds of changes that were found—and those that were not—as Taiwan's economy modernized, we can get some idea of what to anticipate in China in the years to come.[2]

The modernization hypothesis, and possibly some effects of Western media, are at stake alongside the artifact of aging in the Taiwan survey. Modernization and Western media influences are probably greater in Taiwan than in China; there has been, of course, no counterstructuring in Taiwan.

TABLE 10.4 Communication and Values, by Year, Taiwan, 1964-1978

Item	1964 (%)	1978 Panel (%)	1978 After-only (%)
Television: watch regularly	0	88	83
Radio: own receiver	52	95	93
Radio: listening	87	42	41
Newspaper: reads	29	32	50
Reads every day (readers only)	13	58	69
Reads natl news (readers only)	4	46	51
Movies: seen in last 6 months	72	11	19
Prefers Taiwanese dialect	56	33	8
Prefers Mandarin dialect	8	57	69
Prefers Japanese movies	21	0	0
Reads novels	44	12	16
Reads agricultural magazine	16	66	56
Interpersonal contact last month:			
I consulted with someone	40	8	6
Someone consulted with me	25	3	4
By appointment	13	52	64
Ideal family size: 7+ children	24	6	6
One must believe in deity	59	44	33
It is all right to be Christian	61	72	91
Deity rewards gifts to temple: No	49	64	67
Ancestor's tomb affects family	45	34	29
No banquet needed Pai-pai festival	45	34	29
Must continue to worship ancestors	83	87	74
OK: boy/girl friends premarriage	65	57	66
Woman capable of supporting family	37	30	34
(N)	(317)	(185)	(70)

SOURCE: Chu & Chi (1984a).

Rural Taiwan in the period 1964-1978 experienced the introduction of a new channel, television, that means more than just the input of Western media content. The impact of television's introduction on older media generally follows a principle of functional equivalence. As an entertainment medium, TV has tended to displace other entertainment channels such as movies, radio, and the reading of fiction; it has left largely untouched habits of nonfiction reading (Parker, 1961, 1963). Table 10.4 shows data for several measures of media use that strongly indicate the same pattern of functional equivalence in Taiwan as elsewhere.

A number of changes in media habits, reflecting cultural changes of various sorts, can be inferred from Table 10.4. The period in question, 1964-1978, saw not only the introduction of television but also a general process of modernization. Still, the shifts in behavior are remarkable and in some measure must be tied to TV. The expected decline in other entertainment media use (radio listening, movie attendance, reading novels) is evident. This occurs despite an increase to near-ceiling in media availability (radio set ownership, newspaper subscription). It is worth noting too that these shifts in media habits occur within the same individuals; old dogs seem quite capable of learning new tricks— even aging farmers in a remote region of a developing country, when TV arrives.

Media use itself is not particularly cultural in nature, but some of the other measures in Table 10.4 bespeak a correlative shift from a provincial orientation to a national one. Newspaper readers are much more attuned to national news by 1978, and moviegoers have grown more attracted to Mandarin than to Taiwanese dialect films. To be sure, these trends are stronger in the after-only sample, but there are also unmistakable changes over time within the panel respondents themselves. One way to read the newspaper results for the panel is to say that although few nonreaders became readers over the 14-year period, among the readers use of the newspaper became much more frequent and focused increasingly on national news. Some 40% of the newspaper readers changed their consumption patterns in these ways during this time period.

Were these changes in communication accompanied by changes in cultural values? The lower portion of Table 10.4 details some relevant findings, which break down mainly into two areas. First are several items on interpersonal relations and family size that show dramatic change over time, as strong within the panel respondents as in the two cross-sections. It is obvious that in this period of modernization, farmers in this rural Taiwanese region became markedly less interpersonal in their habits of behavior. They were less likely in 1978 to consult one another, more likely to make appointments than simply to drop in on people, and did not value large families.

The second group of items, though, illustrates the holding power of normative values in the realms of religion and marital relations. There is some shift in the panel, and more in the after-only cross section, toward liberalized and less ritualistic religious beliefs. But these are trends, not bespeaking a cultural change of a dramatic order. Large numbers continue to hold traditional religious beliefs of various kinds.

There is also some evidence of aging effects in the panel respondents in Table 10.4. They have become more concerned about ancestors (perhaps sensing themselves nearer to that status), less tolerant of young people experimenting with potential marital partners, and less supportive of the idea of a woman as head of household. No such trends occur in the cross-sections when we compare 1964 with the 1978 after-only sample. Neither, however, has cultural change moved in the other direction, toward more "modern" views of these matters. That is, there has apparently been no modernization effect on issues of close familial relations even though modernization has meant a depersonalization of society beyond the range of family and generational ties.

These shifts (and continuities) in Taiwan give us some idea of what might have happened to Confucian values in China had economic modernization, rather than political counterstructuring, been the order of the day in recent decades. Confucianism tends to hold to its core, as witness values involving the family and intergenerational ties to ancestors, even while loosening gradually in other ways as modernization progresses. Religion retains a fairly strong hold over time, although younger people coming of age in a more modern setting are less imbued with traditional religious beliefs and there is some secularization even within the same person, as the panel data in Table 10.4 illustrate.

CONCLUSIONS

The central purpose of our analyses is to form a general picture of the cultural changes China has been undergoing. Counter-structuring has been an undoubted success in breaking down gender differentiation and discrimination. Women in China are today almost as well educated as men, and their equal access to jobs, pay, and other considerations of society seems to be widely and firmly accepted as a norm in China. This is an achievement that probably would not have occurred without the severe counterstructuring effort. Women's equal place is certainly not so secured in Taiwan. Indeed, the Taiwanese villagers seem not to have changed their views on gender-related issues.

Education, a Confucian value that was submerged during the most severe years of counterstructuring, is surfacing again in China. We find a remarkable willingness there to send one's children to college, even though few adults have had that chance. Religion too may be only sub-merged by counterstructuring. It did not dwindle rapidly in Taiwan as a result of modernization and Western media, and in China it appears to be making something of a comeback in Shanghai as strictures against it are relaxed. Respect for seniors may not be as pervasive as it once was in China. In the workplace, deference to authority seems an unpop-ular principle, eroded further by rising education levels.

Western entertainment media, with their individualistic themes, may in the future erode the interpersonal script of China's Confucian society as much as counterstructuring has. In Taiwan, we see the influx of mass communication associated with marked declines in interpersonal con-tact and in the desire for a large family. In China, Western entertain-ment is a strong predictor of altered perceptions of male-female relationships. But we should not say that China is thereby becoming Westernized. Gender egalitarianism has probably progressed further in China than in the West,[3] and gender relations there are far from what they would have been under traditional Confucian practices.

Survey interviewing is one of many imperfect methods of evaluating cultural change. In this chapter we have been able to identify, through somewhat cumbersome comparisons of survey data, several features of Chinese culture that have been transformed by the government's radi-cal counterstructuring program, and others that have been affected by the more gradual processes of modernization and the incursions of Western media. Further validation of these conclusions awaits further evidence, particularly future survey research in China as its modern history continues to unfold.

NOTES

1. The workshop participants included the authors; Francis L. K. Hsu, anthropologist, Northwestern University; Ambrose King, sociologist, Chinese University of Hong Kong; Anthony Yu, professor of religion, University of Chicago; and Wang Gungwu, historian, University of Hong Kong. Results of this session were later reviewed by Chu with col-leagues at Fudan University, including Ju Yanan, Xu Zhen, Wu Shenling, and Hu Zheng E. Following pretesting, the survey questionnaire was revised in Honolulu by Chu, Ju, and Wu.

2. The results of the panel study alone were reported in English by Chu and Chi (1984b); the full comparative analysis including the after-only sample has heretofore been reported only in Chinese (Chu & Chi, 1984a). The main reason for not reporting the after-only results in English as well was that they did not differ much from the panel

findings, or else they showed even greater change than would have been inferred from the panel data. That is, there was very little evidence of aging effects that could have been mistaken for real change.

3. This statement is corroborated by analyses by Pan and others (in preparation) of surveys conducted in the United States that were modeled on the Shanghai questionnaire. Collaborating investigators, all professors of communication or journalism, include Diana Tillinghast, San Jose State University; Pamela Shoemaker, University of Texas at Austin; Jack McLeod, University of Wisconsin-Madison; Jae-Won Lee, Cleveland State University; Gary Heald and John Mayo, Florida State University; and Leslie Snyder, University of Connecticut.

REFERENCES

Boas, F. (1938). *The mind of primitive man* (rev. ed.). New York: Macmillan.

Chu, G., & Chi, G. Y. (1984a). *Cultural change in rural Taiwan*. Taipei, Taiwan: Shangwu Press. (in Chinese)

Chu, G., & Chi, G. Y. (1984b). *Cultural change in rural Taiwan: A fourteen-year old longitudinal study*. Unpublished manuscript, East-West Center, Institute for Communication and Culture, Honolulu.

Chu, G., & Hsu, F.L.K. (Eds.). (1979). *Moving a mountain: Cultural change in China*. Honolulu: University Press of Hawaii.

Chu, G., & Hsu, F.L.K. (Eds.). (1983). *China's new social fabric*. London: Kegan Paul International.

Chu, G., & Ju, Y. N. (1990). *The Great Wall in ruins: Cultural change in China*. Unpublished manuscript, East-West Center, Institute for Communication and Culture, Honolulu.

Cooper, E., & Jahoda, M. (1947). The evation of propaganda: How prejudiced people respond to anti-prejudice propaganda. *Journal of Psychology, 23,* 15-25.

Dorfman, A., & Mattelart, A. (1971). *Para leer al Pato Donald*. Valaparaiso, Chile: Ediciones Universitarias de Valaparaiso.

Houn, F. W. (1961). *To change a nation: Propaganda and indoctrination in Communist China*. New York: Free Press.

Howking, J. (1982). *Mass communication in China*. New York: Longman.

Hsu, F.L.K. (1970). *Americans and Chinese: Reflections on two cultures and their people*. Garden City, NY: Doubleday.

Hsu, F.L.K. (1971). *Under the ancestors' shadow*. Stanford, CA: Stanford University Press.

Katz, E., & Liebes, T. (1984). Once upon a time, in Dallas. *Intermedia, 12,* 3.

Kluckhohn, C., & Kelly, W. H. (1945). The concept of culture. In R. Linton (Ed.), *The science of man in the world crisis* (pp. 78-105). New York: Columbia University Press.

Kroeber, A. L., & Kluckhohn, C. (1952). *Culture: A critical review of the concepts and definitions* (Vol. 47, No. 1). Papers of the Peabody Museum of American Archaeology and Ethnology, Harvard University, Cambridge, MA.

Lee, C. C. (1980). *Media imperialism reconsidered: The homogenizing of television culture*. Beverly Hills, CA: Sage.

Lerner, D. (1964). *The passing of traditional society.* New York: Free Press.

Liu, A.P.L. (1981). Mass campaigns in the People's Republic of China. In R. Rice & W. Paisley (Eds.), *Public communication campaigns* (pp. 199-223). Beverly Hills, CA: Sage.

Murdock, G. P. (1941). Anthropology and human relations. *Sociometry, 4,* 140-150.

Pan, Z. D., Chaffee, S., Chu, G., & Ju, Y. N. (in preparation). *To see ourselves: Comparing cultural values in the U.S. and China.* Honolulu: East-West Center manuscript.

Parker, E. B. (1961). Changes in the function of radio with the adoption of television. *Journal of Broadcasting, 5,* 39-48.

Parker, E. B. (1963). The effects of television on public library circulation. *Public Opinion Quarterly, 27,* 578-589.

Rogers, E. M. (1983). *Diffusion of innovations* (3rd ed.). New York: Free Press.

Rogers, E. M., Zhao, X. Y., Pan, Z. D., Chen, M., & Beijing Journalists Assn. (1985). The Beijing audience survey. *Communication Research, 12,* 179-208.

Rosen, S. (1989). Public opinion and reform in the People's Republic of China. *Studies in Comparative Communism, 23*(2/3), 153-170.

Schiller, H. (1976). *Communication and cultural domination.* New York: International Arts & Sciences Press.

Wong, S. L. (1979). *Sociology and socialism in contemporary China.* London: Routledge & Kegan Paul.

Yu, F.T.C. (1964). *Mass persuasion in Communist China.* New York: Praeger.

Yu, F.T.C. (1971). Campaigns, communications, and development in Communist China. In W. Schramm & D. Roberts (Eds.), *Process and effects of mass communication* (rev. ed.) (pp. 836-860). Urbana: University of Illinois Press.

Zhao, X. S., Zhu, J. H., & Li, H. R. (1990). *Effects of communication campaigns on knowledge and attitudes—The case of China in reform.* Unpublished manuscript prepared for *China Report* dated 9/24/90. Chapel Hill: University of North Carolina School of Journalism.

Zhao, X. Y. (1989). Effects of foreign media use, government and traditional influences on Chinese women's values. *Revue Europeene des Sciences Sociales, 27,* No. 84, 239-251.

Chapter 11

THEORIES ON INTERPERSONAL COMMUNICATION STYLES FROM A JAPANESE PERSPECTIVE: A SOCIOLOGICAL APPROACH

Youichi Ito

MORE THAN ONE HUNDRED books and articles have been written that touch upon the unique characteristics of Japanese interpersonal communication style. Many of them were written by Japanese or Americans, not only by experts from the fields of interpersonal and intercultural communication but also by social psychologists, anthropologists, sociologists, business management experts, and political scientists.

Most of the work by Japanese scholars was published in Japanese, but this area is also blessed with an abundant English language literature written by Japanese experts (cf. Doi, 1974; Ito, 1989; Midooka, 1990; Minami, 1971; Nakane, 1970, 1974; Naruke, 1974; Nishida, 1977; Okabe, 1983; Tsujimura, 1987; Yoneyama, 1973; Yoshikawa, 1987, 1988a, 1988b). Many studies of Japanese communication style use American communication style as their basis of comparison.

In contrast to the extensive literature of Japanese and American comparisons, there are far fewer comparisons of other combinations such as Japanese and Europeans, Japanese and Chinese, Europeans and Americans, and so on. Edelstein, Ito, and Kepplinger (1989), for example, searched the German communication literature, but found that "very few

AUTHOR'S NOTE: The author thanks Professors Karl Erik Rosengren, William B. Gudykunst, and Jay Blumler for helpful comments on an earlier draft.

comparative studies have been conducted in West Germany on aspects of interpersonal communication" (p. 219). One reason may be that, at least among advanced industrial societies, the United States and Japan show the sharpest contrast in interpersonal communication styles. It is likely that the communication styles of many other countries are located somewhere between these two extremes.

The sharp contrast in Japanese and American interpersonal styles, discerned empirically by Barnlund (1975, pp. 50-54), has been attributed to differences of values, world views, beliefs, psychological tendencies, and even to physiological differences (Yoshikawa, 1988b).

A distinctive difference exists between the Japanese and American literatures on this subject. Most American literature is satisfied with indicating social and cultural variables as explanatory factors without further discussion as to where these social and cultural differences come from. Few American experts have discussed causal relationships even briefly, or where those factors come from and why and how they determine interpersonal communication styles.

The volume of literature describing Japanese and American communication styles is more than sufficient. Those descriptions, therefore, will not be repeated in this chapter. Instead, discussion will center on factors determining interpersonal communication styles. Historical, sociological, climatological, and geographical backgrounds of determinants will be examined. Further, the chapter analyzes current trends and makes predictions as to what may happen to the Japanese and American communication styles in the future. Future predictions, especially for American communication style, have rarely been attempted by American experts. Two reasons can be advanced for this neglect:

(1) Most American experts in this area regard such determinant factors as static and not dynamic; and

(2) They are inclined to psychological determinism.

MAJOR THEORIES
TO EXPLAIN THE DIFFERENCES

There are a number of approaches to accounting for differences in interpersonal communication styles. Most of them may be differentiated by means of three basic dimensions: individualistic-collectivistic, homogeneous-heterogeneous, and human relations-ideology. In this section, each of the three dimensions will be discussed and some additional approaches will be examined.

INDIVIDUALISTIC VERSUS COLLECTIVISTIC SOCIETIES

The individualistic-collectivistic approach is dominant among Western experts on interpersonal and intercultural communication. American scholars, in particular, believe that communication styles are deeply rooted to whether people in a society are "individualistic" or "collectivistic" (Barnlund, 1975; Condon, 1980; Gudykunst, 1987, 1989; Gudykunst & Nishida, 1989, 1990; Gudykunst & Ting-Toomey, 1988; Ting-Toomey, 1989). They have scarcely discussed *why* people in individualistic societies tend to be more talkative, straightforward, frank, self-assertive, opinionated, abrupt, and aggressive than people in collectivistic societies; however, in this writer's view, the following reasons are plausible:

(a) How to talk and to express one's opinions and feelings are taught in the early stages of education at home and school.

Socialization at home and school in collectivistic societies emphasizes values necessary to produce "good members" of groups, organizations, and societies. Children are taught first that people are interdependent with each other. Therefore, they are taught to be pleasant, kind, cooperative, helpful, and polite to other people. They are also taught to respect social order, senior people, and authority.

In contrast, in individualistic societies, early education at home and school emphasizes values necessary to make "strong, independent individuals." Children are taught first that society consists of independent individuals. Each of them must become a strong, independent individual. They are expected to have their own opinions and to express them in public without hesitation. They are expected and encouraged to think for themselves, to decide for themselves, and to do whatever they think right. What other people would think of them is not important. Those "collectivistic" values that are necessary to become "good members" of groups, organizations, and societies may be respected but are of only secondary importance.

(b) Horizontal social mobility is lower in collectivistic societies than in individualistic societies.

This means that people in collectivistic societies cannot change their communities, organizations, or societies as easily as do people in individualistic societies. This makes the maintenance of good human relations and group harmony essential in collectivistic societies. Therefore, to be cautious not to offend others by careless, harsh, abrupt, impolite, or other types of inappropriate remarks is not only a matter of adhering to social norms but also has a practical outcome.

Due to the two conditions above, people in collectivistic societies pay more attention to other people's feelings and possible reactions to what they say and thus become more cautious as to what they say than do people in individualistic societies. This makes them less self-assertive, less talkative, less aggressive, and more ambiguous or evasive.

Although this individualism-collectivism approach is emphasized by American scholars, there are at least seven fundamental problems with this model:

1. *Is individualism-collectivism unidimensional?* Many American experts assume either (1) that all societies in the world can be roughly dichotomized between individualistic and collectivistic societies, or (2) that all societies in the world can be placed on a unidimensional scale with extreme individualism and extreme collectivism as the two ends of the scale. These two assumptions may be applicable to primitive or to premodern societies. They are too simplistic and misleading, however, when applied to complicated modern societies.

This seems obvious if we examine the historical, social, economic, and political backgrounds of individualism and collectivism. Triandis et al., (1988) recognized two distinctive forms of individualism. "Proto-individualism" is found in primitive societies that have not yet formed nation states or other sophisticated social organizations common in "neoindividualistic" societies.

Triandis and his group are arguably the only experts who have paid sufficient attention to these complexities. Even they, however, failed to note the essentially different kinds of individualism found in North America and Europe. North America has always been individualistic; its immigrants arrived as independent individuals and then formed communities, organizations, societies, and states. The same is true for the historic development of Australia.

The opposite sequence is true in Europe, however. When people began to have a sense of individuality, their communities, societies, organizations, and states had been in existence for several hundred years. In other words, European societies *have become* (e.g., U.K., France, and the Scandinavian countries), *are becoming* (e.g., Germany and Austria) or *have not yet become* (e.g., Spain, Portugal, and Greece) individualistic societies according to their scores on Hofstede's individualism-collectivism scale (Hofstede, 1980, 1983). In summary, North America and Australia have developed from "protoindividualistic societies" to "neoindividualistic societies," whereas European societies are at various stages along a path from "collectivistic societies" to "neoindividualistic societies."

What was said about individualism also can be said about collectivism. As Triandis et al. (1988) did in recognizing two kinds of individualism, the writer proposes two different kinds of collectivism: "premodern collectivism" as found in medieval Japan or in medieval Europe and "modern collectivism" as seen in present-day Japanese corporations. Whereas premodern collectivism was maintained chiefly because it was a tradition, modern collectivism is a rational strategy to achieve specific goals.

It is true that modern Japanese corporations have many characteristics of traditional collectivism. In modern collectivism, however, the decision-making process is supposed to be democratic and the distribution of collective interests among individual members is supposed to be fair and equitable. Under these two basic conditions, individuals willingly join these collectivistic organizations believing that it will be the most efficient way to maximize their individual interests. In other words, under modern collectivism each individual tries to maximize his or her own interest by maximizing the collective interest.

It is the case that Americans usually do not have these expectations of business corporations. They do, however, have similar ideas about their own country in being loyal and dedicated to the United States, believing that they can maximize their individual interests by maximizing the interests of the United States. If you replace the United States with Toyota, Sony, NEC, and so on, you should be able to understand the Japanese psychology. This psychology is called in Japan *kigyo nashonarizumu* (corporate nationalism) or *aisha seishin* (corporate patriotism). From whatever cause, this kind of rationalized modern collectivism is essentially different from premodern collectivism in farming villages in Indonesia or among nomadic tribes in Arabia. Whereas pre-modern collectivism is a tradition, modern collectivism is a strategy.

Reflecting these complexities, Triandis et al. (1988) found little evidence to support their hypotheses regarding collectivism, especially with Japanese subjects. Thus they concluded: "It has [been] shown that some of the simpler ideas about what collectivism means must be discarded and that a more complex understanding of the construct is possible. . . . In short, the empirical studies suggest that we need to consider individualism and collectivism as multidimensional constructs" (p. 336).

2. *Are individualism and collectivism value-free, neutral concepts?* Issues regarding individualism and collectivism tend to be easily "ideologized" among scholars and researchers who are supposed to be neutral, objective, and value-free. As a result, empirical studies as well as theoretical discussions tend to be distorted by researchers' biases. This is true for both American and Japanese scholars. Generally speaking, American scholars tend to have the bias that individualism is superior to collectivism. On the other hand, conservative Japanese researchers tend to idealize Japanese tradition and cultural characteristics.

To avoid these problems, American scholars should not ignore the defects of "extreme individualism," and Japanese scholars should not ignore the defects of "extreme collectivism." Quoting Cobb (1976) and Naroll (1983), Triandis et al. (1988) write: "Extreme individualism may be linked to several forms of social pathology, such as high crime, suicide, divorce, child abuse, emotional stress, and physical and mental illness rates" (p. 216). They show that empirically the heart attack rates are higher in individualistic societies than in collectivistic ones, and they suggest that higher stress levels in the individualistic societies may have something to do with that. Many other American scholars, however, ignore negative aspects of individualism, whereas many conservative Japanese scholars ignore negative aspects of collectivism such as authoritarianism, suppression of individual rights, lack of privacy, and so forth.

3. *National leaders and mass media in individualistic societies tend to emphasize collectivistic values, and those in collectivistic societies tend to emphasize individualistic values.* National political leaders in each type of society often express values characteristic of the opposite type. This is not necessarily true in all societies at all times, but it does happen sometimes. Recognition of defects of the extreme forms of

individualism and collectivism make political leaders adopt opposite policies to remedy those defects.

"Ask not what the country can do for you, but ask what you can do for your country" is a famous phrase used by the late President John F. Kennedy in his inaugural address. It would be impossible for postwar Japanese prime ministers to make such a statement because it would sound too strong in the postwar Japanese situation. In postwar Japan, political leaders and central governmental agencies have propagated individualistic values.

The national flag and the national anthem have played far more important roles in the United States than in postwar Japan (Sugimoto, 1983, pp. 70-71). Probably for these reasons, recent international comparative surveys have repeatedly confirmed that Americans and the British are now more nationalistic and patriotic than are the Japanese and the Germans (see Ito & Kohei, 1990, pp. 113-115; Leisure Development Center, 1983; Prime Minister's Office, 1984; Public Opinion Research Institute, NHK, 1982). If nationalistic and patriotic tendencies are indications of collectivistic tendencies, it is possible to argue that Americans and the British are more collectivistic than are the Japanese and Germans.

Public service advertisements in the United States often advocate collectivistic values such as cooperation, teamwork, loyalty, and dedication. This is not true in postwar Japan. On the contrary, Japan IBM has conducted a public relations campaign in Japanese mass media with the headline, "We Respect our Employees as Individuals." Therefore, if researchers content-analyze speeches of political leaders or mass media content, they are very likely to get the result that the United States is a collectivistic society and that Japan is an individualistic one.

4. *People in individualistic societies tend to be more conforming to other people than those in collectivistic societies under the same circumstances.* As repeatedly emphasized by Gudykunst (Gudykunst, 1987, 1989; Gudykunst & Nishida, 1989, 1990; Gudykunst & Ting-Toomey, 1988), "People in individualistic cultures tend to be universalistic and to apply the same value standards to all" (Gudykunst, 1989, p. 227). On the other hand, people in collectivistic cultures tend to be particularistic and apply different standards to different kinds of people. As a result, values in individualistic societies tend to become more uniform than do those in collectivistic societies. These uniform values function as strong social pressures on individuals.

It is well known that in Asch-type experiments on conformity, Japanese subjects have always been less conforming than American subjects (cf. Frager, 1970). The reason is that experimental subjects are not "ingroup members" by Japanese standards. In a different type of study, Triandis et al. (1988) found that, contrary to their hypotheses, Japanese subjects were *less* conforming to the ingroup's wishes than were American subjects.

Nobody will doubt that Americans are generally more sociable than are Japanese or Germans. According to Triandis et al. (1988), the reason is "because [people in individualistic societies] have to work hard to get into and remain in their ingroups" (p. 333). There exist only two or three major political parties in the United States and the U.K. but six or seven in Japan and Germany. These examples and findings indicate that under certain circumstances people in individualistic societies can be more conforming than people in collectivistic societies.

Although individualism may bring universalism, universalism forces all individuals to conform to fewer social norms. Ironically, individualism as a slogan *is more needed* in universalistic than in particularistic societies.

5. *People in individualistic societies tend to be more obedient to authorities than people in collectivistic societies under some circumstances.* Whitehill and Takizawa (1968) found that American workers in their survey were more obedient to their supervisors than were Japanese workers. This result was repeatedly supported by other international comparative surveys (e.g., Leisure Development Center, 1983; Public Opinion Research Institute, NHK, 1982). Whitehill and Takizawa (1968) suggested that in the United States, role differentiation is more developed than in Japan. American workers, therefore, readily follow their supervisors' orders even when they do not agree with them. In comparison, Japanese organizations are still immature, and role differentiation is not yet fully developed. Japanese workers, therefore, do not necessarily follow their supervisors' orders if they do not agree with them.

Like many other American scholars, Whitehill and Takizawa seem to think that the American system is always more advanced than the Japanese system. The writer's answer as to why American workers tend to be more obedient than Japanese workers is that the latter have always been encouraged to participate in and influence the decision-making process, because the company is (supposed to be) *their* company (because workers consider themselves as *"belonging to"* the company).

Conversely, American workers are conditioned to think that the company is *not theirs.* The company belongs to top executives and stock holders. Workers come to the company just for money. Then who cares what will happen to the company that may lay them off at any time? Who cares what the order may mean to the company? So, whatever the order is, they just "obediently" follow it without thinking of its meaning to the company.

6. *The degree of individualism-collectivism may differ from one level to another.* As mentioned above, Americans and the British at present are quite "collectivist" at the national level. Postwar Japanese are no longer collectivist at the national level but are strongly collectivist in their workplaces. People in many developing countries are not collectivist at the national or corporate levels but are so at the family and local community levels. In many underdeveloped countries, people's concerns are still with the small communities around them and not with the state. Political leaders of underdeveloped countries, therefore, tend to think that their people are too "individualistic," because they are not loyal to the state. Managers of Japanese companies operating in underdeveloped countries often lament that workers there are too "individualistic," because they are not loyal to their companies and are not good at cooperating with each other in the factory.

It is "common knowledge" in East Asia that the Japanese are more collectivistic than are the Chinese, Koreans, and most other Asians. The Japanese themselves admit that they are more collectivistic than most other Asians (cf. Hamaguchi, 1977; Hamaguchi & Kumon, 1982; Iwata, 1980; Matsumura, 1984; Minami, 1980; Murakami, Kumon, & Sato, 1979; Nakane, 1970; and many others). Just as individualism is a part of American cultural identity, collectivism may be a part of Japanese cultural identity.

According to Hofstede's (1983) frequently quoted ranking of countries by degree of individualism, however, Japan is 46, close to the median. This figure is higher than that of the Philippines (32), Malaysia (26), Thailand (20), Singapore (20), South Korea (18), Taiwan (17), and Indonesia (14). Those scores contradict both the "common knowledge" in East Asia mentioned above and the Japanese self-image as well. This result would puzzle many Japanese and other Asians.

It is understandable that East Asians have an image of Japan as collectivistic, because the Japanese military invaded those Asian countries before World War II, and Japanese corporations are "invading" them again economically in more recent years. In their eyes, the source of

Japanese strength is their "collectivism." They say that they themselves cannot become as strong as the Japanese, because they are more
"individualistic."

Lee Seung-man, South Korea's first president after World War II,
adopted severe anti-Japanese policies, because he had been tortured by
the Japanese military police while Korea was under Japanese rule. He
has reportedly lamented, however, that Koreans are too "individualistic" and said, "Although Japanese are barbarians, there is one thing that
we should learn from them. That is the spirit of solidarity." A Japanese
professor of business management, Kageyama (1988, p. 14), who studied the business management system in Korea, concluded:

> As individualistic tendencies are stronger in Korea, there must be some
> reason behind "harmony" in Korea. Spontaneous harmony and group
> consciousness as seen in Japan are not easy to create and maintain in
> Korea. . . . To what extent the Japanese model in business management or
> industrialization can be applied to Korea is a difficult question faced by
> Korean government bureaucrats and business leaders.

Then why are the Japanese less collectivistic than other Asians in
Hofstede's study? The reason may be that "Japanese collectivism," famous in Asia, is really "modern collectivism" as seen in the Japanese
military prior to World War II and in Japanese corporations after the
War. On the other hand, the Japanese are probably more "individualistic" than other Asians in more traditional areas such as the family and
the local community. It is likely that Hofstede's scale is comparing
"neoindividualism" (Triandis et al., 1988) and "premodern collectivism," whereas the "modern collectivism" as seen in Japanese corporations as well as in American nationalism is ignored.

7. *The degree of individualism-collectivism is determined not only by
culture but also by social conditions. Therefore, in most complicated
modern societies, individualism and collectivism coexist in the same
culture.* Although good empirical studies are not yet available, it is
likely that individuals' scores on the individuality-collectivity scale are
strongly influenced by the respondents' backgrounds: occupation, social class, level of education, marital status, and place of residence.
These social and educational factors determine to what extent each individual can afford to be, or has to be, individualistic or collectivistic.
A highly educated, single Japanese journalist living in Tokyo is very
likely to be more individualistic than a poorly educated Caucasian
American rural farmer living with his or her family.

The seven problems discussed above indicate how complicated are the relationships between individualism and collectivism. If we see studies dichotomizing "individualistic" and "collectivistic" societies, or putting all societies on a unidimensional scale of individualism-collectivism, we had better doubt their validity. This writer agrees with Triandis et al. (1988), who wrote regarding these problems: "Clearly, the picture is very complex, and it will take decades of research to unravel it" (p. 329).

HOMOGENEOUS VERSUS HETEROGENEOUS SOCIETIES

Whereas the individualism-collectivism approach dominates among American scholars, the homogeneity-heterogeneity approach is more popular and common among Japanese scholars (cf. Kato, 1973; Kitamura, 1977; Kunihiro, 1973, 1976; Suzuki, 1980; Toyama, 1976; Tsujimura, 1987). One reason why American scholars are fond of the individualism-collectivism approach may be that they are proud of American individualism and think that individualism is superior to collectivism. Similarly, one reason why Japanese scholars are fond of the homogeneity-heterogeneity approach may be that they are proud of their racial and cultural homogeneity and think that homogeneous societies are superior to heterogeneous societies. Of course, these are subconscious matters, but it would be interesting if these latent psychologies affected their choices of academic approaches.

That is not the only difference, however. Whereas the individualism-collectivism approach is chiefly concerned with "the extent to which the speaker is concerned with the reactions of the listener and the possible influence on their human relations," the homogeneity-heterogeneity approach is mainly concerned with "the extent to which the speaker expects the listener to infer and understand the meaning without complete verbal explanations."

Many Japanese scholars claim that among people who share common values and knowledge, verbal communication is not important. They can communicate anyway through many nonverbal communication channels including overt behavior. In such a culture, verbal explanation is redundant and often unnecessary. Verbal communication tends to become less frequent, and expressions become ambiguous and indirect.[1]

The tendency to talk ambiguously and indirectly is what Hall (1976) described as "high-context culture." Gudykunst and Ting-Toomey (1988, pp. 39-59) and Gudykunst and Nishida (1990, p. 8) associate "high-context culture" with collectivistic culture and "low-context culture" with individualistic culture. They define high-context cultures as those societies whose individualism scores on Hofstede's individualism-collectivism scale are above the median; low-context cultures are those below the median. They do not explain why the communication culture in individualistic societies tends to be "high context," nor why in collectivistic societies it tends to be "low context."

In order to answer the above questions, we must ask why in general some people talk more ambiguously and indirectly than do others. There are at least seven possibilities:

(1) The speaker is afraid of hurting the listener's feelings.
(2) The speaker is trying to defend his or her ego, or wishes to avoid "losing face" (this happens in situations such as apology, request or confession of love).
(3) To speak clearly or directly is not necessary, because the listener will understand anyway.
(4) The speaker is unintelligent or poorly educated.
(5) The speaker was educated in a field where objectivity or "communicability" is not so important (e.g., poetry, existentialism, phenomenology).
(6) The speaker's culture does not respect logical discussion and rational approaches to problem solving.
(7) The speaker is speaking a foreign language.

It is important to confirm these points, because researchers with PhDs in cultural anthropology or other fields often go to another country, talk with ordinary people, force them to speak English, compare them with him- or herself and colleagues who are highly educated, and conclude that what these people say is not clear enough. From this they decide that the communication culture is high-context. This kind of "research" and its conclusions are really absurd, but in fact there are a number of "research reports" of this sort published by Western anthropologists and communication experts.

If people in individualistic cultures speak more clearly and directly than people in collectivistic cultures, several reasons are conceivable:

(1) People in individualistic societies pay less attention to listener's feelings.

(2) People in individualistic societies have a stronger, more independent self; therefore, their need for ego defense is less, having been educated to be less face-conscious than people in collectivistic societies.

(3) People in individualistic societies are better educated.

Differences in degrees of homogeneity and heterogeneity probably have much to do with the third condition listed on page 247: that is, the speaker does not have to speak so clearly or directly because the listener will understand anyway. Because many people share common values and knowledge, many kinds of nonverbal signs as well as ambiguous expressions are used in homogeneous societies. Therefore, people can take advantage of them when they do not wish to speak too clearly or directly for whatever reason.

Actual reasons for the differences between high- and low-context communication cultures, however, are probably far more complicated. Those differences are obviously caused by a combination of the seven reasons mentioned previously. In order to clarify them, the seven reasons should be checked more closely one by one.

HUMAN-RELATIONS VERSUS IDEOLOGICAL SOCIETIES

This model may be considered as a variation of the homogeneity-heterogeneity model discussed above. According to Clark (1977), major countries in the Eurasian landmass, including China and India, became ideological societies by going through many intertribal conflicts, conquests, and by being defeated. People in the Eurasian landmass and in the Americas and Australia, which are extensions of European civilization, therefore have a tendency to stick to rules, principles, and ideologies and also tend to seek identity in such principles and ideologies.

In comparison, in island societies detached from the Eurasian landmass such as Japan, the Philippines, Indonesia, and the South Pacific islands, people have not experienced many severe intertribal conflicts in their histories. It is true that there were a number of wars within Japan, but Japanese cultural identity was never threatened, because these were civil wars, and people did not have to justify their culture. In island societies, therefore, people are more loose, tolerant, and flexible about rules, principles, religions, and ideologies, and they tend to seek their identity in common blood. Japan is a typical example of a "human relations society." No matter how many years you live in Japan, however well you may speak Japanese, and even if you are naturalized, you will never be accepted as an insider. You must be born Japanese.

It is true that the Japanese are very surprised to see Americans and Europeans adopt children of different races. It is extremely difficult for Japanese to do that, far more difficult than interracial marriage. On the other hand, Americans and Europeans are very surprised to see how many Japanese celebrate the birth of a child at a Shinto shrine, get married at a Christian church, and have a funeral at a Buddhist temple. Why do Japanese do that? It is because to the Japanese the Christian wedding ceremony looks most romantic, the Buddhist funeral looks most solemn, and a Shinto shrine makes Japanese feel nationalistic. When asked, "Why the Buddhist funeral?" a Japanese answered, "I wouldn't feel really dead without it."

Whereas the ideological society is leadership oriented, the human relations society is consensus oriented. Whereas the ideological society needs great leaders and heroes, the human relations society has no need for them, because important decisions are made, not by great heroes or leaders, but through invisible processes of compromise and consensus building. In the human relations society, compromise and consensus are important, and basic rules, principles, and ideologies have only secondary importance.

Quoting Ito (1989), Gudykunst and Nishida (1990) suggest that this human relations versus ideological society explanation can be seen as "a modified version of individualism-collectivism" (p. 41). This, however, is not correct considering the fact that in Clark's (1977) theory all countries on the Eurasian landmass—including China, Korea, India, and other South and West Asian countries—are classified as "ideological societies." Obviously, most Asian societies on the Eurasian landmass are classified as collectivistic societies in the individualism-collectivism approach; thus supporters of this approach may not like Clark's classification. Clark's theory, however, agrees with common knowledge in East Asia despite the fact, puzzling to most Asian experts, that the individualism scores of Japan are higher than those of most other Asian countries on Hofstede's scale. As mentioned in the individualism-collectivism model section, it is widely accepted in East Asia that the Chinese, Koreans, and almost all other Asians (probably excepting the Javanese in Indonesia) are more talkative, expressive, straightforward, aggressive, and even individualistic than are the Japanese.

The only difference between this model and the homogeneity-heterogeneity model is that even if a society maintains racial and cultural homogeneity, it cannot help becoming an "ideological society" as it comes to have much more contact with other cultural groups. Korea, a homogeneous society, is an example (Clark, 1977). It is true that Koreans have taken religions and ideologies more seriously than have the Japanese. According to Yoda (1989, p. 13), what most surprises Koreans who visit Japan is the fact that old Buddhist temples and old Shinto shrines coexist in the same city. In Korea, where Confucianism has been dominant, Buddhist temples are all in the mountains.

According to Clark (1977), pure "human relations societies" now can be seen only in island countries that have not had much contact with other cultural groups until after their cultures were firmly established. Therefore, Clark predicts that Japan also will be obliged to become an "ideological society" as "internationalization" of Japan proceeds. This means that the Japanese also will have to become more talkative, self-assertive, and eloquent than they are at present.

OTHER VARIABLES

The three explanations following are less systematic as social theories than are the three models above but are worth noting as independent variables.

Influence of Religion

Whereas Christianity and Islam encourage active and sometimes aggressive ways of life, Oriental religions such as Buddhism, Confucianism, and Taoism all encourage passive, quiet, and modest ways of life. Confucianism emphasizes politeness, respect for seniority, harmony, and social order. Buddhism denounces secular desires, while emphasizing peace, *jihi* (love and mercy), and harmony, especially harmony with nature. These teachings tend to suppress frank expression of individual opinions. For example, Chu (1988), Ju (1989), and Chaffee and Chu (Chapter 10, this volume) emphasize the strong influence of Confucianism on the Chinese communication culture, claiming that these characteristics in the Chinese interpersonal style have not changed even under Communist rule.

In contrast, according to Barnlund (1975), the United States "resembles a nation of missionaries" (p. 165). Each individual has his or her own opinions regarding many kinds of lessons and is highly motivated to persuade other people to change their opinions. These attitudes and behaviors remind people in non-Christian countries such as the Japanese of those aggressive Christian missionaries of earlier times.

Influence of Climate

Haga (1979) writes, "if you take a train in Tokyo and go westward" (actually, "westward" means southwest in Japan), "you will notice that the train gradually becomes noisy" (p. 19). Spectators of baseball games or horse racing sometimes become excited and fist fights or riots take place. Interestingly, these incidents always occur in southern parts of Japan such as Fukuoka and Hiroshima and seldom take place in northern parts like Sapporo or Sendai.

In Europe, Italians and Spaniards are considered to be more talkative, expressive, passionate, and short-tempered than are Swedes and Norwegians. In Asia, Filipinos, Thais, Indians, and Pakistanis are thought to exhibit these same behaviors more than are the Chinese, Japanese, and Koreans. In Asia, people joke, "Bind the hands of Indians, then they cannot talk." Are these only unscientific stereotyped images that are not true at all?

The difference between northern and southern Japan has often been explained by saying that in northern Japan the temperature in winter is so low that people try to avoid opening their mouths so as not to lose heat. This explanation is rather humorous, but there may be some truth in it: Northern Japanese dialects do require less mouth movement than southern dialects. In addition, high temperatures may stimulate people's motivation to talk.

Population Density

Reischauer (1977) points out that land productivity of grain in East Asia, where the climate is warm and humid, has always been higher than that in colder and/or drier West Asia and Europe. This explains why the density of population has always been higher in East Asia than in West Asia and Europe. Reischauer thinks that "collectivistic" values such as group harmony, good human relations, cooperation, and team work tend to be more important where the population density is higher. This may explain why these values are more respected in East Asia than in West Asia or Europe and relatively less respected in North America and Australia than in the other areas.

CHANGE OF COMMUNICATION CULTURE

It is the writer's belief that all good social theories should be able to explain historical changes and to predict future trends. Cultures change, and communication culture is no exception. Many experts on communication culture have discussed correlations between interpersonal communication styles and various other cultural factors. Very few of them, however, have dealt with causal relationships and made predictions based on them.

Clark's (1977) theory is one of the few exceptions. From his theory he predicted that all societies start as homogeneous "human relations societies" but gradually become "ideological societies" as they have more contact with tribes with different cultures. Identities change from being based on common blood to being based on common ideologies. Therefore, it is possible to predict from this theory that a human relations society like Japan will gradually become an ideological society. Japanese communication culture will inevitably change as a result.

The homogeneity-heterogeneity theory has the same implications. The number of foreigners living in Japan is steadily increasing. They may be workers, students, entertainers, refugees, or businessmen. Rural farming villages are importing Filipinos, Thai, and Sri Lankan "brides" due to the shortage of Japanese girls who are willing to marry farmers. Although it is less prominent, basically the same phenomena seen earlier in West European countries are now taking place in Japan. If Japanese society becomes more heterogeneous racially and culturally, the traditional Japanese communication style may also change.

Very few supporters of the individualism-collectivism model have described historical trends or made future predictions. Quoting the study by Murdock and Provost (1973), Triandis et al. (1988) suggested a "U-shaped function" to explain the differences of human societies in terms of individualism and collectivism. It is not clear if this idea was proposed as a developmental theory. If we may interpret it as such, the function may be stated as follows:

> In societies where sophisticated social organizations have not yet formed, people are basically individualistic in their behavior and ways of thinking. This stage is called "proto-individualism" and is seen in many primitive societies. As sophisticated social organizations form and develop, collective interests begin to dominate individual interests and people become "collectivistic" in their behavior and thinking. However, as the economy develops further, it becomes possible to liberate individuals from collective suppression enabling them to pursue individual interests. This third stage is called "neoindividualism." At this stage, people can pursue individual interests at the same time as sophisticated social organizations are being maintained. (Triandis et al., 1988, p. 324)

If this function is correctly interpreted as a developmental theory, Japan *still* remains at the level of collectivism. As the Japanese economy develops further, Japan will eventually reach the state of neoindividualism as found in North America. Two problems with this prediction are:

(1) The Japanese economy is already fully developed; and
(2) The Japanese seem to have chosen modern collectivism instead of neoindividualism.

In modern collectivism, the decision-making process is supposed to be democratic, the distribution of collective interests among individual members is supposed to be fair and equitable, and basic rights are supposed to be respected. Without these basic democratic conditions, modern collectivism would function less effectively than expected. Whereas neoindividualism emphasizes the effects of the division of labor and specialization, modern collectivism stresses the effects of cooperation and teamwork. Thus, unlike premodern collectivism, individuals are supposed to join social organizations willingly in order to maximize their individual interests by maximizing the interests of the organizations that they belong to. The form of competition in modern collectivism is *intergroup* rather than the *interindividual* competition of neoindividualism.

The "developmental theory" of Triandis et al. (1988) is clearly Anglo-American-centric. It wisely differentiates neoindividualism from protoindividualism, but it fails to distinguish the essential differences between premodern collectivism (collectivism as a tradition or for purposes of security and survival) and modern collectivism (rationalized and democratized collectivism to increase collective efficiency). It also pays insufficient attention to the key differences between North America and Australia (from protoindividualism to neoindividualism) on the one hand, and European societies (from collectivistic societies to neoindividualistic societies) on the other.

What, then, determines the interpersonal style of a society? In the writer's view, it is determined by a combination of several factors, the most important being the extent to which human relations in important ingroups are regarded as critical by individuals. (Here *human relations* does not refer to "connections" or "human networks." It refers to good or bad human relations in major ingroups such as family, workplace, and local communities.) In societies where human relations in this sense are not so important, people can talk in any way they like. This lack of restriction tends to make people talkative, verbose, aggressive, expressive, opinionated, and self-assertive. They can also talk more directly and clearly. The more important human relations in this sense become, the more cautious, reticent, evasive, passive, and ambiguous people tend to become. Of course, this is only one of many factors that create differences that are further reinforced by other factors such as educational background, social class, and occupation.

Let us see how these characteristics have developed in Japan and elsewhere.

HUMAN RELATIONS AND COMMUNICATION CULTURE IN PREMODERN SOCIETIES

The importance of human relations in premodern societies very much depended upon the kind of sustenance activities they relied on. In societies that relied on agriculture, human relations were very important, whereas in those depending on stock farming, nomadism, fishing, or hunting, human relations—except those within the immediate family—were less important. Commerce may be located somewhere between these two ends. Further distinctions could be made among these rough categories depending on the mode and scale of production.

Japanese experts believe that within the same plant agriculture, the Japanese type of rice production was most demanding in terms of the need for cooperation. For example, climatic conditions required that Japanese farmers had to plant, transplant, and harvest rice according to a strictly prescribed schedule. A few days' delay in the schedule could mean failure and starvation. Calendars and making schedules were extremely important to Japanese farmers.[2] This made them time-conscious, schedule-conscious, and industrious. When Japan began industrialization, these farmers became factory workers, and their traditional traits contributed a great deal to the success of Japan's industrialization.

Nakano (1982) finds a prototype of Japanese organizational communication in meetings called *yoriai* held in traditional villages in Japan. When something important to the village members occurs, *yoriai* is held, and all in attendance are asked to express their opinions. Discussions or debates never take place in the first meeting, however, the purpose of which is that members get to know what other people think about the issue. Through intrapersonal communication and informal communication with close friends, family members, or even competitors, each person is expected to modify his or her opinion and cooperate to create a consensus. Discrepancies among members are thus diminished prior to the second meeting, where people are again asked to express their revised opinions. If serious discrepancies still exist, the second meeting adjourns without substantial discussion. This process continues until the discrepancies among the members diminish further and a consensus is achieved.

Feudal Europe also depended heavily on plant agriculture, and human relations have been very important, especially in farming villages. Although American scholars have always wanted to put Europe in the same category as North America so far as interpersonal communication style is concerned, Europeans—especially Northwest Europeans—are often more similar to the Japanese than to Americans. Although North America and Europe share the same "Western civilization," Japan and Europe share two important factors that North America does not have: (1) feudalism in their pasts and (2) small-scale labor-intensive plant agriculture in which cooperation was critically important.

In fact, Naozuka (1980) translated into English many day-to-day conversations by Japanese housewives that she thought uniquely Japanese and investigated the reactions of subjects of many nationalities. One of the findings of this study was that Northwest Europeans, especially the British, were much less resistant to hinting and circumlocutions used in Japanese daily conversations than were Americans and other groups such as South Asians and Latin Americans. Toyama (1976, pp. 302-306) points out that the Japanese and the British resemble each other in that they both dislike verbosity and are inclined to silence and prefer reserved expressions to exaggerated ones.

On the other hand, North America, Australia, and many areas in West Asia depended heavily on stock farming, nomadism, and large-scale labor-intensive agriculture. Under these production systems, human relations or cooperation are not so important (except within the immediate family). In other words, there have been few constraints on the way people talk. This made people from these areas more talkative, straightforward, opinionated, self-assertive, and aggressive. It would be difficult to explain from the individualism-collectivism model why West Asians such as Arabs, Jews, Indians, and Pakistanis are more aggressive and talkative than Europeans, but this theory provides such predictions.

HUMAN RELATIONS AND COMMUNICATION CULTURE IN MODERN SOCIETIES

As a result of the Industrial Revolution, plant agriculture and stock farming declined in North America, Europe, and East Asia, and their influence on people's communication patterns has decreased drastically. Now it is modern economic organizations, particularly private business corporations, that have strong influence on people's communication patterns. If modern economic organizations were to become more similar to each other in North America, Europe, and Japan, communication patterns among these industrialized areas should also become more similar.

Interestingly, however, modern economic organizations in these three major industrial areas have inherited characteristics from their earlier industrial patterns. Yoshikawa (1988b) describes the basic philosophy behind American organizations and business management:

> The American organization basically functions like a machine. It is a composite of separate individuals who are relatively easily separable and replaceable. When something goes wrong with some part of the organization, that part, whether individual or no, is considered a problem area to be remedied. If it gets worse, it is replaced by another part. Individuals in the organization are then primarily interchangeable parts and units of production.

The human relationships in the organization are not generally based on the trust and goodwill of the people as in Japanese organizations, but are generally based on contractual agreements. Thus, it is not a personal bond, but a legal bond that exists between employer and employees, and the legal bond is not generally a lifetime commitment. It is easily broken when circumstance changes on the part of either employer or employee. Both employer and employee regard each other as an object to be used to achieve his own purposes. This common interest serves as a unifying force. The organization, like a contractual society, is built on this type of temporal legal bond, not on the long term personal bond of mutual trust. (p. 156).

The Japanese approach in large organizations is just the opposite of the above description, and the European model is probably somewhere between these two extremes.

According to a recent news report, 2,400 workers of a Japanese automobile company in the United States (Nissan U.S.A. in Tennessee) voted against the proposal to join the United Automobile Worker Union (UAW) (*Asahi Shimbun,* 1989; *Sankei Shimbun,* 1989). This is reportedly the second failure for the UAW after the unsuccessful attempt to unionize the Honda factory in Ohio. The basic idea behind the traditional industrial relations in the United States has been confrontation between manager and workers based on strict interpretations of contracts and laws. For managers and stock holders, workers are just one of the resources for production. For workers, the company is just a place to earn money and nothing more than that.

Layoff and discharge for company reasons harm the mutual trust between managers and workers. As a result, Nissan U.S.A. and Honda U.S.A. both promised that they would never lay off or fire workers for company reasons. This was a major reason why American workers in these companies sided with their companies and rejected the UAW.

Although Americans may not agree, from the Japanese viewpoint the American organization looks like a collection of selfish people who are only pursuing their self-interests. The Japanese organization has tried to become more like a "community sharing the same destiny." In that sense, it is more like a family or a state in North America or Europe. Just as modern states must be democratic, modern business corporations must also follow this pattern. Collective interests must be equally or reasonably distributed among individual members. The image of a person who changes companies many times in Japan is like that of a person who changes wives, husbands, or countries many times in North America or Europe. Just as a person who is loyal to one wife, husband, or country is considered more desirable even in the United States, a person who is loyal to one company is much preferred in Japan. A person who changes companies usually has to start with a lower salary and status.

As a result, the tendency for people to remain in one company affects interpersonal communication style. If horizontal mobility is low and you are likely to work with your existing colleagues for a long period of time, perhaps until retirement, you had better maintain good relationships with them. In order to maintain good relationships, you had better be careful about what you say and the way you say it. Outspoken and aggressive persons in Japanese organizations tend to create and accumulate many enemies and antagonism against themselves in the long run. Such people, if very competent, may be successful temporarily but are not likely to succeed in the long run, for people burdened with antagonism are unlikely to be promoted in Japanese organizations, which emphasize harmony and consensus rather than leadership. Most Japanese are aware of this situation. According to a survey conducted in Japan, 76% of respondents believed that a "silent" man is more likely to succeed in Japan than an "eloquent" one (Klopf, Ishii, & Cambra, 1978).

Conversely, horizontal mobility is very high in societies like those in North America. If a person can easily quit a company whenever he or she wants, human relations within the company are not so important. The person can talk about anything or in any way he or she likes. If the boss does not like it, just quit and find another company. In societies where there are few human relations restraints, people can be more talkative, aggressive, straightforward, opinionated, and self-assertive.

Then what will happen in the future? Modern economic organizations are playing survival games domestically and internationally. Strong and efficient companies survive; weak and inefficient companies disappear from the market. Due to *johoka* or informatization, this survival game is becoming more and more international. In this competitive process, any strengths or secrets of strength held by a company tend to be imitated by its competitors. Therefore, it is very likely that the differences that exist between North American, European, and Japanese economic organizations will decrease in the future.

Until some 20 years ago, Western and Japanese experts both believed that almost all Japanese or Asian cultural characteristics were legacies of their feudal past. People thought that as Japan became modernized, it would become more and more like the United States. Communication experts thought that as Japan became more modernized, the Japanese communication pattern would become more similar to that in North America. However, we are not so sure anymore. One major reason is the combination of Japan's economic strength, its social and political stability, and its relative economic equality.

If certain Japanese cultural characteristics contribute to its economic strength, stability, and relative equality, the Japanese will try to preserve these characteristics, and other nations may try to imitate them. Even if they do not try to imitate them, they will be influenced by the ideas.

For example, American company executives are today criticized by other Americans for paying too much attention to short-term profits and too little attention to long-term gains. One reason why American managers are more concerned with short-term than long-term advantages is that they are not sure where they themselves will be 10 years from now. Some of them plan to sell themselves to another company by bringing a huge short-term profit to the company. That action, however, may be harmful to that company's long-term interest. If the company is only a place to earn money, however, and neither company executives nor employees have any emotional attachment to it, who cares what will happen to it after they leave? To do harm to the company for one's own profit is unethical even under the individualistic American system. Under pure individualism, however, to ignore the company's long-term interest for one's own personal interest is not unethical even for those in top management. The higher horizontal mobility is, the more prominent those tendencies become.

In the ongoing Structural Impediments Initiative (SII) to improve the trade imbalance between the United States and Japan, both sides are demanding of each other the kind of changes that traditionally have been considered as "interference in domestic affairs." One piece of "advice" that the Japanese side is giving the American side at SII negotiations is that the U.S. government should do something to make American company executives pay more attention to their companies' long-term interests rather than to their own short-term interests. If these practices are changed or modified in the future so that American managers become more concerned with the company's long-term interest, it may be considered in a broad sense as Japanese influence.

Most American experts on business management admit that the old American management philosophies, such as Taylorism or McNamaraism that pursued rationalism to the extreme by treating factory workers like parts of a machine, have been almost completely abandoned in recent years. More humanistic approaches to business management are now emphasized. In a public service advertisement broadcast several years ago on major networks in America, Walter Cronkite appealed for the increasing importance of teamwork and cooperation in American factories, using Japanese factories as an example. If the horizontal mobility of American managers and workers decreases and teamwork and human relations in factories are given greater emphasis, the American communication style may come closer to the Japanese style.

SUMMARY AND CONCLUSION

In this chapter, different interpersonal and organizational communication styles were compared and the reasons for differences were discussed. Many past studies have provided detailed descriptions of differences and suggested possible psychological variables behind them. The questions why and how those differences were created and maintained have been ignored, however. Concerns were often microscopic, and little attention was paid to historical and social backgrounds that might have created those differences. Without considering the macroscopic backgrounds, real understanding of the present state and, above all, prediction of the future are impossible.

Therefore, several important models with variables considered to determine or heavily influence interpersonal communication styles were discussed. It has been emphasized, by American scholars particularly, that interpersonal communication styles are determined by the extent to which the society is individualistic or collectivistic. Several fundamental problems regarding the concepts of individualism and collectivism were pointed out and discussed in detail. In relation to these discussions, a new concept of "modern collectivism" was proposed.

As indicated earlier, modern collectivism is supposed to be democratic and equitable. If it fails to meet these conditions, however, there is a danger that it will become fascism or another type of oppressive totalitarianism. Apart from those well-known classical problems of "excessive collectivism," a rather new phenomenon regarding modern collectivism is what Japanese call *shuudan ego* or "collectivistic egoism." This means people's "selfish" tendency to maximize their collective interests at the cost of other groups' interests.

This is not the same as classical ethnocentrism. Postwar Japanese foreign policies have not been particularly ethnocentric. Japanese prime ministers and other top government officials were all sincere in their efforts to settle Japan's trade and investment frictions with other nations. There have never been any conspiracies or plans on the government level to have Japanese industries dominate the world market. Despite that, certain behaviors of Japanese corporations are becoming a nuisance in many countries. One of the reasons is this collectivistic egoism. Just as individual egoism is a problem in individualistic societies, collectivistic egoism is a problem in collectivistic societies even under modern collectivism.

The degrees of homogeneity and heterogeneity also change as time goes by. Japan is obviously becoming less homogeneous than before due to the increase of foreign students, laborers, refugees, and international marriages. Japan is also becoming a major player in world politics and economy. The Japanese must explain their systems, beliefs, and culture to foreigners. In this sense, as Clark (1977) pointed out, Japan will eventually have to change itself from a human relations society to an ideological society. This change may make the traditional Japanese communication style more like the American.

Conversely, in North America the horizontal mobility of managers and employees, the practices of easy layoffs and selling of companies for short-term profits may decrease in the future, because these practices are considered to be among the reasons for the loss of competitiveness of American corporations. In addition, "new frontiers" have been lost that could have allowed Americans to restart businesses.

It is becoming clear that corporations that mechanically connect capital, labor, roles, and obligations by matter-of-fact contracts cannot beat corporations containing more "humane" elements such as loyalty, protection, benevolence, *aisha seishin* (corporate patriotism), solidarity, and mutual trust. This should be understandable if you think of competition between states. States based on solidarity, patriotism, and mutual trust are mightier than states without them. Americans understand this on the national level; then, why can they not understand this at the level of industry? Also, if population density affects people's communication styles, it is likely that the traditional American communication style may become more Japanese in the future.

Therefore, all things considered, Japanese communication style is likely to become more American, and American communication style is likely to become more Japanese. Although this conclusion may sound overly simple, Yoshikawa (1988b), who has lived in the United States for many years, writes: "While in the American culture, the holistic world view has gradually gained a place, so the atomistic world view has gained some prominence in Japanese society" (p. 178). Therefore, Americanization of Japanese communication style and Japanization of American communication style are both probable. The reasons are:

In the case of Japan: tendencies toward more heterogeneity and the resulting "ideologization" of Japanese culture and further democratization.

In the case of the United States: the change in management style in corporations, "loss of frontier," decrease in horizontal social mobility, and the increase in population density.

These are the grounds for convergence.

NOTES

1. Gill (1985, pp. 27-28) is critical of the popular Japanese claim that in a homogeneous society like Japan, people are less talkative, less straightforward, and less self-assertive, because they can understand each other relatively easily without verbal communication. He insists that in homogeneous societies people should feel more at home and comfortable and thus should be more talkative. It is true that one can become more frank, candid, and straightforward in one's family, because the relationship with one's family members is easier to cure than with neighbors or colleagues. Therefore, homogeneity may not necessarily explain why people are less talkative and straightforward. Homogeneity, however, seems to explain why people use ambiguous and indirect expressions.

2. Ben-Dasan (1972) called Japanese farmers "neighbor farmers." That referred to the tradition that Japanese farmers planted rice when their neighbors started to plant, transplanted into paddies and harvested when their neighbors started to do so. That was the safest way of life. "The cruelly exacting schedule imposed by campaign-style rice production" made it important for Japanese farmers to cooperate with each other. Through mutual cooperation, farmers could finish their work on time. Reischauer (1977, p. 17), Matsubara (1980), and Matsumura (1984, p. 184) also emphasize how important cooperation was in the Japanese style of rice production.

REFERENCES

Asahi Shimbun. (1989, July 28). Rohso kessei ni "no": Beikoku Nissan ["No" to unionization: Nissan U.S.A.], p. 8.

Barnlund, D. C. (1975). *Public and private self in Japan and the United States: Communicative styles of two cultures.* Tokyo: Simul Press.

Ben-Dasan, I. (1972). *The Japanese and the Jews.* New York: Weatherhill.

Chu, L. L. (1988). Mass communication theory: A Chinese perspective. In W. Dissanayake (Ed.), *Communication theory: The Asian perspective* (pp. 126-138). Singapore: Asian Mass Communication Research and Information Centre (AMIC).

Clark, G. (1977). *Nihonjin: Yuhkusa no gensen* [The Japanese tribe: Origins of a nation's uniqueness]. Tokyo: Saimaru Shuppankai.

Cobb, S. (1976). Social support as a moderator of life stress. *Psychomatic Medicine, 38,* 300-314.

Condon, J. C. (1980). *Ibunkakan komyunikeishon: Karuchah gyappu no rikai* [Cultural dimensions of communication]. Tokyo: Saimaru Shuppankai.

Doi, T. (1974). Some psychological themes in Japanese human relationships. In J. C. Condon & M. Saito (Eds.), *Intercultural encounters with Japan: Communication—contact and conflict* (pp. 17-26). Tokyo: Simul Press.

Edelstein, A. S., Ito, Y., & Kepplinger, H. M. (1989). *Communication and culture: A comparative approach.* New York: Longman.

Frager, R. (1970). Conformity and anticonformity in Japan. *Journal of Personality and Social Psychology, 15,* 203-210.

Gill, T. (1985). *Han Nihonjin ron* [Anti-Ninonjin ron book]. Tokyo: Kohsaku-sha.

Gudykunst, W. B. (1987). Cross-cultural comparisons. In C. R. Berger & S. H. Chaffee (Eds.), *Handbook of communication science* (pp. 847-889). Newbury Park, CA: Sage.

Gudykunst, W. B. (1989). Cultural variability in ethnolinguistic identity. In S. Ting-Toomey & F. Korzenny (Eds.), *Language, communication and culture: Current directions* (pp. 222-243). Newbury Park, CA: Sage.

Gudykunst, W. B., & Nishida, T. (1989). Theoretical perspectives for studying intercultural communication. In M. K. Asante & W. B. Gudykunst (Eds.), *Handbook of international and intercultural communication* (pp. 17-46). Newbury Park, CA: Sage.

Gudykunst, W. B., & Nishida, T. (1990). Communication in interpersonal relationships in Japan and the United States: Overview of a research program. *Bulletin of the Institute for Communication Research.* Keio University (Tokyo, Japan), *35,* 1-48.

Gudykunst, W. B., & Ting-Toomey, S. (1988). *Culture and interpersonal communication.* Newbury Park, CA: Sage.

Haga, Y. (1979). *Nihonjin no hyohgen shinri* [Psychology of Japanese expressions]. Tokyo: Chuo Kohron-sha.

Hall, E. T. (1976). *Beyond culture.* Garden City, NY: Doubleday.

Hamaguchi, E. (1977). *"Nihonjin rashisa" no saihakken* [The rediscovery of "Japanese-ness"]. Tokyo: Nihon Keizai Shimbun-sha. (Paperback published by: Tokyo: Kohdan-sha, 1988.)

Hamaguchi, E., & Kumon, S. (Eds.). (1982). *Nihonteki shudanshugi* [Japanese collectivism]. Tokyo: Yuhikaku.

Hofstede, G. (1980). *Culture's consequences: International differences in work-related values.* Beverly Hills, CA: Sage.

Hofstede, G. (1983). Dimensions of national cultures in fifty countries and three regions. In J. Deregowski, S. Dziurawiec, & R. Annis (Eds.), *Explications in cross-cultural psychology* (pp. 335-355). Lisse, Netherlands: Swets & Zeitlinger.

Ito, Y. (1989). Socio-cultural background of Japanese interpersonal communications style. *Civilisations* (Brussels, Belgium), *39*(1), 101-127.

Ito, Y., & Kohei, S. (1990). Practical problems in field research in Japan. In U. Narula & W. B. Pearce (Eds.), *Cultures, politics, and research programs: An international assessment of practical problems in field research* (pp. 89-121). Hillsdale, NJ: Lawrence Erlbaum.

Iwata, R. (1980). *Nihonteki sensu no keieigaku* [Japanese-style management]. Tokyo: Toyo Keizai Shimpo-sha.

Ju, Y. (1989). Chinese culture, yesterday and today: From a communication perspective. In G. Osborne & M. Madrigal (Eds.), *International communication: In whose interest?* (pp. 533-542). Canberra, Australia: University of Canberra, Centre for Communication and Information Research.

Kageyama, K. (1988, December 11). Nihongata no teichaku ka ridatsuka, magarikado no kankokushiki keiei [Is the Japanese management system settled in Korea? Korean management at a crossroad]. *Nihon Keizai Shimbun*, p. 14.

Kato, H. (1973). Nihon bunka to komyunikeishon [Japanese culture and communication]. In Y. Uchikawa, K. Okabe, I. Takeuchi, & A. Tsujimura (Eds.), *Kohza: Gendai no shakai to komyunikeishon, 5, Joho to seidatsu* (pp. 177-195). Tokyo: Tokyo Daigaku Shuppankai.

Kitamura, H. (1977). Komyunikeishon [Communication]. In T. Umesao (Ed.), *Kohaz: Hikakubunka, dai 5 kan, nihonjin no gijutsu* (pp. 263-285). Tokyo: Kenkyu-sha.

Klopf, D. W., Ishii, S., & Cambra, R. (1978, July 5). How communicative are the Japanese? *The Hawaii Times.*

Kunihiro, M. (1973). Nihonteki komyunikeishon no heisasei [Closed nature of Japanese communication]. In Y. Nagai & H. Rosovsky (Eds.), *Nichibei komyunikeishon gyappu* (pp. 133-160). Tokyo: Saimaru Shuppankai.

Kunihiro, M. (1976). *Ibunka ni hashi wo kakeru* [Bridging across cultures]. Tokyo: Eigo Kyoiku kyohgikai.

Leisure Development Center. (1983). *Nichi bei ou kachikan chohsa, dehta-hen* [Research on values in Japan, the United States, data book]. Tokyo: Author.

Matsubara, J. (1980). Chiiki shakai no ningen kankei [Human relations in local communities]. In H. Minami (Ed.), *Nihonjin no ningenkankei jiten* [Handbook of Japanese human relations] (pp. 182-193). Tokyo: Kohdan-sha.

Matsumura, T. (1984). Nihonteki komyunikeishon to fuhdo [Japanese communication and natural features]. In A. Tsujimura & T. Mizuhara (Eds.), *Komyunikeishon no shakai shinrigaku* (pp. 171-189). Tokyo: Tokyo Daigaku Shuppankai.

Midooka, K. (1990). Characteristics of Japanese-style communication. *Media, Culture and Society, 12*(4), 477-489.

Minami, H. (1971). *Psychology of the Japanese people.* Toronto: University of Toronto Press.

Minami, H. (1980). *Nihonjin no ningenkankei jiten* [Handbook of Japanese human relations]. Tokyo: Kohdan-sha.

Murakami, Y., Kumon, S., & Sato, S. (1979). *Bunmei to shiteno ie shakai* [Clan society as a civilization]. Tokyo: Chuo Kohron-sha.

Murdock, G. P., & Provost, C. (1973). Measurement of cultural complexity. *Ethnology, 12*, 379-392.

Nakane, C. (1970). *Japanese society.* Berkeley: University of California Press.

Nakane, C. (1974). The social system reflected in interpersonal communication. In J. C. Condon & M. Saito (Eds.), *Intercultural encounters with Japan: Communication-contact and conflict* (pp. 124-131). Tokyo: Simul Press.

Nakano, O. (1982). Nihongata soshiki ni okeru komyunikeishon to ishikettei [Communication and decision-making in Japanese style organizations]. In E. Hamaguchi & S. Kumon (Eds.), *Nihonteki shuhdanshugi* (pp. 143-168). Tokyo: Yuhikaku.

Naozuka, R. (1980). *Ohbeijin ga chinmoku suru toki: Ibunkakan no komyunikeishon* [When Westerners become silent: Communication across different cultures]. Tokyo: Taishumkan.

Naroll, R. (1983). *The moral order.* Beverly Hills, CA: Sage.

Naruke, N. (1974). Selected characteristics of Japanese communication. *Speech Education, 11,* 12-20.

Nishida, T. (1977). An analysis of a cultural concept affecting Japanese interpersonal communication. *Communication, 6,* 69-80.

Okabe, R. (1983). Cultural assumptions of East and West: Japan and the United States. In W. B. Gudykunst (Ed.), *Intercultural communication theory: Current perspectives* (pp. 21-44). Beverly Hills, CA: Sage.

Prime Minister's Office, Seishohnen Taisaku Hombu. (1984). *Nihon no seinen: Sekai seinen ishiki chohsa (dai 3kai) houkokusho* [Report of the third worldwide survey of youth's consciousness]. Tokyo: Printing Bureau, Ministry of Finance.

Public Opinion Research Institute, NHK. (Ed.). (1982). *Nihonjin to Amerikajin* [The Japanese and the Americans]. Tokyo: Nihon Hoso Shuppan Kyokai.

Reischauer, E. O. (1977). *The Japanese.* Cambridge, MA: Harvard University Press.

Sankei Shimbun. (1989, July 28). Nissan no UAW kamei wo hiketsu (Nissan rejects joining UAW), p. 10.

Sugimoto, Y. (1983). *Choh kanri rettoh Nippon* [Super controlled archipelago, Japan]. Tokyo: Kohbun-sha.

Suzuki, T. (1980). Gengo seikatsu [Language life]. In H. Minami (Ed.), *Nihonjin no ningen kankei jiten* (pp. 346-364). Tokyo: Kohdan-sha.

Ting-Toomey, S. (1989). Identity and interpersonal bonding. In M. K. Asante & W. B. Gudykunst (Eds.), *Handbook of international and intercultural communication* (pp. 351-373). Newbury Park, CA: Sage.

Toyama, S. (1976). Nihongo no tokushitsu [Characteristics of the Japanese language]. In S. Takashina (Ed.), *Kohza: hikakubunka, dai 7 kan, Nihonjin no kachikan* (pp. 301-324). Tokyo: Kenkyu-sha.

Triandis, H. C., Bontempo, R., Villareal, M. J., Asai, M., & Lucca, N. (1988). Individualism and collectivism: Cross-cultural perspectives on self-ingroup relationships. *Journal of Personality and Social Psychology, 54*(2), 323-338.

Tsujimura, A. (1987). Some characteristics of the Japanese way of communication. In D. L. Kincaid (Ed.), *Communication theory: Eastern and Western perspectives* (pp. 115-126). New York: Academic Press.

Whitehill, A. M., & Takizawa, S. (1968). *The other worker.* Honolulu: East-West Center Press.

Yoda, Y. (1989). *Nihon no kindaika: Chuhgoku tono hikaku ni oite* [Modernization of Japan: Comparisons with China]. Tokyo: Hokuju Shuppan.

Yoneyama, T. (1973). Basic notions in Japanese social relations. In J. Bailey (Ed.), *Listening to Japan* (pp. 91-110). New York: Praeger.

Yoshikawa, M. J. (1987). The "double swing": Model of Eastern-Western intercultural communication. In D. L. Kincaid (Ed.), *Communication theory: Eastern and Western perspectives* (pp. 319-329). New York: Academic Press.

Yoshikawa, M. J. (1988a). Cross-cultural adaptation and perceptual development. In Y. Y. Kim & W. B. Gudykunst (Eds.), *Cross-cultural adaptation: Current approaches* (pp. 140-148). Newbury Park, CA: Sage.

Yoshikawa, M. J. (1988b). Japanese and American modes of communication and implications for managerial and organizational behavior. In W. Dissanayake (Ed.), *Communication theory: The Asian perspective* (pp. 150-182). Singapore: Asian Mass Communication Research and Information Centre (AMIC).

PART III

CONCLUSIONS

Chapter 12

COMPARATIVE
COMMUNICATION RESEARCH:
FROM EXPLORATION TO CONSOLIDATION

Karl Erik Rosengren, Jack M. McLeod, and Jay G. Blumler

THE BODY OF THIS BOOK offers 10 comparative chapters by 14 authors of international standing from three continents and seven countries. What can we learn from their work?

WAYS FORWARD
FROM THE INDIVIDUAL STUDIES

In our introductory chapter we stressed the potential for creative, pathbreaking work inherent in comparative communication research. Even a cursory review of the preceding essays, with an eye to new questions and directions for further research, offers ample support for our thesis.

In his presentation of a comparative investigation of communication in the French and U.S. presidential election campaigns of 1988, *Swanson* reports that almost all the theoretically diverse analyses undertaken "explained features of campaign messages by pointing to the self-interests of actors . . . situated in roles and contexts defined within institutions of politics and mass communication that both cooperate and compete for dominance." This should spur fresh theorizing about (a) similarities and differences across a wider range of political communication systems as to how crucial actor roles are defined *and* (b) the consequences that may follow for the production of public knowledge about civic affairs in differently organized systems (cf. Blumler, Dayan, & Wolton, 1990, p. 277).

Although *Burgoon* expects many features of her theoretical model of nonverbal communication expectancy violations to be pancultural, she also suggests that:

> so-called human relations societies should tolerate a wider range of violations than ideological ones;
>
> there should be more room for ambiguity in interpreting violations in homogeneous cultures than in heterogeneous ones;
>
> violations may be more salient in collectivstic than in individualistic cultures.

Obviously these and similar hypotheses all have merit and call for a series of follow-up studies offering support or suggesting revisions, as the case may be. In short, they beg to be tested, by Burgoon and other scholars in the field.

Dutton and Vedel find that the development of cable television passed through essentially the same four stages in Britain, France, and the United States, even though the timing was different. How widespread and general is this evolutionary sequence? Could it reflect structural and/or cultural affinities shared by these three Western nations that might not apply to countries in other parts of the world?

Liebes and Livingstone report that the notion of entertainment television serving as a "cultural forum" for the exploration of significant social issues (Newcomb & Hirsch, 1984) seems to fit British soap operas better than their American counterparts. This invites (as the authors conclude) a similarly comparative analysis of audience reception. It also opens the door to a major hypothesis about how broadcasting system differences might affect the crucial relationship of entertainment to politics: In commercially competitive systems, television fiction will focus less often on contemporary social and moral issues and will present a narrower range of perspectives on them than in public service systems.

Hallin and Mancini attribute cross-national differences in Italian, American, and Soviet coverage of superpower summits to media system influences and factors of political context. As they point out, however, "we are just beginning to build up a large enough body of case studies to begin thinking about how to understand . . . interactions" between such factors. Clearly more such studies are needed—across other coverage occasions as well as other countries.

Rosengren presents evidence to suggest that a change in media structure, in particular the introduction of VCR, may be upsetting hitherto existing structural invariances in the relationship between class, gender, and mass media use in Sweden. As a guide to future research, he consequently asks the more encompassing question: "Is the structural invariance of individual media use (including causes and effects of that use) strong enough to survive the change of the media structure presently going on in Sweden and many other European countries?"

Nowak finds similarities and differences in the rhetoric and themes of magazine advertising in Sweden and the United States from the 1930s to the present day, both of which have implications for future research. His provisional conclusion—that the stable levels of informational appeals and nonrational persuasive techniques found are related to the basic functions of commercial advertising in a free enterprise market economy—needs to be examined in other capitalist societies. Much further research into advertising trends could also be based on his ideas about how advertising messages—although modified by an ever-present avoidance of controversial and divisive matters—respond to societal changes in "things to communicate about" and "what people/supposedly/want to hear about."

Chaffee and Chu present evidence to suggest that the purposive counterstructuring that has taken place in China has been successful to a considerable extent. Gender equality, for example, appears further advanced in China than in Taiwan or the United States. Because some other features of the old Confucian culture pattern seem to be living on beneath the surface, however, questions for future analysis arise from the possible impact of continuing modernization and an increasing exposure to Western mass media.

Following a critical review of other perspectives, *Ito* outlines a theory of the determinants of the interpersonal communication styles of different societies that emphasize certain differences in modern economic organization, particularly in the private sector. Because modern economic organizations are now increasingly involved domestically and internationally in what he calls "survival games," where secrets of the strength of one side are likely to be imitated by its competitors, Ito predicts a moderating of differences in modes of (economic) organizational communication in the future, with corresponding potentials for interpersonal communication convergence as well.

In addition to bringing forth many specific concepts, findings, propositions, and questions that deserve to be pursued, the chapters also raise a number of more general issues, with important implications for future comparative communication research. We now turn to some of these implications.

STRATEGIES AND OPTIONS
IN COMPARATIVE RESEARCH

Despite the heterogeneity of the research collected here, the diverse set of authors share common interests. Above all, those interests include the development of theory. None appears to do comparative research simply for the sake of comparison. Each has used a larger than usual increment of comparison, seeking more striking variation in space and time context than in the usual place and time-point comparisons. This requires them to adopt strategies:

to expand existing theory or build new theory,
to construct research teams to conduct comparative research, and
to find ways and means to deal with the problems and pitfalls involved in making larger comparisons.

OVERALL STRATEGIES
FOR COMPARATIVE RESEARCH

In his interesting chapter, "Managing Theoretical Diversity," David Swanson lists three main strategies for conducting comparative research:

forming teams of like-minded scholars (e.g., Converse & Pierce, 1986);
starting with a more diverse team of theorists united by a common specified formulation of research questions (e.g., the more than a dozen researchers from nine EC nations described in Blumler, 1983b); and
to begin with researchers intentionally chosen so as to represent diverse theoretical perspectives (e.g., the U.S.-French 1988 campaign study of which Swanson himself is a member).

What Swanson offers us is actually a typology *in nascendi.* What would be the relevant dimensions of such a typology?

We could certainly think of a number of such dimensions, but a closer look at Swanson's chapter reveals that the dimensions actually

TABLE 12.1 Four Strategies for Comparative Research

		Theoretical Diversity	
		Yes	No
	Yes	1. Multitheoretical	2. Unitheoretical
Primarily Theory-Driven			
	No	3. Theoretically open	4. Atheoretical

implied by him could be labeled "degree of theoretical diversity," and "degree of theoretical drivenness." Although both dimensions could be regarded as continua, it is obvious that Swanson regards them as dichotomies. As is so often the case, by crossing the two implicit dimensions of a list such as Swanson's, we arrive at that simplest of two-dimensional typologies, the fourfold table. We thus obtain four, rather than his three, different types of comparative research (cf. Table 12.1). In terms of this typology, Swanson's three examples will be found in cells 2, 3, and 1 respectively.

Although Table 12.1 may be regarded as the outcome of a somewhat pedestrian exercise of taxonomy, it does possess heuristic value of its own. For instance, an attempt to classify the eight substantive chapters of this volume quickly shows that Cell 4 represents an empty set. Contrary to the provocative assumptions made by Beniger in Chapter 3, then, comparative communication research is not always atheoretical. Lack of theory may have been predominant once and is probably not uncommon today, but it certainly no longer is the dominant characteristic of contemporary comparative communication research. Cell 4 thus represents an early stage of comparative studies: the dominant mode of comparative study in the 1950s and 1960s.

Some scholars would even question whether an atheoretical, data-driven stage has ever existed at all in serious scholarly and scientific endeavors. According to this view, we always have some sort of theory, albeit our theories are sometimes implicit and, therefore, less amenable to discard, revision, or extension. The implicit theories, of course, need to be made explicit. When it comes to comparative studies between countries, the trick seems to be to translate the names of national units into terms of more theoretically fruitful dimensions, a tactic explicitly recommended 20 years ago by Przeworski and Teune (1970) and more or less spontaneously reinvented many times since then. The tactic is put to good use in many chapters of this volume (see, for instance, the chapters by Ito and by Dutton and Vedel).

Asking for explicit theory, comparative research thus has something to offer compilers of media statistics. For one thing, it tells the naive compiler that there is a world outside Verona, and that there were heroes long before Achilles. Actually, without the widened perspective offered by comparative research, even the best collection of statistical indicators may sometimes function much like a prison to communication studies. Spurred by the comparative perspective, however, the researcher may find ways and means of escaping from that prison, often by combining in an innovative way sets of indicators traditionally not regarded as mutually relevant. The three chapters by Nowak, Ito, and Chaffee and Chu offer good examples of such innovative combinations, allowing their authors to break successfully out of a prison built by ever so benevolent compilers of statistical indicators.

Where would those three chapters by Nowak, Ito, and Chaffee and Chu be located in the typology presented in Figure 12.1, one may ask. All three chapters more or less systematically apply different theoretical approaches to the phenomena under study. They thus fit in best with Cell 1, representing the *Multitheoretical* approach.

Different as they may appear on the surface, the chapters by Burgoon, and by Liebes and Livingstone are similar in the sense that both apply one single theoretical perspective: theories of interpersonal communication and feminist theory, respectively. These two chapters, then, are best classified as *Unitheoretical* (Cell 2). The two chapters by Dutton and Vedel and Hallin and Mancini are probably best classified as *Theoretically open* (Cell 3). Both teams draw upon a set of different hypotheses and theories that may be used to explain and/or interpret their findings, while they choose not to bind themselves to any one among these at least partly conflicting sets of hypotheses and theories—at least not within the framework of a single book chapter.

Before ending our little taxonomic exercise we would like to stress that the four cells of Table 12.1 are, of course, best regarded as ideal types, in reality only seldom met in their pure form. A case in point is represented by Rosengren's chapter, which draws on more than one theory for explanation and interpretation. But as a rule he does not systematically confront different theories with one and the same set of data in order to eliminate—or find support for—one among those theories. Instead, he uses different theories one at a time, for different subproblems. Rather than multitheoretical, therefore, his approach may be best characterized as "sequentially unitheoretical." Streaks of the same approach may be discerned in some other chapters as well, e.g., in those by Ito and Nowak.

Typologies are one thing, then; living reality, another. In reality, we often meet with continua rather than with dichotomies. And in reality, the dimensions are many more than the two or three dimensions made explicit in our typologies. All the same, without typologies—however primitive they may appear—reality would overwhelm us by her sheer richness in variation. Typologies may thus provide the overview necessary to raise our choices of research strategies from the level of intuitive hunches to that of explicit decision-making. For instance, although each one of the three theoretically oriented cells in Table 12.1 has its value, and although in some situations only one of them may be applicable, it is nevertheless the case that Cell 1 represents the intuitively most appealing alternative. So the question becomes: How do we get there?

There are two main paths: from Cell 4 via Cell 2 or Cell 3, respectively. It would seem that the choice depends very much on the circumstances. Actually, in many cases it may well be that the problem chosen, the stage of theoretical development, the availability of data will not offer the individual researcher much choice. But for the field as a whole it might all the same be worthwhile to discuss a strategy. We believe that the overall situation of today's comparative communication research invites a theoretically open approach, later on to be followed up at the multitheoretical level. We hypothesize, therefore, that purely unitheoretical research is probably the exception rather than the rule in contemporary comparative communication studies. Furthermore, if in the unitheoretical case the theory should not be very precisely articulated, it may well be that the road from Cell 2 to Cell 1 should—and will—go by way of Cell 3.

The road to Cell 1 from Cell 2 by way of Cell 3 may turn out to be especially rewarding if jointly used by fellow travelers otherwise working within the confines of distinctly different research traditions. Such undertakings may yet be few and far between, but some examples do exist. For instance, although themselves belonging to radically different research traditions within the broader field of audience research, Jensen and Rosengren (1990) managed to hammer out a systematic description of the five traditions that they were able to discern within that broad area. Almost by definition, such theoretically open research overviews should have more to offer than more unitheoretical undertakings and thus may well pave the way for future, multitheoretical, comparative studies. If nothing else, the example shows that the composition of a research team working in comparative studies is well worth some reflections of its own.

TEAMS AND STRATEGIES

The typological exercise presented in the previous section was not undertaken for its own sake. The four cells of the typology, of course, represent ideal types. They are abstractions, in reality only seldom—if ever—found in their pure form. Nevertheless, the actual organization of comparative research is heavily dependent on the type of research undertaken, and vice versa. It may therefore be advantageous to relate the typology of the previous section to the schema for comparative teams presented by Dutton and Vedel in Chapter 5.

Dutton and Vedel distinguish between two basic types for the organization of comparative research teams:

> One team of scholars conducts a number of cases studies of foreign nations; several national teams cooperate on studies of their own countries.

Although both types have their advantages and disadvantages, they are more or less fit for implementing the different types of strategies presented in Table 12.1. Obviously, the single team (and, a fortiori, the single scholar) is best fitted for a unitheoretical strategy, whereas the multiteam project or research program is better fitted to realize the theoretically open or multitheoretical strategies. As Dutton and Vedel point out, however, both approaches also have their disadvantages. As a matter of fact, the two authors maintain that whereas the latter organization runs the risk of producing only a juxtaposition of a number of descriptive national studies, the former approach runs the risk of ending up in pure ethnocentrism. They strongly recommend, therefore, the tactic used by themselves: that each study be conducted by at least two investigators, one native to the country under study, the other a foreigner. Especially in cases where the collaborators have equal status, this will lessen the danger of one person or perspective dominating.

Yet another team variant is exemplified by the tactic used by the group studying the 1979 elections held simultaneously in nine nations to elect the first European parliament (Blumler, 1983a). In addition to their national diversity, the group of researchers was also characterized by considerable variation in theoretical interests. The obvious solution was thus to let each scholar or group of scholars work on data from all the countries under study, focusing, however, on different and yet related topics and theoretical problems. This seemingly inconsequential organizational solution proved to have profound consequences on many levels of the scholarly work undertaken by the group. Manifestly, it brought about a more explicitly theoretical approach, rather than just a descriptively comparative one. In addition, it had the latent function of creating a closer contact between members coming from different countries and different research traditions. Altogether, the simple organizational decision thus proved to exert a decisive influence on the overarching structure of the whole research endeavor, including the way in which the presentation of the final report was organized.

Obviously, there is no handy rule of thumb available for the organization of comparative research teams. Each comparative problem, and each team, will call for its own solution. But it may well be that some variant or combination of the solutions found by Dutton and Vedel and the team working on the European election study will represent a fruitful organizational counterpart to Cell 3 in the typology emanating from Swanson's chapter. In the final analysis, the main task is to ensure that the approach be not atheoretical, and not a number of juxtaposed unitheoretical studies, but actually a set of theoretically open studies that will gradually produce mature, multitheoretical comparative research (Cell 1). As is so often the case, practical, down-to-earth organizational matters prove to have quite far-reaching consequences for the theoretical, methodological, and empirical outcomes of our studies.

It may be added, finally, that there is at least still one other distinct way to organize comparative research. A single researcher may carry out retrospective comparisons over time and space, drawing on secondary analyses of outstanding work by a number of previous workers in the field (or adjacent fields). This "single-scholar-many-studies-strategy" is the approach used by Beniger in his interesting chapter: retrospective comparisons of path-breaking studies undertaken in seemingly unrelated fields. In principle, at least, it is also the approach of the traditional review of research within a given area, sometimes developed into more or less full-fledged meta-analyses (Rosenthal, 1991).

In her chapter, Judee Burgoon convincingly shows what important results a theoretically well focused research overview can produce. Actually, Dr. Burgoon was invited by the conference theme organizers to

apply a comparative perspective to her previous theoretical and empirical research on interpersonal communication. The fact that this task
could be so successfully carried out tells us something about the possibilities inherent in the comparative approach. It is also a tribute to Dr.
Burgoon's theoretical creativity, of course. Similarly—and also focusing on interpersonal communication—Youichi Ito in his chapter uses a
research overview in order to create a macro-oriented framework fur-
thering our understanding of different patterns of interpersonal processes at the micro level.

Under felicitous circumstances the overview approach may well be
able to bring about, if not a paradigm shift (if there are such things as
paradigms in the humanities and the social sciences), at least some
change of direction in normal science or scholarship. To the creative
mind, this approach no doubt opens up fascinating possibilities, best
explored, perhaps, by a humanistically-oriented scholar combining
some erudition with the fertile mind of the potential pioneer.

COMPARISONS OF INCOMPARABILIA

The basic question to be put and answered by all comparativists concerns, of course, what to compare. It would seem there is a natural order
in all attempts at comparison. To the unreflective mind (and sometimes
to the very sophisticated mind as well) the natural starting point is the
comparison between things similar to each other in one way or the
other. This is where compilers of statistics start, producing (at considerable costs in terms of time and money) all those valuable figures
about this and that, figures so often missing and incomplete when
needed, so often taken for granted when found—and yet often derided
by laypeople, scholars, and scientists alike.

The next step may be to turn from things to activities: the number of
hours worked, slept, and so on, in different societies and periods of
time, ad nauseam. Following this, perhaps, is a turn from things and
activities to more abstract qualities (say, prices and changes in prices),
and then a step from simple numbers, averages, and percentages, to
rates of change, relations between averages and rates, and so on. And
on it goes.

A decisive step in the natural history of the act of comparison is
represented by the insight that it may be more productive to compare
dissimilar than similar things—and much more fun. The only thing

necessary to do so is the capacity (seemingly innate in most human beings) to raise the level of abstraction. Apples and oranges are fruits, as James Beniger so strongly underlines in his chapter in this volume, and as fruits they are comparable. The level of abstraction can be raised in more ways than one, however. In order to raise the level of abstraction, one may turn from comparisons of isolated things to comparisons of:

> structures formed by things,
> processes going on within structures, and
> functions of seemingly different things, structures, or processes.

Functional comparisons are notoriously risky endeavors, but in the hands of a perceptive and creative scholar, they may be quite revealing (cf. again Beniger's chapter). Not coincidentally, there are a number of explicit or implicit functional comparisons to be found in the chapters of this volume.

At the bottom of all functional comparisons lies the (more or less explicit) creation of some abstract dimensions along which seemingly different phenomena may be compared. A good example of what such dimensions may look like, and how they may be used to "compare incomparabilia" may be found in Figure 5.1 of Dutton and Vedel's chapter on the dynamics of cable television in three countries. By means of a typology based on the two dimensions (promotion/restriction of cable, public-led/market-led cable developments), Dutton and Vedel are able to demonstrate strikingly parallel developments of the otherwise seemingly rather different cable policies of the United States, the United Kingdom, and France—developments that may, of course, take place within sometimes widely different periods of calendar time (cf. below).

Liebes and Livingstone in their chapter look at how superficially identical feminine role functions seem to be quite differentially shaped and located in the role structure of British and American soap operas. They end up with the overall summary that whereas British soap operas offer "a world that is communal, inclusive and systemic," the world of American soap operas is "individualistic, exclusive, and dyadic." This result, convincing as it may appear, raises two different problems touched upon by the authors. One is how results obtained by means of the qualitative analysis adopted by Liebes and Livingstone can be corroborated by means of detailed quantitative analysis satisfying elementary demands for reproducibility, reliability, validity, and so on. The other, and perhaps the more problematic one, concerns the extent to which it is possible to generalize from a sample of two-times-two soap operas. Obviously, case studies of this size should not be based on random sampling. Rather, the sample of cases must be strategic, heeding concepts, dimensions, and levels vital to the theoretical problem in question.

Some such concepts, dimensions, and levels coming to mind when reading Liebes and Livingstone's chapter are related to possible differences in national culture (homogeneous/heterogeneous), media system (commercial/public service), organization of production (small scale/large scale), type of soap opera (daytime/prime time), age of soap opera (cf. p. 282), and audience structure (stratification by way of class versus status). Variation in all of these dimensions might be reflected in any slice of popular culture. Obviously, in order to cover those dimensions, one would need more than four soap operas from two countries. Although argumentation along these lines does make us wary about the type of conclusions to be drawn from case studies, it hardly tarnishes the luster of the Liebes and Livingstone work. It is a dilemma haunting all case studies: "How many cases *do we need?*—And how many *can we cover?*"

Actually, the full burden of resolving this dilemma satisfactorily cannot realistically be shouldered by individual scholars or even teams. It is a responsibility to be shared across the field as a whole, by way of further extending comparative case studies over the fundamental dimensions of both time and space.

DIMENSIONS OF TIME AND SPACE

Different as they may appear, all problems discussed in the previous section refer primarily to the interface between, on the one hand, the personal or intellectual organization of a research endeavor, and on the other hand, the potential outcome of that endeavor. Turning in this section of our chapter to the basic dimensions of comparative communication research, we shall move closer to the heart of the matter.

THE BASIC ROLE OF TIME AND SPACE IN COMMUNICATION STUDIES

In the introductory chapter, we noted that comparative studies may be based on comparisons over time or space, or both. Interestingly, among the primarily substantively oriented chapters in this volume, only Judee Burgoon's chapter can be said to be absent of any reference to temporal comparisons beyond short-term experimental change. The reason for this, we believe, is that Dr. Burgoon's main interest is to seek and find universals in human interpersonal communications. What she is after are characteristics of human communication that transcend societies. For an often experimental science such as interpersonal communication, the simplest way to find universals is comparisons over space.

In this context it is well worth noticing that, regardless of whether we compare over space or time, the important thing is not space and time as such. As a rule, both time and space are just proxies or vehicles for arriving at different social systems (just as age is a proxy for arriving at different stages of development or maturation among human beings). As proxies, they are—at least in principle—equivalent. They both offer the essential thing: the opportunity to compare at least two different sociocultural systems to each other, in order to arrive at a deeper understanding of our results than would have otherwise been possible.

An interesting complication in this connection is the fact that in order to fully understand comparisons over time, we have to make that basic distinction between, on the one hand, calendar time, and on the other, social time (Elias, 1988). There is no need to assume some variant of linear development theory in order to realize that different societies at the same moment of calendar time may be situated in very different social time.

It should also be noted that different chunks of social time usually do not follow the same pace—they proceed at different tempi. This holds true from a grand macro perspective (the difference, say, between the social time of an isolated Amazonian tribe and that of downtown New York), over organizational differences in social time (say, the difference between the development of cable systems in the U.K. and the United States), right down to the micro-level (say, the tempo of interpersonal communication in northern and southern Europe).

A special case of social time is fictional time—a classic problem among historians and analysts of literature (Church, 1963; Higdon, 1977; Kort, 1985; Meyerhoff 1955; Ricoeur, 1984-1988; Thomsen, 1990). Fictional time, be it that of classic literary works or modern soap operas, is different from other forms of social time in that it can be more easily manipulated. There are at least two fictional times (the time of the story-teller and the time of the story) that, each in their own way, have to be related to the calendar and social time of the listeners, readers, and viewers. An additional complication is that some stories are told over very long times. The epos of antiquity, the medieval *chansons de geste*, the Viking sagas were told and retold over centuries. In a related but different way, some soap operas have been running for decades. The span of fictional time covered by them may or may not coincide with calendar time. Obviously, listeners and viewers having stayed with a given soap opera for years or even decades will experience it and its fictional time differentially from newcomers to that soap opera.

All these time-related problems are no doubt well worth considering. As media scholars, we may all have something to learn from those patient, penetrating, and time-consuming literary analyses so common among representatives of more traditional literary erudition (cf. Jensen & Rosengren, 1990).

Finally it must not be forgotten that although calendar and various types of social time are different, they may always be related to each other. Much as geographical and cultural distance may be compared, social time can be expressed in terms of calendar time, and vice versa. Indeed, the fact that this is so is a precondition—actually, a *sine qua non*—for comparisons over time. When comparing different social times we always use calendar time as our yardstick, implicitly or explicitly. To understand difference and change, we need constant and general concepts and parameters, valid over both time and space.

Time and space, of course, are inherently interrelated. Space always rests in time, time in space. Comparisons over space, then, often imply also comparisons over time, in the sense that different societies may be located at differential stages of development and may be moving in the tempi of very different social times. In order to control for this, one may sometimes be forced to compare societies over extended periods of time, as exemplified in the three chapters by Dutton and Vedel, Nowak, and Chaffee and Chu. These are macro comparisons, of course, but in such macro comparisons one may sometimes come very close to the distinctions between cohort (generational), maturational (age), and situational effects developed within longitudinal studies at the micro level and in this volume exemplified by Rosengren's chapter on invariance and change in individual media use.

For instance, the Swedish and American advertising systems studied by Kjell Nowak may have been around for roughly the same number of calendar years. By and large, they are thus equally old. But the effects from the two surrounding societies are not to be neglected and should be expressed in terms of social time. They may be observed only by means of simultaneous comparisons over both time and space—comparisons that could be, speculatively at least, collated with comparisons between panels from different cohorts, with a view to disentangling situational, generational, and maturational effects. In a similar vein, Chaffee and Chu seek comparisons over time and space (China and Taiwan during various phases of the postwar period), allowing them at least tentatively to disentangle the effects exerted on an overall Confucian culture by the traumatic experiences following in the wake of general modernization carried out at differential pace, and under radically different social, economic, and political conditions.

An additional advantage of combined temporal and spatial comparisons, finally, is that simultaneous comparisons between societies located at different stages of development may provide good opportunities to carry out those sophisticated arguments about functional alternatives, functional equivalence, and so on, so eloquently called for in the chapter by James Beniger (cf. also previous arguments in this chapter). As a matter of fact, such functional comparisons may be found both in Judee Burgoon's basically atemporal chapter and in Chaffee and Chu's primarily longitudinally oriented chapter.

A WORLD SYSTEM?

An interesting result turning up in different chapters of the volume has a bearing on the often-discussed problem of the emergence of a communicative world system, appearing in the literature under different names from McLuhan's "global village" to Herbert Schiller's (and many others') "cultural imperialism." The question plays a central role in Hallin and Mancini's chapter, which offers striking illustrations of the tendency toward a global village, interpreted by the two authors in (literally) dramatic terms, their interpretation actually spanning millenia.

The role of the media in this process is seen by Hallin and Mancini as double: "They are both the narrators of the drama and a character in it." The story is told to us from the "walls of journalists," just as more than two thousand years ago the battles outside the scene were told to the audiences of Greek tragedies from the walls of the rotunda. And at the same time the journalists act much as the chorus in a Greek tragedy, "expressing through its fears, hopes, questions, and judgments the feelings of the spectators who make up the civic community," as Hallin and Mancini express it.

Although this *Theatrum mundi* writ large may be interesting as such, to the comparative scholar the tendency toward a communicative world system—a system of shared symbols—does raise an intriguing methodological question. Comparative studies imply comparisons between bounded systems, we noted in our introductory chapter. To the extent, then, that our communicative systems are not bounded any more, they could not be made the object of comparative studies, it might be argued. The processes of flow and diffusion of symbols within that single world system would take the place of comparative studies of a number of bounded systems. The counterargument, however, is obvious.

In the first place—as Hallin and Mancini are, of course, well aware—the communicative world system has not yet quite arrived. On the contrary, it is developing at a very differential pace in different parts of the world, thus actually inviting comparative research in and by itself.

Second, even if and when a world symbol system should be common to all of us, we would no doubt keep the regional, national, and local symbol systems of our own for a very long time to come. The interplay between the common world system and those spatially more restricted systems would actually offer fertile ground for a large number of comparative studies, forerunners of which have, as a matter of fact, already made their entrance upon the scene (cf., for instance, Gurevitch, 1989; Kivikuru, 1988; Liebes & Katz, 1990; Silj, 1988).

Such future studies might do well to heed Hallin's and Mancini's basic distinction between, on the one hand, media events as implying a symbolic constitution of a global community of values, and on the other, media events as building public spheres for sometimes quite lively discussions of central issues of conflicting views. The distinction combines in a fruitful way consensus-oriented Durkheimian sociology of culture with conflict-oriented, Marxist or Marxisant sociology of power and economics. This is a central dimension of the scholarly discussion between various "quasi-paradigms" that has been going on for decades (Rosengren, 1989). The fact that the comparative study of media events brings this problem to the fore, and suggests an approach to it (albeit in a limited area), does bode well for future comparative studies of international communication on a global scale. Such conceptual innovations may then be followed up at the more complex level of explicit hypotheses and theories. We are approaching the fundamental tasks of comparative research.

THREE FUNDAMENTAL TASKS
OF COMPARATIVE RESEARCH

In all comparative studies, be they temporally or spatially oriented, there are three fundamentally different, basic tasks to be carried out—the tasks of:

(1) identifying a set of basic parameters and their structural interrelationships,

(2) measuring the parameter values, as well as assessing the strength of their relationships, and

(3) comparing differences and similarities in parameter values and structural relationships over space, as well as charting the development of parameter values and structural relationships over time.

The first of the three tasks is primarily a theoretical one, the second is an empirical one, and the third represents the essence of comparative research in that the empirical measurements and comparisons involved in the task lead the researcher back to basic theoretical problems, often by way of overcoming fundamental methodological problems (for instance, that of comparing the seemingly incomparable).

In order to be really successful, comparative research demands that—at least in the long run—all three types of tasks be solved. There is a natural order in which to solve the tasks, and it is only in the nature of things that progress is quite differential in varied areas and fields of research. In our case, two widely different stages are represented by the two chapters by Burgoon and Liebes and Livingstone, respectively, with the rest of the chapters falling somewhere in between.

What Liebes and Livingstone do in a relatively unexplored area is to try to identify a set of basic parameters and to offer some informed guesses about their levels and about their structural interrelationships. Burgoon, on the other hand, has at her disposital a number of fairly well organized studies having already solved tasks (1) and (2) above. She is thus able to move on to task (3), often ending up with the suggestion that the parameters and structural relationships identified in the different studies at hand are indeed central to all interpersonal communication, so that what remains is to chart the range of values to be expected for the parameters and their interrelationships within different sociocultural systems.

Burgoon's fascinating results thus suggest that comparative studies may sometimes even let the possibility of universals in communication loom just above the horizon. More institutionally anchored as are, for instance, Rosengren's comparative studies, he must of necessity remain satisfied with producing increased knowledge about the relative stability over time—as well as the generality over space—of a number of parameters and their interrelationships. Similarly, both Nowak's and Dutton and Vedel's results suggest some generality over time and space—granted, of course, the fundamental difference between calendar and social time.

The chapters by Hallin and Mancini (Chapter 7) and Chaffee and Chu (Chapter 10), finally, are closer to the Liebes and Livingstone end of the continuum. They still must wrestle with the difficult tasks of establishing the basic theoretical dimensions and suggesting ways and means of measuring those dimensions and assessing their interrelationships. Yet what measurements are within reach in their pioneering studies do suggest important similarities and differences between communication in different social systems—similarities and differences that will in their turn offer possibilities for continued theoretical and methodological analyses with a view later on to arriving at more specific knowledge about the parameters and their relationships.

We conclude here by pointing out that the theoretical task of comparative communication research at its most highly developed stage will be especially demanding, because it calls for an interplay between theorizing of two kinds. On the one hand, there will be theories about substance, that is, about a specified body of communication phenomena. Thinking illustratively of the interests of a few of our authors, substance-focused conceptualization might include theories about:

> how media construct a political reality that audiences may (or may not) absorb;
> influences on policies for the adoption of a communication innovation, like cable television;
> mechanisms shaping reactions to violations of communication expectancies; or
> explanations of age-related trends in television consumption.

On the other hand, there will be theories about the organization of systems (spatial or temporal), that is, about formal and formative dimensions along which such systems might vary, and how certain substantive consequences could vary with them. The priorities of comparative scholars will naturally vary in these terms. Among our authors, Burgoon seems most substantively driven, and Ito most systematically oriented. Comparative research will be richer, however, when both modes of theorizing are explicitly harnessed so as to fortify each other, not only at the interpersonal level, but at the organizational and societal levels as well (cf. below).

FUTURE DIRECTIONS IN
COMPARATIVE COMMUNICATION RESEARCH

Comparative communication research—just as so much other communication research—could be likened to a number of commodities in a supermarket, lying beside each other, ordered after some measure of similarity, but with few other relations between them. The traditional organization of conventions and conferences in the field strengthens this impression. Indirectly, at least, this rather unimaginative lack of intellectual structure is probably one of the causes behind the lack of cumulativity that unfortunately still characterizes much comparative communication research—and some other traditions in the field as well, we note in passing and with rather mixed feelings. In its turn, the lack of cumulativity has important consequences for our possibilities to assess the level of generality obtained by our results or—differently put —the degree of specificity to be expected from them.

In the following sections we will discuss some problems related to cumulativity, generality and specificity.

CUMULATIVITY

What are the causes of restricted cumulativity, one might ask. We feel there are at least two different types of causes: organizational and intellectual. Let us start with the former.

At many conferences in our field, the presentations are organized in terms of rather traditional divisions between more or less taken-for-granted areas of research delimited by way of institutions (politics, culture, etc.), levels (interpersonal, organizational, etc.), or media (TV, radio, cable, satellites). In its way, this may be quite functional, of course—especially in the short run and in an initial phase of the intellectual organization of an emerging discipline.

In the long run, however, these traditional divisions have to be transcended, we feel, or at least be given a shaking up from time to time. One way to move in that direction is to increase the number of thematically organized sessions or symposiums, transgressing the usual borders between divisions prevailing between the more conventional program items offered at our conferences. A good theme for such sessions, for instance, has been and will be for some time to come, comparative studies. (This theme, it may be noted, has already become a recurring feature of some conferences in the field.) Another step in that direction may be an increased cooperation between international organizations in the field (IAMCR, ICA, IIC, etc.). Perhaps the promotion of world regional organizations in the field undertaken by UNESCO may also be of some help in this respect, but all this will no doubt call for considerable time to be realized fully.

An important institutional factor of vital importance to any field of research is the organization of its funding. The fact that a substantial portion of the monies for communication research is intended primarily for applied research may have some unfortunate consequences here, because grantors of money for applied research quite naturally tend to think in terms of short-term solutions to narrowly defined practical problems, rather than in terms of long-term research focusing on abstract, generally conceived research problems. There is actually an educational problem here that may be solved only by sustained efforts from the professional organizations in our field.

Regardless of its institutional organization, we must not forget the obvious fact that the amount of funding available for travel and international research projects shows considerable variation between countries and over time. For instance, funds for such purposes in the United States have diminished markedly as compared to the relatively abundant support available in the first decades after World War II. The failure of development projects, the scars of Vietnam, and the political situation during the past decade have made the present U.S. political climate less conducive to generating funding from either governmental agencies or private foundations. Although most of the world's governments are not sufficiently affluent to support comparative research, there is perhaps more hope for support for comparative studies from, say, the European Community, as well as from rapidly growing nations such as Germany, Japan, and perhaps other nations on the Pacific Rim. On the positive side, we should also note recent developments within technologies such as electronic mail and rapid delivery systems that at least make the "nitty-gritty" of intellectual exchange more efficient.

Although it is no argument against trying them, the organizational avenues to an increased cumulativity in our field by and large seem to offer prospects of only rather modest progress. What about the more intellectually oriented avenues?

Paradoxically, one way to achieve increased cumulativity in comparative communication studies may be to try to increase the heterogeneity of the field. We thus need to *broaden the range of cases under study.* This may be done in a number of ways, one of which is strikingly simple: to increase the number of spatial units to be compared.

Although the chapters in this volume build on comparisons of communications in a number of countries on three continents, all chapters except Rosengren's have at least one leg planted in U.S. soil. This may be methodologically well motivated by the fact that the United States could be taken to be one of the technologically most advanced countries in the world, thus to be fruitfully used as a source of benchmark data to be compared with technologically less advanced countries. Yet it is a sad fact that most comparative communications studies cover just a small number of countries in Northwestern Europe and North America. There are some signs, though, that this will change in the not too distant future, so that we will be able to learn from a number of comparative studies including countries in Eastern Europe, the Pacific Rim, and some developing countries. In-region collaboration might be less costly to fund, and freedom to explore in-region patterns without reference to U.S. conditions might inspire new and fruitful conceptualizations.

Such comparisons between widely different and yet in some respects similar countries will no doubt have much to offer, not least for descriptive purposes. Especially the first comparisons between countries formerly not compared do possess an "exoticism value," the importance of which should by no means be underestimated. In order to become theoretically really fruitful, however, these comparisons must gradually leave the stage of regarding countries as units interesting per se, regarding them instead as cases representing different values on theoretically central and fruitful dimensions (see Blumler & Gurevitch, 1975; Gurevitch, 1989; Kohn, 1989).

The sooner this difficult but extremely important change comes about, the better (cf. above). It has its natural counterpart in comparisons over time, in which periods of different and/or identical calendar time may be regarded as representing different and/or identical chunks of social time, in their turn representing different values on theoretically central dimensions. (There is a strong need for *temporal classification* here: we still lack a reasonable communicative periodization. For a daring attempt in that direction, however, see Namenwirth & Weber, 1987.)

A second, quite different way of broadening the range of cases under study would be comparisons over levels of society. Comparisons over levels, of course, represent a classic methodological problem in sociology (individual versus ecological correlations), but it would be a serious mistake to reduce it to just a technical problem. Greater sensitivity to levels of analysis is of considerable importance in correctly identifying sources of difference and similarity in comparative research (Eulau, 1986; Pan & McLeod, 1991; Price, 1988).

To pick just one example from the many opportunities for level comparisons offered in the chapters of this volume: As we have already mentioned, it would be very interesting to see whether the analyses presented in Liebes and Livingstone's chapter would hold up at the audience level. What one could envision here is no less than a whole new series of comparative reception analyses combining insightful content analyses (quantitative and qualitative) with equally insightful audience analyses.

Generalizing the argument, nations as units, objects, or contexts of analysis can be seen as composites of structures and processes at various levels: total society (e.g., the stratification system), states and local communities, formal organizations and social movements, and microsocial systems (e.g., families and work groups). Two societies might be relatively similar at certain levels and quite different at others. In addition, institutions and structures in any given society are apt to be changing at differing rates. A careful unpacking and understanding of levels, therefore, should be quite instrumental in helping to reduce the confounding of variables in analyses over space and time.

The interplay between different levels, between macro and micro, structure and agency, society and individual, is indeed central to all social science, and not least to communication studies. For instance, the relationship between culture regarded as a macro phenomenon ("societal culture") and as a micro phenomenon ("internalized culture") represents the broad fields of socialization, enculturation, and acculturation research. In communication research these fields have a whole series of important counterparts, in terms of a temporal perspective ranging from:

Habermasian "Oeffentlichkeit" studies (centuries and decades), to
cultivation studies (decades and years), to
research on the spiral of silence (years and months), to
agenda setting research (months and weeks), to
diffusion of news research (days and hours),

and including also such broad research traditions as effects research, uses and gratifications research, and reception analyses (Jensen & Rosengren, 1990; Rosengren, 1985, p. 39; Rosengren 1988, p. 13). Moving down to the intraindividual level, we would arrive at even more finely tuned temporal studies, working within the range of minutes, seconds, and parts of seconds (see, for instance, Reeves, 1989). Very probably there is a parallelism to be found between the units of time and space. The larger and the more complex the system, the longer the unit of time appropriate to its study.

A third way of broadening the range of cases under study would be to regard the same cases in light of different theoretical approaches. In this respect, and at least for the time being, the "theoretically open" type of comparative studies seems to offer the most promising vistas (see Table 12.1). If teams of comparative researchers could be made strongly heterogeneous with respect not only to their national origins but also to their theoretical origins, so that they would represent radically different quasi-paradigms (for instance, conflict versus consensus orientation, objectivistic versus subjectivistic approaches), no doubt the theoretical productivity of comparative studies would be considerably enhanced.

Serious theoretical confrontations carried out in a positive spirit would very probably lead to considerable clarification of certain problems now blurred because of their having been approached only through the prism of one theoretical perspective. And only theoretical clarification will enable us to reach that ultimate goal of comparative research—to be able to see the specifics of the general, and the general in the overwhelming number of seemingly specific phenomena meeting the untrained observer's eye.

Finally, cumulativity could be furthered by more sustained involvement in prior theorizing about the organization of communication systems per se (see our remarks about substantive, formal, and formative dimensions above). The present collection is uneven in this respect. Although preliminary theorizing of such a kind is ventured by Burgoon, Hallin and Mancini, Ito, and Nowak, it is nowhere elaborated in extended terms (with the possible exceptions of Ito and of Nowak). An inductive approach, in which similarities and differences in the communication phenomena concerned are first plotted and system explanations are sought after the fact, seems popular. Such a use of data for theory building may be natural to an exploratory research phase. As we are advancing beyond this exploratory phase, toward a more formative one, however, more "system-sensitive" theorizing—theorizing that can itself be criticized, tested, and modified by others—seems to be in order.

Of the various branches of communication studies, it seems to be mainly in the two literatures of cultural and political communication that relatively extensive theorizing about the organization of systems can be found. In the former, empirical studies of systemic influences on cultural and societal change over time have been inspired by conceptualizations of linkages between mass media institutions, cultural, and other societal subsystems (Melischek, Rosengren, & Stappers, 1984; Namenwirth & Weber, 1987; Rosengren, 1985). In the latter, theorizing about differences in the degree and form of political system control over mass media systems and vice-versa (in, e.g., Blumler & Gurevitch, 1975; Kepplinger, 1985; Seymour-Ure, 1974; Wolton, 1990) has spurred an expanding number of empirical studies of cross-national consequences of distinctions at that level for political mass media content and its reception by audiences (in, e.g., Cohen, Adoni, & Bantz, 1990; Mazzoleni, 1987; Semetko, et al., 1991).

GENERALITY VERSUS SPECIFICITY

The question of generality and specificity lies right at the heart of comparative research. Small wonder, then, that it turns up in virtually all the chapters of this volume. For striking examples, the interested reader is invited again to consider some of the short summaries of the chapters offered in the first section of this chapter, contemplating them from the crucial perspective of generality versus specificity. Here are some illustrative questions raised by some of the chapters:

How general is *Dutton and Vedel's* model—for instance, over small and large, poor and affluent countries, and over different media? What are the different combinations of social and calendar time implied by the model?

Will *Rosengren's* "structural invariances" in individual media use be strong enough to survive the restructuring of media institutions going on right now in many countries? Will it survive the slower but perhaps more basic change of family structures already under way in many countries?

And what about the temporal generality of *Hallin and Mancini's* work on summitry? Is it challenged by the rapidly changing pattern of power arrangements promising (or threatening) to take international discourse into uncharted waters? Will they still be studying the same phenomena when the rules of the game are being so markedly changed?

Can *Ito's* intriguing relationships between culture and communication at the individual, organizational, and societal levels be tested in strictly empirical, quantitative, and qualitative research? If so, what results could be expected?

Only by systematically trying to seek and finding answers to these and a host of similar questions about generality and specificity will comparative communication research arrive at some degree of cumulativity.

CUMULATIVITY, GENERALITY, AND SPECIFICITY

We firmly believe that there is an intricate balance to be sought between the three basic concepts discussed in this final section of this concluding chapter: the concepts of cumulativity, generality, and specificity. On the one hand, we need to achieve cumulativity by way of collecting detailed knowledge about specifics. On the other hand, we need cumulation by way of reaching for ever higher degrees of generality.

To counterpose the two ways of achieving cumulativity would be rather naive—not to say downright foolish—for there is a true dialectic prevailing between them. Only by carefully observing and comparing a large number of specific cases showing a really broad range of variation will we ever be able to cumulate our results by discerning the general in all that otherwise overwhelming specificity prevailing out there. Wherever general theory and appropriate methodology meet social and cultural realities in empirical comparative research, however, the chances are good that relevant—but always tentative—answers to those important questions about specificity and generality may at long last be found.

We are convinced that comparative communication research is right now heading in that direction. The exploratory phase of comparative research has indeed been a long one. It is now about to be succeeded, we believe, by a more formative phase. The chapters in this volume give testimony to our belief. What might be the criteria for elaborating this formative stage?

First, research questions are now being formulated whose answers are particularly or perhaps uniquely provided by comparative research. Second, the concepts used in recent comparative research are sufficiently abstract to permit comparisons across larger stretches of time and space. Third, strategies of research design—articulated game plans—are involved that make use of cultural and intellectual differences rather than letting such differences be an awkward impediment to comparison. Fourth, the evidence from the analyses informs us not only about the similarities and differences of nations and time periods being compared, but much more about the structural contexts and dynamic processes within the various units. Finally, comparisons are now being carried out cumulatively in such a way as to raise new questions as well as to answer old ones, thus pointing the way to forming new issues for comparative investigation.

Comparative communication research started with seemingly naive but always necessary "comparisons of the first order": "How much, how many of this and that in this and that social system?" Comparative researchers are now turning to "comparisons of the second and third order": "What relations between communicative phenomena are specific to different systems? Which ones are invariant over time and space, between systems, and over levels?"

When a decade and a half ago Blumler and Gurevitch overviewed comparative communication research, they maintained that "there is neither a settled view of what such studies should be concerned with, nor even a firmly crystallized set of alternative options for research, between which scholars of diverse philosophical persuasions could choose" (Blumler & Gurevitch, 1975; cf. Gurevitch, 1989). Since then, the whole situation has undergone a sea change: from tentative exploration to formative consolidation.

We hope this book will further that development.

REFERENCES

Blumler, J. G. (Ed.), (1983a). *Communicating to voters. Television in the first European parliamentary elections.* London: Sage.

Blumler, J. G. (1983b). Election communication: A comparative perspective. In J. G. Blumler (Ed.), *Communicating to voters: Television in the first European parliamentary elections* (pp. 359-378). London: Sage.

Blumler, J. G., Dayan, D., & Wolton, D. (1990). West European perspectives on political communication: Structures and dynamics. *European Journal of Communication, 5,* 261-284.

Blumler, J. G., & Gurevitch, M. (1975). Towards a comparative framework for political communication research. In S. H. Chaffee (Ed.), *Political communication.* Beverly Hills, CA: Sage.

Church, M. (1963). *Time and reality: Studies in contemporary fiction.* Chapel Hill: University of North Carolina Press.

Cohen, A. A., Adoni, H., & Bantz, C. R. (1990). *Social conflict and television news.* Newbury Park, CA: Sage.

Converse, P. E., & Pierce, R. (1986). *Political representation in France.* Cambridge, MA: Belknap Press of Harvard University Press.

Elias, N. (1988). *Time: An essay.* Oxford and New York: Basil Blackwell.

Eulau, H. (1986). *Politics, self and society: A theme and variations.* Cambridge, MA: Harvard University Press.

Gurevitch, M. (1989). Comparative research on television news. *American Behavioral Scientist, 33,* 221-229.

Higdon, D. L. (1977). *Time and English fiction.* London: Macmillan.

Jensen, K. B., & Rosengren, K. E. (1990). Five traditions in search of the audience. *European Journal of Communication, 5,* 207-238.

Kepplinger, H. M. (1985). Systemtheoretische Aspekte politischer Kommunikation. *Publizistik, 30,* 247-264.

Kivikuru, U. (1988). From import to modelling: Finland—An example of old periphery dependency. *European Journal of Communication, 3,* 9-34.

Kohn, M. L. (1989). Cross-national research as an analytic strategy. In M. L. Kohn (Ed.), *Cross-national research in sociology* (pp. 77-102). Newbury Park, CA: Sage.

Kort, W. A. (1985). *Modern fiction and human time.* Tampa: University of South Florida Press.

Liebes, T., & Katz, E. (1990). *The export of meaning: Cross cultural readings of "Dallas."* New York: Oxford University Press.

Mazzoleni, G. (1987). Media logic and party logic in campaign coverage: The Italian general election of 1983. *European Journal of Communication, 2,* 81-103.

Melischek, G., Rosengren, K. E., & Stappers, J. (Eds.). (1984). *Cultural indicators: An international symposium.* Wien: Österreichische Akademie der Wissenschaften.

Meyerhoff, H. (1955). *Time in literature.* Berkeley: University of California Press.

Namenwirth, J. Z., & Weber, R. P. (1987). *Dynamics of culture.* Boston: Allen & Unwin.

Newcomb, H. M., & Hirsch, P. M. (1984). Television as a cultural forum: Implications for research. In W. R. Rowland & B. Watkins (Eds.), *Interpreting television: Current perspectives* (pp. 58-73). Beverly Hills, CA: Sage.

Pan, Z., & McLeod, J. M. (1991). Multi-level analysis in mass communication research. *Communication Research, 18,* 140-173.

Price, V. (1988). On the public aspects of opinion: Linking levels in public opinion research. *Communication Research, 15,* 659-679.

Przeworski, A., & Teune, H. (1970). *The logic of comparative social inquiry.* New York: John Wiley.

Reeves, B. (1989). Theories about news and theories about cognition: Arguments for a more radical separation. *American Behavioral Scientist, 33,* 191-198.

Ricoeur, P. (1984-1988). *Time and narrative, I-III.* Chicago: University of Chicago Press.

Rosengren, K. E. (1985). Media linkages of culture and other societal systems. In M. L. McLaughlin (Ed.), *Communication yearbook 9* (pp. 19-56). Beverly Hills, CA: Sage.

Rosengren, K. E. (1988). The study of media culture: Ideas, actions and artifacts. *Lund Research Papers on the Sociology of Communication, 10.*

Rosengren, K. E. (1989). Paradigms lost and regained. In B. Dervin, L. Grossberg, B. J. O'Keefe, & E. Wartella (Eds.), *Rethinking communication. Volume 1: Paradigm issues* (pp. 21-39). Newbury Park, CA: Sage.

Rosenthal, R. (1991). *Meta-analytic procedures for social research.* Newbury Park, CA: Sage.

Semetko, H. A., Blumler, J. G., Gurevitch, M., & Weaver, D. H. (1991). *The formation of campaign agendas: A comparative analysis of party and media roles in recent American and British elections.* Hillsdale, NJ: Lawrence Erlbaum.

Seymour-Ure, C. (1974). *The political impact of mass media.* London: Constable.

Silj, A. (1988). *East of Dallas: The European challenge to American television.* London: British Film Institute.

Thomsen, H. H. (1990). *Litterær tid.* Odense, Denmark: Odense universitetsforlag.

Wolton, D. (1990). Political communication: The construction of a model. *European Journal of Communication, 5,* 9-28.

ABOUT THE CONTRIBUTORS

JAMES R. BENIGER is Associate Professor at the Annenberg School for Communication, University of Southern California. His research interests include information technology, communication theory, and societal change, with particular attention to the implications for social control, popular culture, and the arts. His most recent book, *The Control Revolution: Technological and Economic Origins of the Information Society* (1986), won an annual Association of American Publishers award for "the most outstanding book in the social and behavioral sciences" and the *New York Times Book Review* "Notable Books of the Year" designation. He is Associate Editor of *Communication Research* and author of its regular "Far Afield" section.

JAY G. BLUMLER is Associate Director of the Center for Research in Public Communication, College of Journalism, University of Maryland, and Emeritus Professor at the University of Leeds, where for many years he directed its Centre for Television Research. He is Founding Editor of the *European Journal of Communication,* International Editor of the *Journal of Communication,* and Past President and a Fellow of the International Communication Association. In recent writings he has developed comparative perspectives on political communication systems and policies for public television in a multichannel environment, including: *Communicating to Voters: Television in the First European Parliamentary Elections* (1983); *The Formation of Campaign Agendas: A Comparative Analysis of Party and Media Roles in Recent American and British Elections* (1991); *Broadcasting Finance in Transition: A*

Comparative Handbook (1991); and *Television and the Public Interest: Vulnerable Values in West European Broadcasting* (in press).

JUDEE K. BURGOON is Professor of Communication and Director of Graduate Studies at the University of Arizona. Her areas of specialization include nonverbal communication, interpersonal relations management, research methods, and mass media. She has authored or coauthored five books and monographs: *The Unspoken Dialogue: An Introduction to Nonverbal Communication*; *Nonverbal Communication: An Unspoken Dialogue*; *Introduction to Small Group Communication: A Functional Approach*; *Mexican Americans and the Mass Media*; and *The World of the Working Journalist*.

STEVEN H. CHAFFEE is Janet M. Peck Professor of International Communication at Stanford University. He is a past President and a Fellow of the International Communication Association. His research has included such topics as family interaction, political communication, adolescent socialization, interpersonal coorientation, health and prevention campaigns, and survey research methods. His publications include *Political Communication, Television and Human Behavior* (with George Comstock and others), *Handbook of Communication Science* (with Charles Berger), and *Communication Concepts 1: Explication*.

GODWIN CHU is Senior Research Associate at the Institute of Culture and Communication, East-West Center. His publications include *Radical Change Through Communication in Mao's China*; *Moving a Mountain—Cultural Change in China*; *China's New Social Fabric*; *Cultural Change in Rural Taiwan: Mass Media and Development in Indonesia*; *Social Impact of Satellite Television in Indonesia;* and *Satellite Television and Images in Korea*. His current research focuses on modern communication technologies and social/cultural change in Asia, including China, Indonesia and Thailand. He was formerly Director of the Communication Institute, East-West Center.

WILLIAM H. DUTTON is a Professor at the Annenberg School for Communication and the School of Public Administration at the University of Southern California. He received his doctorate in political science from SUNY at Buffalo in 1974. His research focuses on the social and political aspects of information technology in the communications field. Currently he is conducting cross-national research on communication technology and public policy, primarily in Britain, France, and Japan.

DANIEL C. HALLIN is an Associate Professor in the Department of Communication at the University of California at San Diego. He is author of *The "Uncensored War": The Media and Vietnam* and recently won the Woodrow Wilson Center Media Studies Essay Contest for an article on television and presidential elections. He is now working on a study of the restructuring of the media in societies in transition from authoritarian to pluralist rule, focusing on Eastern Europe and Latin America.

YOUICHI ITO is Professor in the Department of Policy Management at Keio University, Fujisawa. His recent English-language publications include *Communication & Culture: A Comparative Approach* (1989); "Mass Communication Theories from a Japanese Perspective" in *Media, Culture & Society, 12*(4) (1990); "The Trade Winds Change: Japan's Shift from an Information Importer to an Information Exporter, 1965-1985" in *Communication Yearbook, Vol 13* (1990); and "Practical Problems in Field Research in Japan" in U. Narula and W. B. Pearce (Eds.), *Cultures, Politics, and Research Programs: An International Assessment of Practical Problems in Field Research* (1990). He is editor of *Keio Communication Review* and editorial board member of *Communication Theory, Media, Culture & Society* and the *Journal of Development Communication*.

TAMAR LIEBES is Lecturer in the Department of Communication at the Hebrew University and is an Associate of the Guttman Institute of Applied Social Research in Jerusalem. She is coauthor, with Elihu Katz, of *The Export of Meaning: Cross-Cultural Readings of Dallas* (1990) and is currently studying the role of television in the process of political socialization in families, under a grant from the Spencer Foundation. Together with Sonia Livingstone, she is launching a new project on the advice young women receive from mothers and media.

SONIA M. LIVINGSTONE is a Lecturer in Social Psychology at the London School of Economics and Political Science. Her research interests include the active and critical viewer, the social cognition of the television audience, the soap opera, the psychology of consumption, reader-reception theory, and issues of genre and gender. She is author of *Making Sense of Television: The Psychology of Audience Interpretation* (1990) and of a number of articles in communication and social psychology journals. She is currently working on a project investigating viewers' critical reception of and participation in television debates.

PAOLO MANCINI is Associate Professor at the Instituto di Studi Sociali, Universita de Perugia, Italy. Mancini is a specialist of political communication; several of his works deal with comparative analysis of social systems. He is author of *Il manifesto politico. Per una semiologia del sonsenso* (Torino, 1980); *Videopolitica. Telegiornali in Italia e in USA* (Torino, 1985); and *Come vincere le elezioni* (Bologna, 1988). His work has appeared in *Theory and Society, European Journal of Communication,* and in edited monographs. With Dan Hallin, he wrote *Friendly Enemies: The Reagan-Gorbachev Summits on US, Italian and Soviet Television* (Perugia, 1990).

JACK M. McLEOD is Maier-Bascom Professor of Journalism and Mass Communication and Chair, Mass Communications Research Center, at the University of Wisconsin-Madison. He is a Fellow of the International Communication Association and the Midwest Association for Public Opinion Research. His interests have centered on the effects of audience orientations and news media use on political learning. His recent work has examined "Multilevel Communication Research" (with Z. Pan, *Communication Research,* 1991), "On Understanding and Misunderstanding Media Effects" (with G. Kosicki and Z. Pan, *Mass Communication and Society,* 1991), and "Learning from Political News: Effects of Media Images and Information Processing Strategies" (with G. Kosicki, *Mass Communication and Political Information Processing,* 1990).

KJELL NOWAK is Professor of Mass Communication at Stockholm University, Sweden. His published work includes research on audiences and communicators, on content as well as effects. Much of his research has been cross-disciplinary. Apart from the advertising research reported here, he has recently studied images of social stratification in Swedish television programming and is presently working on TV reception as a cognitive and sociocultural process.

KARL ERIK ROSENGREN, previously a Research Fellow of the Swedish Social Science Council and Professor of Mass Communication at the University of Gothenburg, is Professor of Sociology and Communication at the University of Lund in Sweden. He has published a number of books and articles in the sociology of communication and culture. Recent publications of his include *Media Matter. TV Use in Childhood and Adolescence* (with S. Windahl and others, 1989) and *European Communication Research: The State of the Art* (with J. Blumler and D. McQuail, 1990, a special issue of the *European Journal of Communication*). Together with J. G. Blumler and D. McQuail, he is a founding coeditor of *EJC*.

DAVID L. SWANSON is Professor of Speech Communication, University of Illinois at Urbana-Champaign. His interest in comparative research grew out of participation in a study of political communication in the 1988 presidential elections in the United States and France. His research concerns the social and political effects of public communication, critical analysis of public communication, and theoretical and metatheoretical issues in communication research. His work appears in various journals and volumes, and he is coeditor of *New Directions in Political Communication* and coauthor of *The Nature of Human Communication.*

THIERRY VEDEL is a Research Fellow with the National Center for Scientific Research and works at the Centre d' Etude de la Vie Politique Française, a research center based at the Fondation Nationale des Sciences Politiques in Paris. He is a former student of the Ecole Normale Superieure and a graduate of the Institut d' Etudes Politiques de Paris (1980). He holds a master degree in economics from the Universite de Paris 1—Sorbonne (1978) and received doctoral degrees in communications studies (1981) and in political science (1981). His current work deals with the politics of telecommunications in industrialized countries.